D0904159

NEFESH SHIMSHON

Gates of Emunah

Rav Shimshon Dovid Pincus

Nefesh Shimshon

Gates of Emunah

The Principles of Faith:
The Fundamentals of Jewish Belief in Hashem and Divine Providence

FELDHEIM PUBLISHERS
JERUSALEM NEW YORK

For cassettes and CDs of the Rav's talks: +972 (527) 625-966

ISBN 978-1-59826-503-3

FELDHEIM PUBLISHERS
POB 43163 / Jerusalem, Israel

208 Airport Executive Park
Nanuet, NY 10954

www.feldheim.com

10 9 8 7 6 5 4 3 2 1

Printed in Israel

Contents

Introduction to the English Edition

It is with feelings of great joy and gratitude to *Hashem Yisbarach* that we proudly present this English translation of *Nefesh Shimshon: Sha'arei Emunah* on the topics of *emunah* and the Rambam's Thirteen Principles of Faith, by our father, *zt"l*.

After our father's passing, we were blessed by Heaven with the opportunity to publish a series of *sefarim* adapted from his taped lectures. These touch on a wide variety of subjects including *emunah, bitachon,* and living one's life connected with Hashem. Published originally in Hebrew, these *sefarim* enjoy wide circulation and are embraced by *b'nei Torah,* as well as by the Jewish public in general. Many people's lives have been illuminated by these books.

The material on the Rambam's Thirteen Principles of Faith presented in this *sefer* is unique: it originated as a series of classes delivered to a group of select *kollel* men, in which each Principle was elucidated on its own. As is known, every Jew is obligated to know the basic principles of the Jewish faith. The beautifully clear explanations in this book enable the reader to gain this essential knowledge.

We received many requests over the years to translate these *sefarim* into English so that these teachings could reach a larger audience. Approximately one year since its publication, the first volume in the English series, *Nefesh Shimshon: Shabbos Kodesh*, has already established itself as a popular bestseller. *Baruch Hashem*, we are now presenting the second volume in this series, *Nefesh Shimshon: The Principles of Faith*. It is our hope that this book will educate the public regarding this important topic.

In truth, the topic of *emunah* divides into two parts. The first is understanding Torah faith and its principles, and bringing it into one's heart. This naturally leads to the second part, which is living one's life with Hashem. This English book focuses on the first part; the second will be treated in a book to come. (Both parts were included in the lengthy Hebrew volume titled *Sha'arei Emunah*.)

Our father had an original and enlightening way of explaining matters of *emunah*. His lively approach placed an indelible impression on the thousands of people around the world who heard him address this important topic, one that was so close to his heart.

Parts of this book touch on profound issues. Our father's firm grasp on the meaning of Hashem's Oneness enabled him to clarify even the most difficult points with amazing simplicity.

As this edition goes to print, we wish to express our gratitude to our friends R' Yehonasan Posen and R' Yaakov Posen, who after the passing our father, *zt"l*, took upon themselves the task of publishing his lectures, working day and night toward this end. Thanks to them, we have merited to see the lectures of our illustrious father published in more than ten impressive volumes. This is an eternal *zechus* for them; may they be blessed by the Source of all blessings in this world and the next.

In the same vein, we wish to thank R' Aharon Schwartz, who has been of invaluable assistance in everything connected to publishing the *sefarim*, and who has devoted himself to disseminating the teachings of our father, *zt"l*, by means of audio cassettes as well. Now he has undertaken the task of preparing the books for publication in English. He worked without rest to complete the impressive volume that we see before us today.

We also wish to mention and thank R' Tzvi Yosef Shechter and R' Shlomo Hoffman who masterfully prepared the lectures for the Hebrew edition. We also thank R' Ilan Greenwald for his work in preparing the Hebrew edition for publication.

With the appearance of the English edition, we wish to express our deep gratitude to the translator, R' Shmuel Globus. His abundant understanding graced this English edition with the tasteful and thoughtful form that we see before us today. We also wish to mention Feldheim Publishers' talented editorial staff for enhancing and perfecting this edition. And we thank all the others who assisted with the publication of this book in any way.

May all of them be blessed by Hashem. May Hashem reward them with much *nachas* and happiness, blessing and joy, all the days of their lives in this world and the next.

We hereby offer our apologies in the name of all the people who took part in this work. The process of adapting the lectures and translating them was done with great emphasis on precision and on translating according to the original text. However, translation is known to be a very difficult task and it is possible that there are deviations from what was originally said. And it is surely possible that we have failed to comprehend the full depth of the subjects discussed, due to their great profundity. Therefore, any mistake that is found in this book should certainly be attributed to us.

In conclusion, we extend our hands in prayer to the Master of all: Just as Your mercy has helped us until now, so may You never abandon us. May it be Your will that this *sefer* be an *illui neshamah* for our father HaRav HaGaon Shimshon Dovid ben Rav Chaim Avraham, *zt"l,* and our righteous mother Chayah

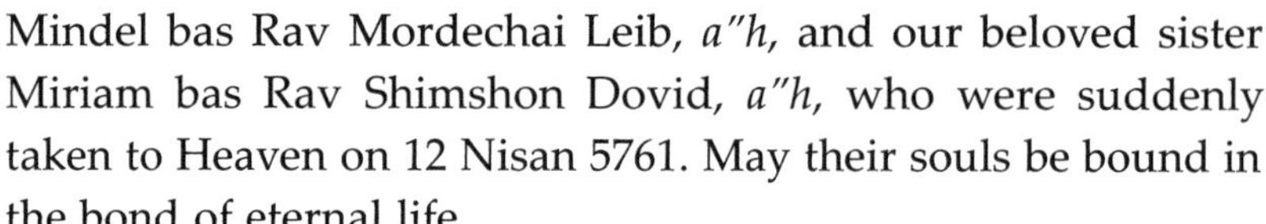

Mindel bas Rav Mordechai Leib, *a"h,* and our beloved sister Miriam bas Rav Shimshon Dovid, *a"h,* who were suddenly taken to Heaven on 12 Nisan 5761. May their souls be bound in the bond of eternal life.

The Pincus Family
Kislev 5770

NEFESH SHIMSHON

Basics of Emunah

מצות האמונה – דביקות בהשי"ת

1

How to Achieve Emunah

The "Mitzvah" to Believe in Hashem

LET US START WITH some very basic questions: What is *emunah*? How do we acquire it? What effect does it have on our life? The Rambam in his *Sefer HaMitzvos* counts *emunah* as the very first mitzvah:

> The first mitzvah that we were commanded is to believe in God. This means to believe there is a Source and Cause that brings about everything that exists. Regarding this it was said,[1] *"I am Hashem your God."*

Some *Rishonim* objected to counting *emunah* as one of the mitzvos. They argued that *emunah* is so basic that it cannot be called a mitzvah.[2] In order to fulfill any mitzvah, a person first has to be a believer. This is because there is no such thing as a commandment without He Who commands. And once we believe in the existence of He Who commands, we already have *emunah*! Thus, it does not make sense to call *emunah* a mitzvah.

1. *Shemos* 20:2.
2. *Hasagos HaRamban* ad loc., citing *Ba'al Halachos Gedolos*.

In this vein, the Ramban quotes the following teaching of *Chazal:*[3]

> *"You shall not have other gods in My presence."*[4] Why does it say this? Because just before it said, *"I am Hashem your God."* This may be compared to a human king who enters a city, and his ministers say to him, "Make decrees upon the people." The king responds, "No. When they accept my kingship, I will make decrees upon them. If they don't accept my kingship, they won't accept my decrees either."
>
> And so Hashem said to the Jewish people: *"I am Hashem your God... You shall not have other gods in My presence."* Hashem was saying, so to speak: "Am I the One Whose Kingship you accepted upon yourselves in Egypt?" The Jewish people responded, "Yes!" He then said: "Since you accepted My kingship upon yourselves, accept My decrees."

This shows that accepting Hashem's kingship is a prerequisite to all the mitzvos. First we must accept His kingship; He is the One Who commands. This means to believe in God. Only then are we capable of accepting His other mitzvos.

There is another objection to counting *emunah* as one of the mitzvos: it is not something that a person can be told to do. If a person does not believe in God, how can you "command" him to believe? This objection is also raised regarding the mitzvah of *ahavas Hashem,* which the Rambam counts as the third mitzvah. It does not make sense to "command" someone to love. Let's say there is a certain type of candy that I don't particularly care for. If I don't like it, what will it help to "command" me to like it? The same goes for the mitzvah of *yiras Hashem*, which the Rambam counts as the fourth mitzvah. How can you "command" someone to fear?

3. *Mechilta, Yisro*, chap. 6.

4. *Shemos* 20:2.

The answer regarding *ahavas Hashem* is well known: There is such sweetness and pleasantness, such beauty and splendor surrounding Hashem that a person is naturally inspired to love Him. In fact, it is impossible not to. Whoever knows Him, loves Him. And whoever does not love Him, it is because he does not have contact with Him. So what is the mitzvah of *ahavas Hashem?* In truth, the mitzvah is more technical than emotional. It involves performing actions by which "love will necessarily follow," as the Rambam says in mitzvah 3. In other words, the mitzvah is not to love Hashem, as that comes automatically. The mitzvah is to do things that *bring* us to love Him.

What about *yiras Hashem?* It makes no difference whether we are speaking about fear of punishment or awe of Hashem's greatness. Hashem is so fearsome and awesome that it is impossible not to have *yiras Hashem.* Whoever knows Him, has *yirah.* So what is the mitzvah? It is to perform those actions by which *yirah* will necessarily follow.

The same applies to *emunah.* If a person would simply have contact with Hashem, he would believe in Him. So what does the mitzvah of *emunah* entail? It involves performing actions by which *emunah* will necessarily follow. *Emunah* starts with a simple, though weak, knowledge that there is a God. One does not fulfill the mitzvah of *emunah* with this piece of knowledge, but at least he recognizes Hashem. It doesn't really matter how a person gains this initial awareness, for the mitzvah is not to believe in theory; rather, the obligation is to do things that bring us to true *emunah.* Just as the mitzvah of *ahavas Hashem* is not "to love," but rather to perform actions that bring about feelings of love, so too, the mitzvah of *emunah* involves doing actions. Belief in Hashem is an automatic consequence of these actions.

This is how the *Acharonim* explained the Rambam's counting of *emunah* as one of the mitzvos. The belief in God that is a prerequisite to mitzvah observance is a weak belief. It is a mere awareness that there is a God. This is not yet *emunah*! The

mitzvah of *"I am Hashem Your God"* is instructing us to do things that will bring us to full *emunah.*

Every Mitzvah Is a Level of Connection to Hashem

Let us take a deeper look at this matter. *Ahavas Hashem* is a certain type of connection, of relationship, to Hashem. It represents a certain *madreigah.* And the same is true of *yiras Hashem.* The Brisker Rav said that nowadays, there is no more *yirah.* Some people are more careful in their mitzvah observance than others, but true *yirah* does not exist anymore.

What is true *yirah?* There is an anecdote about the Brisker Rav who was once in Switzerland during the month of Elul. The person accompanying him noticed that the Rav had suddenly begun to tremble. He asked him: "What's the matter?" The Rav answered: "It says, 'We are in fear and trembling of the day of Your arrival'!"[5] For the Brisker Rav, what the prayer says is a reality. If it says, "We are in fear and trembling," he trembles! This is *yiras Hashem.*

Every mitzvah in the Torah is another level of connection to Hashem. Take the mitzvah of wearing tefillin, for instance. We experience no difficulty putting on tefillin. For other people, however, laying tefillin is as hard as learning a whole hour without interruption is for us. They just can't manage it.

Keeping kosher, too, is a level of connection to Hashem. I know a certain man, an observant Jew, who bears the titles of both rabbi and professor. He regards himself a great Torah scholar and an equally great professor. During our conversation he told me of a number of food products that have serious *kashrus* problems despite the fact that they bear a certain rabbinical supervision. He went into detail about the problems

5. *Selichos,* first day.

with these products. But when I visited his house, what did I see? The very same products that he had spoken about! Then I realized what was going on: He was not on the *madreigah* to refrain from eating those products. He knew they were problematic, but could not bring himself to give them up. This is because keeping kosher is a certain *madreigah*, level, of connection to Hashem.

Keeping Shabbos is a level of connection to Hashem. We, *baruch Hashem*, have that level of connection; we are on the *madreigah* of keeping Shabbos, so it is not hard for us to keep the halachos. But let's take a non-observant Jew who shows interest in Torah and wants to start keeping Shabbos. He typically finds this step very difficult to manage. It is so hard for him to keep Shabbos! This is because Torah and Hashem are one; they are inseparable. Every mitzvah in the Torah is a certain level of connection to Hashem. We do not feel that basic mitzvah observance is a towering challenge because we are already at that level of connection to Hashem.

Emunah and Intellect

Emunah, too, is not a *madreigah* we acquire by amassing knowledge or exerting our intellect. *Emunah* is rather a certain level of connection to Hashem. The closer we come to Hashem and the more connected we are to Him, the more we will truly believe in Him.

From an intellectual point of view, any clear-thinking person will realize that *emunah* is a most basic concept. In fact, it is an open miracle that a person is able to deny Hashem. If we think about it, we will realize that this is the greatest miracle in the world!

When a person notices a table, he understands that a carpenter was involved. When he notices a camera, he understands that it was produced by someone skilled. Let's say a person notices a human eye. This sophisticated "camera" is simply amazing. It has automatic focus, picks up the subtlest shades

of color, and lasts for seventy or eighty years. It washes its own lens. If something more serious happens, it is kept closed for a day, and fixes itself! Why would anyone think that it just came into existence on its own?

How could anyone deny Hashem? How does this happen? It is only because of a person's distance from Hashem. Distance from Him creates the ability to deny Him. And *emunah* is acquired by coming close to Him.

The Vicious Cycle

How does a person grow so far from Hashem that he is capable of denying Him? Again, let us consider mitzvos in general. Just as doing mitzvos causes a person to be enveloped by a spirit of purity, so doing *aveiros* causes a person to be enveloped by a spirit of impurity. Let us consider the prohibition of *yichud,* for instance. A man and woman who are not married to one another may not be secluded in a room with each other, even for a relatively short time. Often, there is no reason to think that a short seclusion will lead to anything. Yet, someone who is in *yichud* is transgressing a Rabbinic prohibition. Furthermore, he is in proximity to a Torah prohibition, and is affected by its powerful spirit of impurity. This impurity attaches itself to him, and as a result, he is liable to slip to depths which he otherwise would never have reached.

There is a story about a tzaddik who found himself alone in a room with an eighty-five-year-old woman. He immediately jumped out of the window. When asked, "Are you afraid of her?" he answered, "I am not afraid of her; I am afraid of the *Shulchan Aruch*!" If it is forbidden, there is a good reason to be afraid. In a different version of the story, he answered: "The *yetzer hara* makes an elderly woman into a young one, and an unattractive woman into a beauty." The *yetzer hara* has this ability, and he wields it especially on someone who is transgressing the prohibition of *yichud*.

Returning to our subject: when a person's *emunah* has a little crack, his foundations have a little crack. But it is more than this. Such a situation brings upon him a spirit of impurity whose effects are progressively more insidious and destructive. The spirit of impurity constantly feeds on itself and intensifies. Just as *emunah* brings a person to *ahavas Hashem* and *yiras Hashem,* so does a lack of *emunah* bring a person to heavy spiritual setbacks.

Along the same lines, there were good, God-fearing Jews who started to lose their faith in Torah after speaking to a non-believer. Why is this? Is it because they were spiritually weak to begin with and their inner inclinations started to emerge? That is not the explanation — it is because of the spirit of impurity that rests on the very words of the non-believer. A word that denies Hashem is like a word that conveys immodesty and indecency. One off-color joke can ruin the purity of a person's thoughts. It infects his mind with a spirit of impurity, even if he is an upright and outstanding person.

Someone who hears the people around him denying Hashem is not immune to the effects just because he knows that what they are saying is nonsense. This kind of speech contains the worst possible degree of impurity and filth that exists. Its powerful, destructive impact goes well beyond the actual subject that was discussed.

The Chassidim have a saying: "'*I have believed, for I have spoken*'[6] — a person acquires *emunah* by speaking about it again and again." *Emunah* is not acquired effortlessly. It is not enough just to know. It is something one must work on, like one works on *kedushah* and *taharah*. We must daven for *siyatta d'Shemaya* and stay far away from elements destructive to *emunah*.

This is the "mitzvah" of *emunah*.

6. *Tehillim* 116:10.

Torah Learning Bestows Emunah

The real force behind our *emunah* is Torah. *Sefer Nefesh HaChaim* teaches us that our connection to Hashem comes mainly through Torah learning. It is important to know that also our *emunah*-connection to Hashem comes by virtue of the Torah's inherent sanctity.

If we feel spiritually heightened when we speak in Torah, it is only because of the power of Torah. It is the power of Torah, together with the *kedushah* and the connection to Hashem that it produces, that brings us to *emunah*. Learning Gemara topics such as *shnayim ochazim b'tallis* brings us to *emunah*. Without such learning, we cannot attain *emunah*. Neither can we attain *ahavah* or *yirah*.

What if we feel that our *emunah* is more enhanced by a good lecture on *emunah* than it is by learning *shnayim ochazim b'tallis*? This is because each area of Torah has a special power to affect us in its unique way. Just as learning *hilchos Shabbos* has a special power to enhance our Shabbos, so does learning *hilchos emunah* have a special power to enhance our *emunah*.

But in truth, increased knowledge is not what brings a person to *emunah*. It is the *kedushas haTorah* that does it. Only *kedushas haTorah* and being connected to Hashem can bring a person to *emunah, ahavah,* and *yirah*. "I created the *yetzer hara,* and I created Torah as its remedy."[7] The only thing that kills the *yetzer hara* is Torah. Exerting oneself in Torah learning brings one to *emunah*. It is not *one* way to acquire *emunah* — it is the *only* way!

Knowledge of Hashem means connecting oneself to Hashem. We work on *emunah* through Torah learning, and the *kedushas haTorah* causes us to become connected to Hashem. It is as simple as that. A person with *emunah* is a person who is connected to Hashem.

7. *Kiddushin* 30b.

As we said, the "mitzvah" of *emunah* is to involve ourselves in attaining *emunah*. *"You shall realize [it] today and impress [it] upon your heart."*[8] It is a mitzvah fulfilled practically, not intellectually. *Emunah* is not something we grasp with our minds: to know that Hashem is everywhere, and so forth. A person can be cognizant of Hashem and still deny Him. Someone who studies the property laws of *maseches Bava Basra* is fulfilling the mitzvah of *emunah* because in this way he draws himself closer to Hashem. He becomes connected to Hashem, so he thereby attains *emunah*.

Torah Breaks Through

An explosive shell tossed against a window has far more force than a simple object does. The shell's explosive power is incomparably greater than its force as a tossed object. This illustrates the difference between knowing Hashem from the world He created, and knowing Him from the Torah.

The sun, the moon, and all the creations testify to us about the One Who created them. They are a great force bringing us to recognize Hashem: *"Raise your eyes to the Heavens and see Who created these."*[9] Regarding the Torah, however, aside from the message it conveys, it is also packed with an "explosive" power. When someone learns Torah, for instance by studying the verse of *"In the beginning, God created,"*[10] the Torah's innate *kedushah* explodes within him. This has an impact going far beyond the meaning of the words he recites.

True, it is possible to learn Torah and remain a non-believer. The Ramchal says that it is possible to empty the Torah of all its

8. *Devarim* 4:39.
9. *Yeshayahu* 40:26.
10. *Bereishis* 1:1.

spiritual content and turn it into a mere body of knowledge.[11] But to do this, one must struggle very hard against Hashem. Very few people learned a lot of Torah and still denied Hashem. Maybe one in a million.

The very act of learning Torah brings a person to *emunah,* even if he misunderstands the topic he is studying and does not arrive at correct conclusions. One might think that every mistake made in Torah learning should be considered a denial of Hashem, since knowledge of Torah is actually knowledge of Hashem. However, Hashem designed the Torah in such a way that "*dilugo alai ahavah* — his deletions are beloved to Me." That is, even if a person makes mistakes when learning Torah, and "skips" important points, Hashem is still pleased with his learning and still loves him.[12] If a person errs in his learning, it is not denial of Hashem.

This is one of the great miracles of Torah. It is beyond our understanding. When a person learns Torah earnestly, with *yiras Shamayim* and *ehrlichkeit,* Hashem considers even his mistakes as Torah learning. When he learns with *kedushah* and *taharah,* and his mind tells him that the matter is so, this is considered Torah even if he has erred in his understanding. If this would be considered a perversion of the truth and a denial of Hashem then we would have to close our Gemaras.

Toiling in Torah Brings Emunah into the Heart

The effort and exertion that a person puts into his learning is the primary factor in the Torah's ability to bring him to *emunah.* Toiling in Torah works the heart and "plows" it, so to speak. It breaks through the hard outer layer of the heart.

When a person struggles to understand a *kushya,* this

11. See *Derech Hashem,* vol. 4, chap. 2:5–6.

12. See *Shir HaShirim Rabbah* 2:15.

"plows" furrows in his heart. This first stage already starts to bring him *emunah* and closeness to Hashem. Then the heart starts to break open, and whatever is closest enters it: *kedushah,* Hashem's words. The Torah is acquired through *kedushah* and *taharah,* holiness and purity. But practically speaking, the first, basic step to acquire Torah is to just sit down and start learning Torah. We know that when a person learns six hours straight, then his *Shemoneh Esrei* is different: his mind is clear, and nothing disturbs his prayers. His *emunah* and closeness to Hashem is greatly enhanced.

The effect of Torah can be seen also from *kiruv* seminars. The most amazing things happen. Some of the participants are totally bereft of Judaism, people steeped in every kind of spiritual impurity. And after three or four days at a *kiruv* seminar they have changed from one extreme to the other. What causes this astounding transformation? Only one thing: the Torah they learned during those days.

Yes, a *kiruv* seminar needs good speakers because the participants need to be drawn into Torah learning and have their appetite for Torah stimulated. But in truth it does not really matter what stories the speakers tell or how they pique the interest of the audience. A few days later nobody even remembers. The main thing is to keep their interest so they continue coming to the Torah lectures straight to the end. In fact, if the speakers could skip all the inspirational introductions and just sit down to learn *shnayim ochazim b'tallis* with them for a few days, the participants would do much more *teshuvah*! And the speakers, too, would become closer to Hashem.

This is because the power of Torah is what truly affects people. If you take someone and feed him Torah for a few days, his heart breaks open and the Torah's *kedushah* fills it.

The power of Torah can be seen also from the seminars held for Torah Jews in America. I have seen people go through startling transformations. I remember a couple that attended who could only be described as "secular Torah-observant Jews." On the one hand they were full members of the *frum* community. Their daughters were in Bais Yaakov, their sons were in yeshivos, etc. But this couple did whatever they felt like. They fully transgressed Torah prohibitions. At the end of the seminar they woke up to Torah. The wife told me, "This is the first time in fifteen years that I said *Shema Yisrael*!"

Another seminar participant was a woman whose whole life revolved around her career. Nothing else was of much importance to her; surely not her spiritual life. A year later she remarked that since the seminar, she has not missed *Minchah* even once. Another example is a Torah-observant man who came with his wife to a seminar and spoke to me privately: "Rabbi, my wife says *Tehillim* every day, but the magazines she has…! Please, mention this topic!" After the seminar he came to say, "Thanks! Everything is okay now."

What influenced these people? It was not the power of persuasion — it was the inherent power of Torah itself. These people grew up in *frum* homes and heard about these things since they were born. They knew very well what the Torah forbids and what the Torah permits. No gifted speaker came and opened their eyes to things they were not previously aware of. So why did they change? Because the power of Torah breaks open the heart.

Torah and its *kedushah* is the way to work on *emunah*. Someone who does not work on it in a way of *kedushah* will not attain *emunah*. A person can read a book on the subject of *emunah* from cover to cover but if he does not recite *birkas haTorah*, he will gain nothing from this study. In fact it will lead him toward denying Hashem. This is because true Jewish *emunah* is acquired only through *kedushah*.

Emunah is being connected to Hashem. Only toiling in Torah brings a person to *emunah* and closeness to Hashem. True, toiling in Torah does not give a person the details of *emunah*; it does not provide training in *emunah*. There are many books devoted to the subject of *emunah*. Toiling in Torah does something much more important: it causes *emunah* to penetrate a man's heart. "*You shall realize [it] today and impress [it] upon your heart.*"[13] Once it enters his heart, he has true *emunah*.

13. *Devarim* 4:39.

"אתה הראת לדעת"

2

The Knowledge that Precedes Emunah

Hashem Revealed Himself at Har Sinai

AT MOUNT SINAI, HASHEM revealed Himself to the Jewish people. Every individual, without exception, saw Hashem with his own eyes:

> *You were shown [things] for [you] to realize that it is the Eternal Who is God; there is none other besides Him!*[1]

In truth, it is easy to see that Hashem exists. We do not need special revelations for this. Everything in the world that He created cries out, "*How manifold are Your works, Hashem*!"[2] Nevertheless, Hashem wanted to "meet" us:

> *Hashem spoke with you at the mountain face-to-face.*[3]

When we see something with our own eyes, face-to-face, it requires no further proof. But this brings us to a practical

1. *Devarim* 4:35.
2. *Tehillim* 104:24.
3. *Devarim* 5:4.

question: We who live today do not remember that Hashem spoke with us face-to-face. If so, how does "You were shown [things] for [you] to realize" apply to our generation? How was Hashem shown to *us*? The answer is that we, too, may attain this level of knowledge by utilizing the sense and understanding with which human beings have been endowed.

There are certain things that are a basic part of human reality. For instance, there are axioms whose truth is self-evident and unchallenged. Similarly, there are certain basic historical facts that have been written about time and again and everyone accepts that they are true. Does anyone question whether Napoleon really existed? Or George Washington? He lived over two hundred years ago, served as the first president of the United States, and was seen in his time by countless people. It is accepted as a fact that George Washington existed, although no one alive today ever saw him.

What about Hashem revealing Himself at *Har Sinai*? What is the historical status of this event? It was witnessed by three million people. We stood at *Har Sinai* about eighty generations ago — that's four thousand years. Egyptian pyramids are older than that; we are not talking about some imaginary era in the nonexistent past.

Furthermore, the Jewish nation which exists to this day was established on the basis of Hashem's revelation at *Har Sinai*. This event forms an intrinsic part of Pesach, a holiday celebrated in our times by millions of families throughout the world, who sit at the table on Seder night to recount the story of the Exodus and what followed. Therefore, we should regard *Har Sinai* as an established historical fact. On Shavuos night, everyone stays up because at *Har Sinai* they slept that night. Again, it is an accepted fact.

There is another logical proof for *Har Sinai*. The Jewish people has plenty of enemies. In past times the Christians posed a serious threat. They felt compelled to annihilate Jews, due to

what their faith told them the Jews did. The Muslims similarly sentenced Jews to death on grounds of faith. Although these religions were bitterly opposed to what Judaism stands for, they never denied that Hashem revealed Himself at *Har Sinai*! Clearly, *Har Sinai* is a fact beyond question. Even our enemies could not deny it. These religions rather based their persecutions on the claim that later on in history, a "prophet" came and announced that God rejected the Jews for their many sins and replaced them with a new "chosen people."

So we see that *Har Sinai* is not a matter of faith. Rather, it is something we know as a fact. If someone would ask you, "How do you know that Hashem exists?" the proper reply would be, "We met Him at Mount Sinai!" If our questioner would press further and say, "If so, tell me what He looks like," the proper reply would be, "It was such an exalted event that there are simply no words to describe it."

Hashem exists, and we saw Him. It does not matter that we cannot describe it in ordinary language. If a blind person would ask, "What is red? Is it hot or cold?" we would answer, "Red cannot be described in terms of temperature. It is a color." If he wanted to be stubborn he could reply, "I'm sorry, but if you cannot describe red in terms of my experience, then I cannot accept that it exists." His inability to comprehend "red" makes no difference at all. Red is a color, and everyone knows it exists.

Three million people who claim that they saw Hashem are not lying. They ate *mann* morning and evening for forty years. It fell from Heaven every day. With this faith we marched through fire and water for thousands of years. Jews are intelligent people; you can't sell them nonsense. Would Jews give up their lives and the lives of their children throughout the generations for a fairy tale?!

When we recite a *berachah* we say, "*Baruch Atah Hashem.*" We speak to Hashem directly, in the second person, as we would to someone standing right in front of us. This is because He is here. We do not see Him with our eyes or perceive Him with our other senses. But if we are clear thinkers and are realistic, we will regard Him as an absolute reality. His existence is an accepted fact that no one denied until about a hundred years ago.

What happened then? Why did people suddenly start to lose their faith in God? It is because nowadays, people have ceased to be people! Modern man lives a life of abandon. The family structure is disintegrating. Values are vanishing. More and more, people forsake the basic elements of humanity. But as long as a person remains committed to what is straight and true, he sees Hashem as a reality.

We have thus established that Hashem exists. How do we know He gave us the mitzvos? Here we rely on the assumption that Hashem did not leave us in the dark. Since He created us, it is logical to assume that He clearly communicated to us what He expects of us. It does not make sense to maintain that God created the world and then said, "Go do whatever you want." Rather, He gave us a guide book instructing us how to live and how to connect to Him.

Everything we have said up to this point is for all of humanity. Hashem did not create just the Jewish people. He created all the nations in the world, and gave them instructions how they should live, too. God does not exist only for Jews.

If so, what is special about Judaism? How are Jews different from everyone else?

Emunah Follows Knowledge

Here we come to something called *emunah.* Jews connect to *HaKadosh Baruch Hu* not just through their knowledge that He exists. They relate to Him not just as the Creator of the world. Rather, they have a relationship of love with Him. We are "married" to Hashem, so to speak. "You chose us from among all the nations;

You loved us and found us desirable."[4] We have a unique relationship of love with *HaKadosh Baruch Hu*.

Indeed, Jews feel they are special and unique, even if they don't understand why. There are Jews who do not observe Shabbos, do not keep kosher, do not even fast on Yom Kippur. But they feel very strongly about the fact that they are Jews. If they would hear that their daughter is to marry a non-Jew, they would be aghast. Why? What is wrong with this?

Let us try to put a finger on what makes Jews different. Are Jews the "best" people in the world? Are they the most upright? What is special about us? The following allegory points to an answer:

A wealthy and successful businessman booked a flight to Europe. He and his wife will be traveling in the first-class section. Imagine we would say to him, "It is understandable that you travel first class. You are very wealthy, you have international business dealings; it is fitting for you to travel first class. But why must your wife go first class? Is she a prominent businesswoman? Is she a famous writer? I can't understand what is special about her." The businessman would answer, "It's very simple. She's my wife!"

So it is with the Jewish people. We may not always behave more exemplarily than everyone else, but we do have a relationship of love with *HaKadosh Baruch Hu*. Before a man gets married, he checks his potential spouse thoroughly before he decides she is the woman he wants to take as his wife. But after marriage, after they have already established their relationship, he doesn't keep "checking." They belong to each other, and that's it! He accepts her the way she is.

Marriage is a covenant that mutually obligates husband and wife to each other. Similarly, Hashem promised that He

4. *Siddur, Amidah of Shalosh Regalim.*

will love us regardless of our relative merits. In His inscrutable wisdom, He chose to establish with us an eternal relationship of love. We love Him and He loves us. When we are in pain, He feels it, and vice versa.

This is the true meaning of the pain we feel on Tishah b'Av. We are not really lacking. We have homes, we have children, etc. But Hashem is lacking, and we are connected to Him. We feel His pain, so to speak. His children are scattered throughout the world. Millions of them are so estranged that they do not even know He is their Father. Such pain! On Tishah b'Av, we feel the pain of *HaKadosh Baruch Hu*.

This also explains why Shabbos is such an important mitzvah. Shabbos is a little bit like a "honeymoon." It is our private time to be with *HaKadosh Baruch Hu*. Let's imagine a husband and wife who both work full-time. All week long, each one is occupied in his own field. But once a week they go to a hotel together. This is their only real time to be in each other's company. One day, just as they reach the hotel, the husband's cellular phone starts ringing. His wife turns to him and says, "Can you please turn off your phone? We've come here to be together with each other. Nothing else exists now, no business matters, nothing! It's just you and me now." On Shabbos, we should put weekday affairs out of mind and focus on spending time with *HaKadosh Baruch Hu*!

This relationship of love is what Shabbos is all about, and what Judaism is all about. Let's say your spouse brings you a cup of coffee or tea. What do you say? "Thank you, dear!" Similarly, when we receive a cup of coffee or tea from Hashem, we say, *Baruch Atah Hashem*. When a person regains consciousness after an operation, he says to the surgeon, "Thank you, Doctor. You saved my life!" Similarly, when we wake up in the morning, we say, *Modeh ani lefanecha*.

This is the difference between Jews and others. The nations of the world know that God exists. It is human nature to believe. But Jews go beyond this basic level of belief, and have a relationship of love with Hashem. Why did He choose us for this relationship? When Hashem wished to give the Torah, He approached all the nations and only the Jews wanted to receive it.[5] Let us consider what this signifies: In a relationship of love, the most important thing is that it is mutual. The husband wants to be desirable to the wife, and the wife wants to be desirable to the husband. The whole relationship depends on the fact that it is mutual.

The first person to seek out Hashem was Avraham Avinu. No one else in the world cared, but Avraham Avinu did. He went looking for Hashem. And Hashem said to him, so to speak: "Since I am desirable to you, you are desirable to Me." The Jewish people did the same when they said, *Na'aseh v'nishma.* They expressed mutual love. They entered into a relationship with Hashem that was sealed in blood. They trusted in Hashem and followed Him out of Egypt into the wilderness. A relationship like this cannot be broken. It is eternal, like the relationship of parent and child. While a couple can get divorced, no one can undo the relationship of parent and child. That is why the first message Hashem communicated to Pharaoh was, *"Yisrael is My firstborn son."*[6]

Relating to Hashem as a Concrete "Personality"

How can we develop this *emunah,* this relationship of love with *HaKadosh Baruch Hu*? It cannot be done if we relate to Him merely as an abstract concept. The *Meshech Chochmah* states an important principle regarding this. He cites early Torah sources who say:

5. *Avodah Zarah* 2b.
6. *Shemos* 4:22.

Just as Hashem's capability is unlimited and infinite, so is He capable of functioning in a finite and limited way.[7]

Many people, including great philosophers, have erroneous views on this very important point. It is so important, in fact, that it is one of the foundations of *emunah*. This seemingly simple idea clears up a lot of issues and answers a lot of questions, because it explains how we can relate to Hashem.

All created beings, humans included, exist within a certain defined framework. We are not infinite and endless. Our very nature is bounded and delineated, and our only way of perceiving things is by limiting and defining them. We cannot understand something that lacks definable qualities.

This is because of *Bereishis bara Elokim*. The Name *Elokim*, as Rashi explains, is *middas ha-din*. In other words, the whole world was created with a Divine Name that expresses the power of limitation, thereby imprinting this nature on everything in the world. If something would lack all limitation and delineation, it would not "exist"! This is a profound matter that we will not delve into.

Our good qualities are all related to our finite and limited nature. For example, a person possesses the faculty of thought, the faculty of sight, and the faculty of hearing. In order to have these good qualities, one needs to have brains, eyes, and ears.

What about Hashem? He is above all human comprehension. He is unlimited, unending, and infinite. When we speak of Hashem, we do not say He has "eyes" or "ears" or "brains." That which is considered a valuable asset for a person, Hashem has no need for.

Does this mean that Hashem cannot think, see, or hear?

7. *Meshech Chochmah, Bereishis* 1:1.

Surely not. For every good quality that we have, Hashem possesses it even more. Indeed, David HaMelech declares:

> *He Who implants the ear, will He not hear? If He forms the eye, will He not see?*[8]

We attribute every good quality to Hashem. He is "wise," He "sees," etc. If we would not attribute good qualities to Hashem, we would not be able to describe Him and relate to Him. This is because we can comprehend only that which is limited and definable.

I once spoke to a group of five-year-old boys and said to them that Hashem has no body. He has no eyes, no ears, etc. One boy jumped up and exclaimed, "It's true! He doesn't have anything!" I explained to the child that this is not so. It's not that Hashem doesn't have anything; He has *everything*. But He does not need eyes in order to see, or ears in order to hear.

Hashem surely has no physical form. Nevertheless, Jews relate to Him as a personality that possesses concrete qualities. We relate to Him as being very close and very real. For us, Hashem is not an abstract philosophical concept. He is a real personality. He hears us right now, He is here with us, He sees us. He is involved with our lives; He loves us.

Many people have trouble with this concept. They feel that by relating to Hashem in this way, by attributing to Him concrete qualities, they are minimizing Him. But just the opposite is true. As I explained when speaking to the children, Hashem has *everything*. We magnify and glorify Hashem by attributing to Him every positive quality that exists — the small ones and the great ones.

This is the point the *Meshech Chochmah* was making, as we mentioned before: "Just as Hashem's capability is unlimited and

8. *Tehillim* 94:9.

infinite, so is He capable of functioning in a finite and limited way." He can see us and hear us and have a relationship with us, despite our smallness. It is not true that Hashem's infinite greatness prevents Him from involvement with that which is small and finite. That would go against the basic principles of faith.

Life Is Different When Hashem Is a Reality

The *Mesillas Yesharim* writes (Chapter 19) that when we pray, we should know that Hashem is with us and hears us. It is like a person speaking to his friend.

A person should know that Hashem hears him and loves him just like he knows that his parents love him, or that he loves his children. It should be just as clear and real to him. Hashem is a very concrete and real personality. He is close to us, and loved by us.

Hashem possesses every positive quality to an unlimited degree. He sees *all.* He loves us *unlimitedly*. Someone who does not live with this awareness is missing an important facet of his Judaism. Jews are always partners with *HaKadosh Baruch Hu*. They have a relationship with Him and work together with Him. For instance, *Chazal* say:

> Whoever prays... and says "*Vayechulu*" is considered as if he became a partner with *HaKadosh Baruch Hu* in the creation of the world.[9]

We relate to Hashem as *Avinu Malkeinu*, our Father and our King. It is hard for us to understand what a king is because we never met one. But everyone knows what a father is. In a child's eyes, his father is someone who is always there for him. When the child goes to sleep and is lost in his dreams, his father is

9. *Shabbos* 119b.

awake and takes care of him. He is a very powerful "friend" and benefactor.

We should relate to Hashem the same way, as if He were a real live person. Hashem is very kind, very caring, very strong and capable, very involved with us, and very interested in us. We should relate to Him as a personality who has all these qualities.

If we don't relate to Him in this way, what we say in *Shemoneh Esrei* makes no sense!

There is no way we can comprehend what Hashem really is. We do not even think about it. We just know that He exists, and then describe how He relates to us. We say, so to speak: "I have a rich uncle, and he is in control of the whole system. Whatever I need, he takes care of. His resources are literally endless! Who is he? Hashem!"

When a person davens the *Shemoneh Esrei,* he is speaking to Hashem Himself. He is speaking to a Being Whose true nature he understands absolutely nothing about. Yet, just as Hashem is boundless and inscrutable, He is also capable of everything. He relates to us, He hears us, He loves us. There are no limits on what He can do. He is close to us, and He is enormously full of kindness!

We view it as a positive quality for a person to allow others to become close to him. Hashem, too, possesses this positive quality, and He wants us to relate to Him in this way.

For us, Hashem is like a good and benevolent friend. This principle is found throughout the Torah. We have no friend like Him. Our father may give us a house, but Hashem gives us our spouse: "*A house and wealth is inherited from fathers. But from Hashem comes a wise woman.*"[10] Hashem gave us our parents, He gives us life, He gives us health. He gives us tremendous gifts. Health is a gift. The faculty of sight is a gift. These gifts are

10. *Mishlei* 19:14.

from Hashem. His care and involvement with us is absolutely astounding.

If we would start to think this way we would be almost beside ourselves with excitement. We never imagined we have a Friend like this, Who gives us such large gifts. His kindness, benevolence and love for us are overwhelmingly powerful. He is a very concrete personality. This is Hashem. Although we have absolutely no comprehension of His true, unbounded nature, we can see very clearly the way in which He relates to us. We are literally surrounded by His gifts of love.

Many people mistakenly view Hashem's relationship with us as an abstract philosophical concept, since Hashem's true nature cannot be defined in human terms. But this is not the way. A person must get into the habit of living with Hashem.

Rabbi Uri Zohar, a renowned Israeli comedian who returned to Torah, recounts that when he took leave of his friends they asked him to tell them a last joke. He told them the following joke: Two religious young men were riding a motorcycle. A policeman noticed them and decided he would catch them violating a traffic law. They rode on and on, with the cop following right behind them, but they did not do anything wrong. He finally stopped them and asked, "How is it that you managed not to break a single traffic law the whole time?"

They answered, "It's simple. Hashem is with us."

"Aha!" the cop exclaimed. "Now I've caught you! You've got three riders on a motorcycle!"

That is how a Jew lives. Hashem is constantly with us. *Chazal* say:

> A man and wife… if they are meritorious, the Shechinah is among them.[11]

11. *Sotah* 17a.

Hashem in His infinite greatness is capable of relating to us in all different ways. He chooses to relate to us as a man relates to his friend. This means that He chooses to "lower Himself," as it says, "*He lowers [His eyes] to look into the Heavens and the earth.*"[12] At the same time, He remains Hashem in all His unbounded and inscrutable greatness. This is *emunah*.

12. *Tehillim* 113:6.

"האלקים עשה את האדם ישר והמה בקשו חשבונות רבים"

3

How to Attain Simple Faith

"Yisrael Was a Child, and I Loved Him"

WHAT IS THE PURPOSE of infancy and childhood? Adam HaRishon was not created as a baby. He opened his eyes for the first time as a fully developed adult. Yet, the rest of us have to grow up. For what purpose did Hashem create the slow, gradual development stages that we go through from infancy to adulthood?

When a child is about two years old, we start to teach him simple *pesukim* such as *Torah tzivah lanu Moshe* and *Shema Yisrael.* When he is about five and he can understand a little more, we start to teach him *Chumash.* Little by little, as the years go by, he gains more knowledge and understanding. Why shouldn't a person be born with a fully developed intellect? Then we could offer him a mature understanding of Judaism right from the beginning.

It seems to me that a child's understanding of Judaism is the true understanding of Judaism. When we are forty, fifty, sixty, or seventy, the extent to which we view things with the simplicity of a child is the extent to which we have a proper understanding of Judaism. In fact, the wiser we become, the more likely we are to get confused. We are liable to lose the simple, fresh approach which a child takes to the world, Hashem, and Torah — thereby missing the true meaning of Judaism.

This does not mean that only a child can understand Judaism. Surely an adult can, too, but only if he has the quality of *"Yisrael was a child, and I loved him."*[1] In other words, he needs to maintain the freshness and simplicity of a child.

Just One Word Missing

In our times, we lack clarity regarding some of the basics of Judaism. The following anecdote illustrates this point. I knew a distinguished rosh yeshivah whose ability to lecture in English was quite impressive. He had an accurate translation for every word and an apt definition for every term. People loved to hear him speak.

His son told me that after one of his father's lectures, a man came up and said, "Rabbi, I understood every word you said. I really enjoyed your lecture. There was just one word that I didn't understand, one word you forgot to translate: '*Hashem*.' Aside from that, I understood everything!"

There are many people nowadays who "understand everything." The only word they are missing is "*Hashem*." In earlier times, there only was one word: "*Hashem*." There was nothing else. Now, there are many things.

Today, *baruch Hashem,* there is a great amount of Torah learning. There are many yeshivos and kollelim where people learn uninterruptedly and with depth of understanding. Similarly, mitzvah observance is very careful and meticulous. What is lacking today is simplicity. The simple, clear awareness that Hashem exists and is here with us. This is what we lack most.

How did we come to lose something so simple and obvious?

Scientific Proof

People have a tendency to perceive science and *emunah* as being in conflict with each other. This perception is not as prevalent now as it once was, but it

1. *Hoshea* 11:1.

is still dominant in the world at large. Although today there are doctors and scientists who are Torah-observant Jews, even *talmidei chachamim*, they are the exception rather than the rule. Let's say we hear of Dr. Joseph Goldbergstein, famous professor in the field of optical neurology. How do we picture him in our minds? If we would manage to get an appointment with the doctor and find a man with a beard and *peyos* sitting behind the desk, we would probably be a little surprised.

What exactly is the contradiction between science and *emunah*? Why do we assume that just because someone is a leader in the field of medical science, he probably is not pious and mitzvah observant? Really, the opposite should be true. One can recognize the world's Creator from the structure of a human cell, or from studying the galaxies. Why do we feel that science and *emunah* do not get along? How can it be that science, which is devoted to observing the wonders of the universe, does not readily accept the existence of the world's Creator?

The answer lies in the concept known as "scientific proof." What is "scientific proof"? It is proof based on data discernable by the tools of science. Researchers can examine only data that comes from microscopes, telescopes, radar, etc. By use of such tools they determine what is true and what is not; what is and what isn't. Hashem cannot be observed by means of such tools. Therefore, from a scientific standpoint, Hashem does not exist.

There is a piquant illustration that makes this point clear. A scientist is performing an experiment to determine whether a fish exists whose diameter is half a millimeter. He takes an appropriate net and goes searching throughout the world. He begins his search in Antarctica. He checks the Indian Ocean. He checks the Atlantic Ocean. He takes samples from every body of water in the world, examines them carefully, and does not find such a fish. Has he proven that it does not exist? No, this is not a conclusive proof. It is possible that his search was not comprehensive enough. If he would search more, perhaps he would find his fish. Yet, he has raised doubts as to its existence. We may speculate that there indeed is no such fish.

Now, let us imagine for a moment that it is impossible to make a net whose holes are smaller than a millimeter because water will not pass through the holes. The laws of physics dictate that such a net cannot be constructed. So the scientist takes the finest net possible, with holes of exactly one millimeter, and goes searching for the half-millimeter fish. And he doesn't find it. Has he raised doubts as to the fish's existence? We would not think so. This scientist lacked tools that were appropriate to the experiment he sought to perform, so it is no surprise the results were negative.

Nonetheless, according to the ways of science, this is enough proof that a half-millimeter fish does not exist. Science accepts data only from the tools it recognizes, however limited their capabilities may be, and on that basis determines what exists and what doesn't. Since the tools of science cannot detect the existence of such a fish, as far as science is concerned, the fish does not exist.

The point of this illustration is to show that "scientific proof" is incapable of seeing beyond its own limitations, even though many things are clearly beyond its scope.

Actually, we all do the same thing as the above scientist. It is our nature to ascertain reality using the tools that are at our disposal. Once, when I was five years old, my father sent me to shul to look for one of my brothers. I entered the shul and looked over the tables and under the tables and everywhere possible. In the end I came back home with a definitive answer: he is not in shul! On what basis did I come to this conclusion? What I saw with my own eyes, of course.

Everyone determines thousands upon thousands of facts every day based on what he sees. We are naturally inclined to believe that whatever our eyes see, exists. And whatever they don't see, does not exist.

This is a mistake because there are plenty of real things that we cannot see with our eyes. Let's consider sound waves, for example, which are not visible. If we would be silly enough to judge only on the basis of what we see, when we observe a person talking on the telephone we would regard him as mentally deranged. If we determine reality only on the basis of what is visually perceptible, we are brought to the conclusion that sound waves do not exist.

So it is with the existence of Hashem. Science says, "I looked for Hashem by radar and I did not find Him. I looked for Hashem by telescope and I did not find Him. I went into the lab, split an atom into protons and neutrons and electrons, and I did not find Hashem there, either. I am forced to the scientific conclusion that He does not exist."

Science will never find Hashem because He cannot be detected by radar, tracked by a telescope or dissected in a laboratory. Yet, people get carried away with the idea of "scientific proof." That is why they come to see science and *emunah* as being in conflict with each other. This erroneous attitude is damaging to simple, clear *emunah*.

Just Be a Mensch

There are "tools" by which we can perceive Hashem. All we have to do is utilize the basic human understanding which we all have, and take a realistic look at the wonders of the world around us. When we look at a magnificent, starry sky, we know that Hashem exists. When we observe a grain of sand, we cannot help but recognize the Divine wisdom that created it. The atoms in one grain of sand contain enough energy to blow up the whole world. Who put all that energy into it?

Or, we can look within at the human body. The human eye has 120 million rod cells, and a brain has a trillion support cells. If we are honest with ourselves we must come to the conclusion that such a thing could not have sprung into existence by itself.

Man must have a Creator. The tools of human understanding perceive Hashem very clearly. It is as simple as two and two makes four.

It is just a matter of being realistic. When we see a CD player, we know we are looking at a sophisticated instrument. Yet, one leg of the smallest ant crawling on the sidewalk is more sophisticated than any CD player. It is more sophisticated than the most advanced computer in the world. Another example: a child's brain contains 100 billion neurons (brain cells). Isn't this an impressive capacity? Where did it come from?

The innate tools possessed by every human being perceive clearly that Hashem created the world we see. But let us make sure we know what a "human being" is.

I once met a granddaughter of the Chofetz Chaim, his son's daughter. This woman arrived in Eretz Yisrael from Russia. I joined Rabbi Hillel Zaks, a leading rosh yeshivah and grandson of the Chofetz Chaim, who was going to greet his cousin in the Beer Sheva absorption center.

She recounted that at the age of sixteen she ran away from home, having fallen victim to the *haskalah* which was extremely dominant at that time. When she came home to visit her grandfather the Chofetz Chaim, she said to him: "Zeidy, why do you sit in the darkness? Go out into the illuminated world!" (In her own words: "*Zeide, far vos zitz du in di finsternisht? Gey arois tzu dem lichtige velt*!")

This took place while the First World War was raging. In those days, primitive airplanes were first employed in battle. The pilot would lob explosives from the open cockpit onto the enemy below. The Chofetz Chaim said to her: "You know those planes? They will reach the moon. You know those bombs? A day will come when they will make bombs that can blow up the whole world. That is what *they* make. But *we* make human beings — *mir machen menschen*." This is what the Chofetz Chaim said, almost a century ago.

There is something called a *mensch*, a human being. A human being is one who uses his tools of human understanding. He perceives the truth simply and realistically. A human being is one who "goes in the straight way, as God made him."[2]

A child starts out life with limited intellect. What is the reason for this? We adults are "smart" and "sophisticated." We use our eyes and other senses to determine reality for ourselves. This makes it hard for us to arrive at the truth since we cannot see Hashem with our eyes — and the outside world has convinced us not to believe what we cannot see. To perceive Hashem, we need to employ the tools of human understanding.

But a child does not have these problems. When we tell him in utter simplicity that Hashem created the world, he accepts it as a fact. How could it be otherwise? Being "childlike" means to throw off the big lie that the outside world has sold us, to believe only what our senses tell us. If we would do this we would perceive Hashem without any difficulty at all, and easily attain simple, clear *emunah*.

What It Means to Be Human

What qualities make us human? Some think that the ability to maneuver a ball down a court and throw it deftly through a hoop makes a person worthwhile. Others are convinced that life has no meaning without listening to music. Many see the amassing of wealth as man's goal in life.

There are those who are more high minded and regard doing acts of *chesed* as the mark of humanity. If you are a volunteer ambulance-driver and you rushed to an accident and saved someone's life, you are a *mensch*. Otherwise, you haven't done very much with yourself.

What qualities truly make us human? Shlomo HaMelech

2. See *Rambam, Mishneh Torah, Hilchos Shemittah V'Yovel* 13:13.

summed it up in one pithy sentence: "*God is in Heaven and you are on earth.*"[3] In other words, there is a vast distance separating God from man. A human being is one who can bridge that distance, and connect to God. This is the only valid definition of a human being.

Someone can devote his life to doing countless acts of *chesed* and indeed this is very laudable. But as long as he has not developed a connection with his Creator, he has not expressed his humanity. He has not truly become a *mensch*. Doing *chesed* can be very gratifying. It is surely a very lofty form of self-gratification, but when taken on its own, it is no more than that. In a certain sense, he is just following his nature — some people enjoy other things, and this person enjoys doing *chesed*. Such *chesed* is not what makes a human being special.

A human being is a creature who forms a relationship with Hashem. This relationship is expressed through speech. A human being is characterized by the faculty of speech. (In classic sources, a human is called a *baal chai medaber*, "an animate being that speaks.") A human speaks in Torah and *tefillah*, thus communicating with Hashem.

What does it mean to have a relationship with Hashem?

The following allegory illustrates the point. Someone is sitting at one end of a room and his friend is sitting at the other end. A curtain in the middle of the room separates them; they cannot see each other. When one speaks to the other, he knows that the other hears him. And he knows that the other is aware that he knows this. These two people are communicating with each other and relating to one another.

This is the way a person communicates with Hashem and relates to Him. The person says, "Hashem, You are so wonderful. You are so great." The person knows that Hashem hears him, for

3. *Koheles* 5:1.

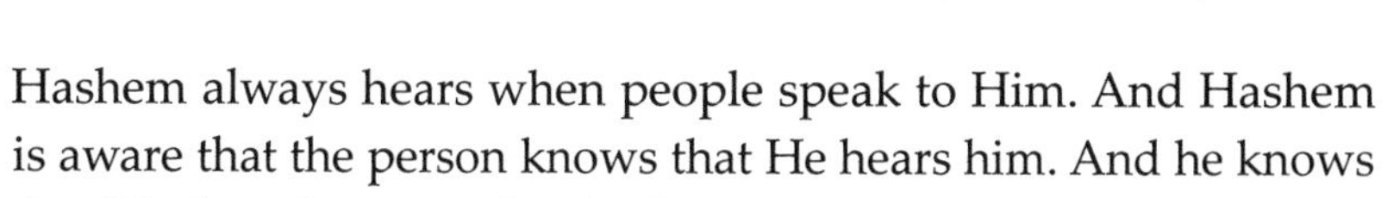

Hashem always hears when people speak to Him. And Hashem is aware that the person knows that He hears him. And he knows that Hashem is aware that he knows that Hashem hears him. In this way communication is formed between them, and the person thereby actualizes his humanity. He becomes a *mensch.*

This is the simple definition of a human being. We have not yet defined a Jew! Prayer, which is communicating with God and relating to Him, is not something unique to Jews.

Hashem Speaks in Worlds

Recognizing that the world has a Creator leads us to the understanding that His capabilities are unlimited. He made *everything.* And, as we explained in Chapter 2, Hashem has a special relationship of love with the Jewish people. Therefore, He bestows His unlimited *chesed* in its entirety upon each and every Jew. This is something a human being cannot do for his loved ones, no matter how much he might want to. When a father brings home a cake, he has to divide it between all his children; each one receives just a small piece.

But Hashem is unlimited. Everything about Him is infinite and eternal. So when He gives His children something, He doesn't have to divide it up — He gives it all. He gives all the *chesed* to each and every Jew. Hashem has no lack of goodness! He will not run out after having given unlimitedly to the first person, or after having so given to the second…

The Gemara (*Sanhedrin* 100a) teaches:

> It is said in Eretz Yisrael, in the name of Rava bar Mari: "In the future, *HaKadosh Baruch Hu* will give 310 worlds to each and every tzaddik, as it says, '*I bequeath 310 (יש) to those who love Me, and fill their treasure-houses.*[4]'"

4. *Mishlei* 8:21.

This requires some explanation. How did our Sages know that the verse refers to 310 *worlds?* Where are worlds mentioned in the verse? Perhaps it refers to 310 rivers of balsam oil, or some other good thing?

The following allegory illustrates the answer. A person walks into a store in the USA and asks, "How much does this item over here cost?"

The salesman says, "Twenty, sir."

The person is confused: "Twenty what?"

But what the salesman meant is clear: twenty dollars! There's no reason for him to say it straight out. In the United States, prices are given in dollars. In England they are given in pounds, and in Israel, in shekels.

So it is with our subject. The verse quoted above is speaking of *HaKadosh Baruch Hu,* Creator of all the worlds. Of course the verse refers to worlds, because *HaKadosh Baruch Hu* speaks in these terms. *HaKadosh Baruch Hu* deals in worlds. So when He wishes to reward the tzaddikim, He gives them entire worlds, with all the eternity this implies.

When a Jew has a true relationship with *HaKadosh Baruch Hu,* he receives unlimited *chesed.* He receives "worlds" of *chesed.*

What It Means to Be a Wife

We have spoken a lot about having a relationship with Hashem. But does this make sense? How can we, who are so puny, have a relationship of love with Hashem, Who is so infinitely great?

The following parable illustrates the point. There is a tremendously powerful and wealthy man named Mr. Grossreich. He chooses to marry the daughter of poor little Mr. Kleinershtub. Thus, young Miss Kleinershtub approaches her marriage penniless. Her assets are zero. She is a "nothing." But the moment her bridegroom puts the ring on her finger, she is as wealthy as he! From now on they both benefit equally from all his billions.

As a child I was puzzled by the teaching of *Chazal* that

Esther sent an order to Mordechai to see to it that all the barbershops and bathhouses in the capital city of Shushan would be closed. "Where did she get such power?" I wondered. The answer is very simple. The moment she had a relationship with King Achashveirosh, the moment she became his wife, she acquired reign over all the countries in her husband's kingdom.

Similarly, Jews have a close relationship with Hashem. We are the people He chose to be His. In many verses in *Shir HaShirim*, Hashem refers to *Klal Yisrael* as *rayasi*, "My beloved wife." If we are "married" to Hashem, so to speak, then we have everything! Such is the nature of the relationship.

We can see this from our very name. When a woman marries, she takes on her husband's family name. When indigent Miss Kleinershtub married the billionaire she became Mrs. Grossreich. What about us?

In Hebrew, a Jew is called יהודי. This interesting name is actually the four letters of Hashem's Name, with an added ד. The ד stands for דל, "poor and impoverished." In other words, a Jew's name is "Mrs. Hashem." We belong to Hashem.

Our generation is so sophisticated and so highly developed that we tend to lose our childlike simplicity. We overlook some of the basics of Judaism we were taught in our early *chinuch*. If we will just grab hold of simple *emunah*, and utilize the tools of human understanding, a wondrous relationship with Hashem is ours for the having — to believe with perfect *emunah* and experience *deveikus* all the days of our lives.

4

When Emunah Penetrates the Heart

Can You Check Your Emunah?

THE SUBJECT OF *EMUNAH* and *bitachon* is a very basic one. At the same time, it is very deep. The Ramchal wrote:

> The better that something is known and the more obviously it is true, the more frequently it is ignored and largely forgotten.[1]

When something is really basic, it tends to escape our attention. Let us focus on a few points that will help us with the practical side of this very basic subject: *emunah* and *bitachon*.

Emunah expresses itself in various ways, among them *yirah, ahavah,* and *tefillah.* The most practical expression of *emunah* is in *tefillah.* If a person knows that God exists, he will speak to Him and turn to Him when he needs something.

We all know and believe that Hashem exists. No one just "goes through the motions" of believing. If someone does not actually believe in his heart, there is no question that he will stop being a Torah-observant Jew. He might not throw off his *yarmulke* right away. It might even take a year or two for his

1. *Mesillas Yesharim,* Introduction.

behavior to visibly deteriorate, but in the end, someone who does not believe will go all the way down. If a Jew keeps Shabbos and learns Torah, it is only because somewhere deep within his subconscious he knows that Hashem exists.

The only question is: How strong is our *emunah*? Is it powerful and clear, or is it weak and sketchy? The main ways to check the strength of our deep-down *emunah* are through *tefillah* and *bitachon*.

Through *tefillah,* we can check our *emunah* by seeing what kind of *kavanah* we have. This point requires some explanation; we will discuss it later.

Through *bitachon,* we can check our *emunah* by seeing how we react in real-life situations. Let me give you an example. I know a man, we will call him Yossi Himmelberg, who frequently travels abroad. His friends back in Israel often ask him to pick up a few small electronic items and other things that would be more expensive in Israel.

The problem is: What happens when he lands in Israel? What he's doing is completely legal — by law, a person can bring in a certain amount of electronic items without paying tax. But who knows what kind of official will be checking at the customs authority? He will have to walk past customs while carrying his two bulging suitcases. Chances are he will be called over for an inspection and the customs official could very well be a stickler. Without receipts, how can he prove the cost of each item? It will look like he's trying to smuggle goods through customs in order to sell them, and he could face an enormous fine!

So he spends eight to ten hours on the flight back to Israel working on his *emunah* and *bitachon*. He repeats to himself over and over that everything is directed by Heaven; no human being can control what will happen to him. If Hashem wants him to succeed, he will. After all, he is just trying to do a little *chesed* for a couple friends and neighbors. It is not for his personal use. So he calms himself with *emunah, emunah, emunah...*

Now he is off the plane. He picks up his luggage and walks down the corridor, through the customs area. He feels very uncomfortable and notices that his hands are shaking. Why? What happened to all the *emunah* that he worked on the whole flight? Everything looked fine until it was tested out in real life.

Here is another example: Let's say you are driving down the highway and a police car signals to you to pull over. The officer gets out of his car and slowly walks toward you. How do you feel? You know he will not send you to Siberia. The worst thing he can do is give you a fine. So why do you have such an uncomfortable feeling? What are you afraid of?

The answer is that we all know Hashem exists, but knowledge alone is not enough for healthy *emunah*. It is crucial that Hashem become for us a real personality. We should feel that He is alive and real, that He is actually here with us right now, like the other real, tangible things that make up our world. He is called "the living God" because we are meant to relate to Him as a real, live personality.

This point is very important for proper *tefillah*. People talk a lot about having *kavanah* in *tefillah*. What is *kavanah*, really? We can understand the meaning of *kavanah* by comparing it to situations in real life.

Sometimes we need to ask a friend for a favor. All of us have been in this kind of situation. We concentrate on the fact that our friend has a warm place in his heart for us, and we make our request.

During the time that I merited serving as a *meshulach* for various Torah institutions, I often faced situations like this. I would pay visits to wealthy Jews and ask for their support. Whenever I met with a potential donor and told him about the specific institution I was fundraising for, on what was I concentrating? Not only was I thinking about what I needed, I was also focusing on the man whom I was speaking to. I would focus on who he is, on his personality and on his good character traits.

I would think to myself: Here I am, sitting in front of a man who can help me with what I need, i.e., funding for the project. My task right now is to find the right way to speak to him and enlist his support.

Now let us apply this to *kavanah* in *tefillah*. Someone has a sick child at home. He cries out to Hashem: *Refa'einu Hashem v'neirafei!* Alternatively, a person is in a tough financial situation. He begs Hashem: *Bareich aleinu Hashem Elokeinu es ha-shanah ha-zos!* What is he focusing on during those moments?

It is likely that he is focusing solely on the sickness or the financial difficulty. Unlike the situations from real life that we just mentioned, here the person in need is not really thinking about to Whom he is speaking. He is not truly communicating with Hashem and relating to Him. All his *kavanah* could be expressed in the words, "I need." For him, a little *kavanah* means, "I kind of need it." A lot of *kavanah* means, "I need it badly!" When he intensifies his *kavanah,* he is really just intensifying his focus on what he needs.

Unfortunately, a person could daven the entire *Shemoneh Esrei* this way. In *Atah chonen l'adam da'as,* he thinks: "I really need understanding in Torah." When he says, *Hashiveinu Avinu l'Sorasecha,* he thinks: "And I need to do *teshuvah*." When he gets to *Selach lanu,* he thinks: "I must get forgiveness." And so forth. All the way through he is focusing on himself and his needs, rather than on Who he is addressing. This is not communication. This is not speaking with Hashem.

True *kavanah* in *tefillah* is to know that you are speaking to the living God. He is alive and real, and He is right in front of you. All the money is His. All the healing is His. He can do literally everything. Just talk to Him, cry to Him, plead with Him — and He will give you! When davening, focus completely on Him. A little *kavanah* goes like this: "Hashem, You are the 'Healer of all flesh.' You have six billion people in Your world. Please, Hashem, can't You give a little healing to me, too?" A lot of *kavanah* goes like this: "Hashem, I am not going to leave You alone. I love You so much, and You love me so much. You are my God. So please, give me healing!"

The main thing is to focus on Whom you are communicating with. *Kavanah* is focusing on Hashem as a real, live personality Who is right there in front of you. The more a person strengthens this awareness, the more he strengthens his *kavanah* in *tefillah*. And when a person has this kind of *kavanah*, he is expressing his deep-down *emunah*.

Yeridas HaDoros

In my opinion, the sense of Hashem as a real personality is what our generation lacks more than anything. We have all heard of the concept of *yeridas ha-doros*. Each generation is on a lower spiritual plane than the one that preceded it. On the other hand, once there were *amei ha'aretz* who really didn't know any Torah — much less than we do — yet they were millions of *madreigos* higher than us. In what way were they higher than us? Some of them did not even know how to read. What did they have that we don't?

The answer is that their greatness lay in their *emunah*. For Jews of former generations, Hashem was as real as their next-door neighbor. Those of us who live in apartment buildings understand how important it is not to cause grief to our neighbors. We meet them every day so we do our best not to make noise late at night, not to hang out our laundry to dry where it bothers them, etc. Similarly, Hashem is real and alive. He is even closer than our next-door neighbor. He knows, feels and even speaks, but in His own special language.

This is what the simple, uneducated Jew of olden times was like. The generations declined, and with them declined our sense of Hashem as a real personality.

The goal in *emunah* is to experience Hashem as something real and concrete. We have difficulty with this because we cannot perceive Hashem with our eyes and ears the same way we perceive our neighbor. However, as we said in Chapter 2, an important aspect of Hashem's greatness is that He is able to show Himself in ways that we can comprehend. He is "wise," He is "mighty," He is "kind." He is a personality with qualities that we can relate to. And He is real — even more real than our neighbor!

This level of *emunah* is not so easy to achieve, as can be seen from the following teaching of *Chazal.* R. Yochanan ben Zakkai blessed his disciples before his death, and said:

> "May it be His will that you should fear Heaven the way you fear people."
>
> His disciples replied: "Should we fear Him only that much?"
>
> He answered them: "If only you would fear Him that much! You may know it is so, because when someone commits a sin, he thinks, 'I hope people don't see me...'"[2]

If Hashem is as real for us as our neighbor is, we have achieved a very high *madreigah.* This is what we are striving for when we work on *emunah.*

Why It Doesn't Work

We spoke before about Yossi Himmelberg and his fears of going through customs even after strengthening his *bitachon.* And we learned from R. Yochanan ben Zakkai that tangible *emunah* is indeed a very high level. Why is this so? Why is it so hard to achieve this?

Actually, we could ask the same question about all of Judaism's three foundations. As we know, there are three *Avos*: Avraham, Yitzchak and Yaakov. They embody the three foundations of Judaism. Avraham is *ahavah,* Yitzchak is *yirah,* and Yaakov is truth and *emunah.*

2. *Berachos* 28b.

First, let us speak about *yirah*. Imagine a man leaning on the counter of a snack bar, buying himself a soft drink. A patient breaks out of the mental institution across the street, and it is clear that he is totally mad. He runs forward and shrieks: "Don't drink, it's poison!" At that moment the men in white coats catch him and carry him back inside.

Does the man at the snack bar have any reason to think his cola is poisoned? No. But for some reason he suddenly doesn't feel like drinking. If a person has a doubt — even one in a million — that his drink has been poisoned, he won't touch it.

Yet when it comes to the existence of *Gehinnom*'s punishments, there isn't even any doubt. We all believe in the World to Come. There is *Gan Eden* and there is *Gehinnom;* we all know it. The *Ba'alei Mussar* say that if a person refrains from food when there is a tiny chance of poison, surely he should refrain from sin if he thinks there is a tiny chance that the Torah's punishments will come true. And all the more if he has full faith!

In light of this, where is our *yiras Shamayim*? Why is it so difficult to attain true *yirah*? We fear all sorts of things large and small, but for some reason, *Gehinnom* does not seem to be one of them. Certainly, we strive to the utmost to stay far from *aveiros*. This goes without question. But let's say a person feels he is on the verge of speaking a little *lashon hara*. Does he start trembling and lose his appetite in fear of the great punishment he is about to incur? If not, he lacks tangible *yirah*.

The same applies to *ahavah*. Every day we recite the blessings of *pokeach ivrim, malbish arumim, matir asurim,* etc. This is because without Hashem, a person would be blind, lacking clothing, and paralyzed. *Roka ha'aretz al ha-mayim* — without Hashem, a person would be floating aimlessly in space. *She'asah li kol tzorki* — thanks to Hashem, he has a spouse, children, and all good things. *Ozeir Yisrael b'gvurah* — Hashem made him a Jew. *Oteir Yisrael b'sifarah* — Hashem made him honored. *Ha-*

Nosein la-ya'eif koach — without Hashem, he would still be sleeping, unable to wake up.

After realizing all that Hashem did for him this morning, why doesn't a person feel an overwhelming love for Him? If a person went to sleep with a slight suspicion that he might not be able to see or move the next morning and then woke up in the morning healthy and sound, he surely would be bursting with love and gratitude to Hashem. His love would be tangible.

And the same applies to *emunah*. When Yossi Himmelberg walks through customs, his hands tremble and he feels very uncomfortable. But what if he would know that the head of customs is his uncle, who can help him out by explaining to the inspectors that he is just bringing in a few innocent little items for his friends? He would feel completely different.

Here is another illustration: A man with an incurable illness is lying in the hospital. The doctors just explained to him that there is absolutely nothing they can do for him, and that he has two weeks and a day to live. Suddenly, a nurse enters and announces that Dr. Vunderovitch, the famed medical specialist from Helsinki, has just arrived at the hospital. He happens to be an expert in the same exact disease this man is suffering from, and has a treatment that offers a thirty percent chance of success. Just hearing such news produces noticeable relief. Now he feels different.

Every day we say in *Shacharis* that Hashem is *Borei refuos*. The Ramban says that the word *bri'ah* means creation that is *yeish mei'ayin*: something that is created out of nothing. Thus, *Borei refuos* means that Hashem creates cures that did not exist before at all. So even if the doctor says all is lost, Hashem can create a completely new cure that did not exist until today. Just knowing this should give a person the inner strength not to treat the doctor's pronouncements as if they were absolute.

All this being so, why don't we feel a burning love for Hashem? Why don't we tremble in fear of Him? Why doesn't our faith in Him make us feel calm in threatening situations?

Some people think this proves we don't really believe.

To me, it is clear as day that this is not so! We all believe in the Torah and in Hashem. As we explained before, someone who doesn't have deep-down faith in Hashem and His Torah will not continue living as a Torah-observant Jew. If so, there is no question that we all have faith. But why don't we feel the *ahavah, yirah,* and *bitachon* that faith in Hashem should produce?

Out of Our Realm

Man, like everything else that Hashem created, has certain inherent rules. We could compare this to a machine. Every machine works in a certain way, and it won't work if you ignore the rules. Your camera will not take a picture if there is total darkness. Combustion will not occur in your car engine if you put water in the tank instead of gasoline. It just doesn't work that way. Man, too, has a certain way in which he works.

Man is composed of two parts: intellect and heart. The intellect acquires knowledge about how a person should live his life. This knowledge, however, is external to a person's being. The heart comprises that which is absorbed into his being and becomes part of his natural feelings. This is what actually motivates a person. Early Torah sources call these two aspects *ohr makif* and *ohr penimi.*

I will give an example. I saw the following marvelous quote from Rav Simchah Zissel Ziv *zt"l*, the Alter of Kelm, posted on the bulletin board in a certain *beis midrash*: "It would be worthwhile to be born, and to live seventy years, just to say *baruch Hu u'varuch Shemo* one time. And [saying] a thousand *baruch Hu u'varuch Shemo*s does not reach the reward for saying one *amen.* And [saying] a thousand *amens* does not reach the reward for

one *amen yehei shemei rabba.* And [saying] a thousand *amen yehei shemei rabbas* does not reach the reward for [learning] one word of Torah." This was hanging on the wall at the entrance to the *beis midrash.*

If a man who studies Torah would read this quote, he surely would comprehend its message and recognize its truth. What practical conclusion should he come to? That he should promptly enter the *beis midrash,* start learning, and not stop for anything. He should not miss a moment of Torah learning. What about all the important things he has to do? What about earning a livelihood? *Na'ar hayisi v'gam zakanti v'lo ra'isi tzaddik ne'ezav.* No one ever died of starvation from staying in the *beis midrash.*

His intellect tells him that every word of Torah is worth the whole world. But this knowledge is external to him. Only a very small percentage of it has become part of his heart and being. Therefore, if someone will come up to him while he is still at the bulletin board, and tell him that he could make a thousand dollars right now if he will just travel to city such and such, he will immediately leave the *beis midrash* and hurry off to get the money. This is despite his knowledge that for one word of Torah, a person merits 310 worlds. What is a thousand dollars compared to 310 entire worlds?

When it comes to having understanding of the value of Torah learning, i.e., *ohr makif,* we can have it in unlimited amounts. But we can have *ohr penimi* only in an amount corresponding to our own level of devotion to Torah learning. The great tzaddikim of the past such as Moshe Rabbeinu, the Tannaim, the Amoraim, and the Rishonim had an *ohr makif* that was also *ohr penimi.* That which they understood to be true became a part of their very lives.

And this is indeed the goal: that our intellectual understanding should become transformed into a natural feeling which is a part of our selves. But until a person reaches this level, he will

not naturally fear *Gehinnom* or love Hashem, or feel calm in threatening situations.

By nature, man's heart does not react to things that are far away and outside his realm. If a person is in Philadelphia he is not terrified when a bomb goes off in Afghanistan, nor is he shaken up when an earthquake strikes Indonesia. He might view these events as significant and concerning, he might sympathize with the victims, but by nature he will not fear and tremble from something that is beyond his realm. That is how man works.

The fire of *Gehinnom* is not in this world. It is not a furnace that we can go and see. It is in a different world, far from our realm. If a person thought there was a slight chance that someone might come and throw him into a boiling cauldron in a local factory if he speaks *lashon hara,* he surely would guard his tongue very well. But the angel who takes people and throws them into the fire of *Gehinnom* after their death is well beyond his realm.

Therefore, we may conclude that our lack of *yirah, ahavah,* and *emunah* has nothing to do with a lack of belief on our part. There is no question that we believe in Hashem. But Hashem's presence in the world is not a physical entity that we can perceive with our senses. Naturally speaking, it is beyond our realm — unless we work on making Hashem real.

There are fine, respectable Jews who live eighty years and more, every morning taking a siddur in hand and reciting *Baruch Atah Hashem Elokeinu Melech HaOlam,* but without feeling even once that Hashem is a real, perceptible reality. They never experience Hashem as an actual personality that they are standing before and speaking to, although they "daven" three times a day. It does not even occur to them that there is a personality named "Hashem." Sadly enough, a Jew could easily go through life without ever having spoken with Hashem, felt love for Him, or had fear of Him. A whole lifetime, cut off from *HaKadosh Baruch Hu*!

Making It Real What can we do to bring Hashem into our everyday reality, enabling us to relate to Him as something tangible and real?

First of all, we must know that there are two parts to the Torah. The first part is the regular mitzvos that make up the framework of our lives. Davening three times a day, Shabbos, Rosh Hashanah, Yom Kippur, etc. These mitzvos are the program that Hashem set up for every Jew to involve him in *avodas Hashem.* We have a *Shulchan Aruch* which we all follow. It tells us that when we reach the *Shemoneh Esrei,* we should stand up, place our feet together, and close our eyes. This is Hashem's program for every Jew. It is a special *mussar* activity: to close our eyes for five minutes and say *Baruch Atah Hashem, Elokeinu Veilokei Avoseinu…*

But this alone is not enough. We need the second part of Torah. If a person wants to acquire *ahavah, yirah,* and *emunah,* if he wants to feel like a Jew should, remaining calm in threatening situations because he knows the Boss is with him and taking care of him, then he needs to work on attaining this.

You shall realize [it] today and impress [it] upon your heart.[3]

What is this familiar verse which forms part of the *Aleinu* prayer telling us? That even after a person knows something to be true; he still has to bring it into his heart. He has to work on it. For instance, when he says *Baruch Atah Hashem,* he should think about the meaning of what he is saying. *Baruch* is from the same root as *breichah,* "pool." *Baruch Atah Hashem* means that Hashem is like a pool of blessing that sustains everything in the world. From Hashem's great pool of blessing emanates everything: me, my eyes, the *beis midrash*, the air that I breathe… everything comes from Him, and He gives and gives.

3. *Devarim* 4:39.

And so a person repeats these words, *Baruch Atah Hashem,* over and over again during the course of the day, until *Baruch Atah Hashem* starts to come alive for him and become real. This brings Hashem into his realm and makes Hashem accessible to his senses. Hashem becomes integrated into his natural perception of the world. When Hashem becomes real for him, he immediately starts to fear Hashem, love Him, and rely on His protection.

This was an important aspect of Chassidus. The Chassidim would work on this tirelessly until Hashem became a concrete reality for them. They exerted themselves greatly to achieve this. Later, the Mussar Movement also devoted itself to working on this point, to a certain extent. The Alter of Kelm would learn the subject of *emunah* for six hours straight. He would do it in the way that R. Yisrael Salanter had taught him: he would close himself in a room and repeat *pesukim* about *emunah* over and over to himself with great concentration.

The Alter of Kelm recounted that once, after he had been studying the subject of *emunah* in this way, "He [R. Yisrael] said to me then… he joked with me and asked if Eliyahu HaNavi had appeared to me. I understood this as follows: since I had just learned a lot of *mussar* and worked on… strengthening *emunah,* that it should be alive to me… he was concerned that I would delude myself and start to think that I had reached exceptionally lofty levels. So he joked with me and asked if Eliyahu HaNavi had appeared to me."[4]

When I was a yeshivah boy, I too would do this, although not for six hours, and not every day. For instance, once on Erev Shavuos I went to a shul and sat alone for forty-five minutes and repeated the following verse over and over to myself: "*Hashem*

4. *Chochmah U'Mussar*, vol. 1, pp. 26–27.

descended upon Mount Sinai."[5] I repeated this verse hundreds of times until the idea of Hashem descending on Mount Sinai started to come alive for me. The Alter of Kelm did this over the course of years, every day for six hours!

There is a similar story about the Vilna Gaon. Once, he spent all night repeating over and over to himself a teaching of *Chazal* about the importance of not neglecting Torah learning: "*Oy lahem, la-briyos, mei-elbonah shel Torah* — Woe to them, to the people, due to [their] insult to the Torah."[6] The Vilna Gaon's neighbor, who was a working man, heard the Gaon's voice through his window and was so influenced that the next morning he abandoned his occupation and devoted his life to Torah learning.

This was the ABCs of Jews of old: They knew that "*You shall realize [it] today*" is not enough. The main thing is, "*and impress [it] upon your heart.*" We need to repeat to ourselves over and over again those things that we know to be true, until they penetrate our heart.

There were Chassidim who lived with a constant sense of Hashem's presence and felt real *yirah* and *ahavah.* This was the goal of Chassidus. R. Chaim Volozhiner describes: "I saw with my own eyes that this had become so prevalent in a certain region that most of their *batei midrash* had nothing but an abundant supply of *mussar* books. They did not even have a complete copy of the *Shas.*"[7] What were these Jews doing all day? They were working on *deveikus,* on being connected to Hashem, to the point that Hashem became alive for them. They spent so much time on it that they neglected study of Gemara and halachah, which R. Chaim Volozhiner rightly criticized, since

5. *Shemos* 19:20.

6. *Pirkei Avos* 6:2.

7. *Nefesh HaChaim* 4:1.

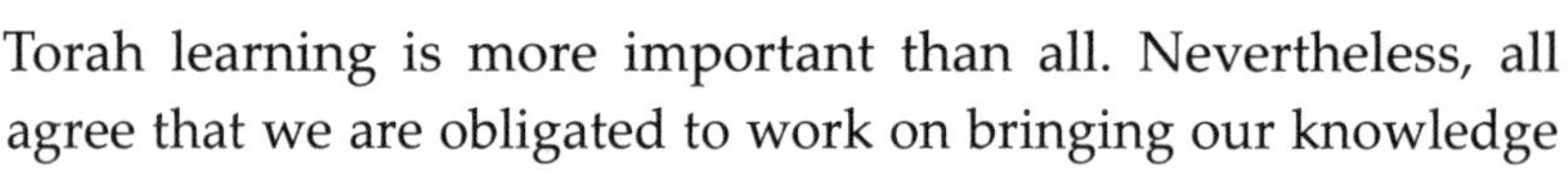

Torah learning is more important than all. Nevertheless, all agree that we are obligated to work on bringing our knowledge into our hearts.

Someone who works on this will, with Hashem's help, see with his own eyes the true meaning of *emunah, bitachon,* and *ahavas Hashem.*

"ואביא אתכם אלי"

5

And I Will Bring You to Me

When Hashem Himself Gets Involved

WE ALL KNOW THAT Hashem Himself came and took us out of Egypt. It says in the Haggadah:

> Not by means of an angel, and not by means of a seraph, and not by means of a messenger. Rather, it was the Holy One, Blessed is He, in His Glory, by Himself![1]

Indeed, Hashem Himself took us out, as it says: "*God brought them out of Egypt.*"[2] What brought Hashem to do it this way? At first Moshe went to Pharaoh and declared, "*This is what Hashem, the God of Israel has said: 'Release My people, [so that] they may celebrate a festival for Me in the desert.'*"[3] But it did not work. Pharaoh just enslaved the people more harshly, depriving them of straw. When Moshe complained about this, Hashem replied: "If you can't do it, then I will do it Myself — '*Now you will see what **I** shall do to Pharaoh.*'"[4] At that point, Hashem Himself went into action, so to speak.

1. *Haggadah shel Pesach.*
2. *Bemidbar* 23:22.
3. *Shemos* 5:1.
4. Ibid., 6:1.

How Do We Merit Hashem's Personal Involvement?

The Jewish people were also involved in bringing about their redemption — in two ways. The first was through their *emunah*. Moshe argued when standing at the burning bush, *"They will not believe me."*[5] Hashem replied that it would not be so — "They are believers and their forefathers were believers."[6] Indeed, the Torah testifies about them, *"The people believed."*[7]

The second way they helped to bring about their redemption was by their *ratzon*, their will and desire. Rashi tells us that only one-fifth of the Jewish people actually left Egypt. The rest died there during the plague of darkness.[8] What was the sin of those who died in Egypt? It was not idolatry, for among those who left Egypt there were also idolaters. Neither was it adultery, for none of the Jews were guilty of this.[9] Those who died were guilty of only one thing: They did not want to go out of Egypt. For this they were considered wicked, and they died during the plague of darkness.[10] The Jews who left Egypt were the ones who wanted to leave.

From this we learn that to merit Hashem's personal involvement in our lives, so that He will take us out of our own "Egypt," two conditions must be met: *emunah* and *ratzon*. Hashem will come and take us out of "Egypt" if we desire it and we believe it is possible. Our problem is that we do not always fulfill these two conditions.

What is leaving Egypt? It is leaving behind the depths of

5. Ibid., 4:1.
6. *Shabbos* 97a.
7. *Shemos* 4:31.
8. *Rashi, Shemos* 13:18.
9. *Rashi, Vayikra* 24:11.
10. *Rashi, Shemos* 10:22.

sin and impurity, and coming back to Hashem. This is actually the process of *teshuvah.* We may compare *teshuvah* to mending a torn garment. If a garment has a hole there are several ways to solve the problem. The simplest is to just take a needle and thread, and sew up the hole. A more thorough way is to take a piece of fabric and make a patch. Yet, this too is imperfect. The garment is likely to come out looking raggedy. It is better to cut the garment with scissors, make a new seam, and reshape the whole garment. If we leave the garment as is and focus only on mending the hole, the garment will not come out looking right. If we want it to be nice and presentable again, we need to reshape it.

So it is with *teshuvah.* We can patch up the weak areas. If we do not pray properly, we can work on our davening. If we do not learn enough, we can stop frittering our time on other matters. And so forth.

This is indeed a valid approach to *teshuvah*. But there is another approach: "Cut and reshape." This way everything comes out looking nice and presentable again. It is a new creation — *"A created people will praise God."*[11]

Yetzias Mitzrayim was not patching up a problem. It was a reshaping of the Jewish people. *Mitzrayim* is called *kur ha-barzel;*[12] a refinery that melts down and reshapes the Jewish people. This profound process was performed by Hashem Himself.

Those who did not want to leave Egypt were defined as "wicked," as we explained. What does it mean they were "wicked"? It means they did not want to change their current state. Leaving Egypt and becoming Hashem's people was a major change, and they did not want this.

We all face the same problem when it comes to our own

11. *Tehillim* 102:19.
12. *Devarim* 4:20.

personal *Yetzias Mitzrayim.* We do not want to change our personality, to become the different type of person called a *ben Torah,* to fundamentally change our reality, to live with Hashem and the Torah. We'd rather hang on to our personality and try to fix it up with all sorts of "patches."

And there is another problem: we need to believe that we can actually leave *Mitzrayim* behind and become transformed into Hashem's people. I would suggest that this is a matter on its own; it is not the same thing as *emunah* in Hashem. We do not find it difficult to believe that God created the world. And we do not have trouble believing that He Who created everything, and Who split the Reed Sea, has the ability to take us as well out of the suffering of *Mitzrayim.*

But we have a problem believing in the culmination of *Yetzias Mitzrayim,* which is: "*I have brought you to Me.*"[13] We have trouble believing that *HaKadosh Baruch Hu* can bring us to Him and transform us into the holy people of Israel. This is not a miracle like turning the Nile to blood or filling Egypt with frogs. This is the miracle of being transformed into a true Jew, a *talmid chacham,* a wonderful being. It means to live a wonderful life of *kedushah,* of *hasmadah,* of Torah. To savor a *sevara,* to take deep enjoyment in *Yiddishkeit,* to be a true *ben Torah.* We simply do not believe this is possible!

These are the two components of *Yetzias Mitzrayim*: the desire to leave, and to believe that we are capable of it.

As we mentioned, eighty percent of the Jewish people said: "Leave us alone! We want to stay here." This was not because life in Egypt was so wonderful. They suffered greatly there. They were oppressed, enslaved, and tortured there.

We also suffer. But we lack the desire to change, to become transformed into different people. Furthermore, we are not

13. *Shemos* 19:4.

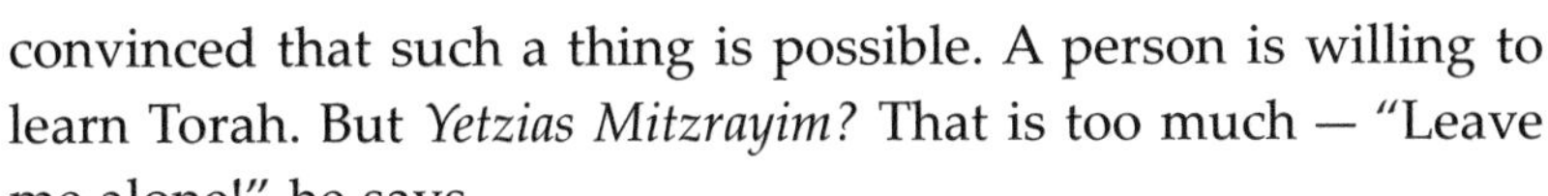

convinced that such a thing is possible. A person is willing to learn Torah. But *Yetzias Mitzrayim?* That is too much — "Leave me alone!" he says.

When we are ready to say that a true life of Torah is for us, when we are willing to accept the reshaping and transformation of our personality, when we believe that we are actually capable of living with the Torah and Hashem, then Hashem Himself gets involved. When this happens, we can achieve things we never imagined.

It is true that the Jews in Egypt needed mitzvos in order to be redeemed. They needed merits, so they were given two mitzvos: the *korban Pesach* and the blood of *bris milah*. But these mitzvos were not the main factor that enabled the Jewish people to leave Egypt. The Jews did not even perform them until Erev Pesach, when everything was already set for them to leave. The true basis for *Yetzias Mitzrayim* was what preceded: *ratzon* and *emunah*. They wanted to leave, and they believed it possible.

A person's first step in doing *teshuvah* is to make a clear decision: I want my life to be as it should be. I want to become a true *ben Torah*. And I believe that I am capable of it. This is what it means to be a Jew.

Shovavim

Early Torah sources tell us that the period of *Shovavim* (the weeks during which the *parshiyos* of *Shemos* through *Mishpatim* are read) especially lends itself to working on matters of *kedushah*, and doing *teshuvah* for mishaps and shortcomings.

We all know that the period of Rosh Hashanah through Yom Kippur is a special time of *teshuvah*, and that there is a distinct *siyatta d'Shemaya* for *teshuvah* at that time. Similarly, in the period of *Shovavim* when we read the Torah's account of *Yetzias Mitzrayim*, there is an abundance of Heavenly blessing and assistance, enabling every person to undergo his own personal

Yetzias Mitzrayim. Each of us is in bondage in his own personal *Mitzrayim*: his unique problems, his unique pettiness and limitations. The Torah teaches us that during this period a person can leave all of this behind and go out to freedom.

What is the special *teshuvah* of the period of *Shovavim?* The *Mesillas Yesharim* teaches us a principle about matters of *kedushah*:

> It begins with man's effort and ends with Hashem's gift.[14]

Someone who lives in this world cannot completely perfect himself by his own efforts. He cannot refine and purify himself to the point that when the time comes, he can stand before Hashem. But he must make the effort. A person must do all that he can. If he does, in the end he will receive *kedushah* as a gift from Hashem.

How did the great tzaddikim that we know achieve their *gadlus,* their greatness? Their *gadlus* was not something manmade. It is written:

> *Hashem, Who made Moshe and Aharon.*[15]

True *gadlus* is something made by Hashem. So it is with all the great tzaddikim that we know: the Vilna Gaon, the Chafetz Chaim, etc. They were all made by Hashem. But one thing is certain: in the beginning, they made the effort.

A period of *teshuvah* is a period of work and effort, but at the same time there is great *siyatta d'Shemaya*. When the Jewish people left Egypt they merited experiencing the involvement of Hashem Himself, which was manifested in tremendous *siyatta d'Shemaya* — above the ways of nature. And so it is with the awakening to *teshuvah* in this special period of *Shovavim* when

14. *Mesillas Yesharim,* chap. 26.
15. *I Shmuel* 12:6.

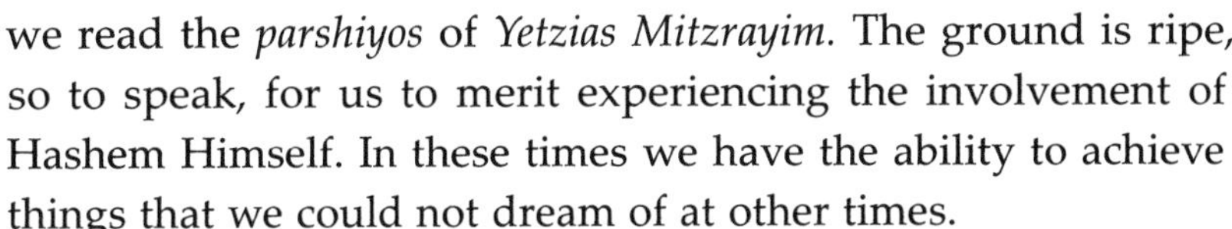

we read the *parshiyos* of *Yetzias Mitzrayim*. The ground is ripe, so to speak, for us to merit experiencing the involvement of Hashem Himself. In these times we have the ability to achieve things that we could not dream of at other times.

Shema Yisrael, and Baruch Shem Kevod

Hashem's involvement in our lives underlies *Keri'as Shema*. After we accept upon ourselves Hashem's Kingship by declaring *Shema Yisrael*, we recite *Baruch shem kevod....* For what reason does this recitation follow *Shema Yisrael*? The Rambam explains:

> Why do we recite this? We have an oral tradition that when Yaakov Avinu gathered his sons in Egypt before his death, he commanded them and exhorted them about Hashem's Oneness and about the way of Hashem which was followed by Avraham and Yitzchak, his father.
>
> He asked them, "My sons, perhaps there is improperness among you; someone who is not in accord with me as regards to Hashem's Oneness?" They all answered, "*Shema Yisrael, Hashem Elokeinu Hashem Echad*." In other words: "Listen to us, our Father Yisrael. Hashem is our God, and He is One." Their venerable father responded, "*Baruch shem kevod malchuso le'olam va'ed*." This is why all Jews have the custom of reciting this praise, said by the venerable Yisrael, after the verse of *Shema Yisrael*.[16]

The halachah states that these words of *Baruch shem kevod...* are to be recited in a whisper. Why is this? *Chazal* explain:

> The Rabbis said: How shall we conduct ourselves [regarding *Baruch shem kevod...*]? Perhaps we should recite it? But Moshe did not recite it [as it is not written in the Torah]. Perhaps we

16. *Rambam, Mishneh Torah, Hilchos Keri'as Shema* 1:4.

should not recite it? But Yaakov did recite it. Thus it was instituted to be recited quietly.

This may be compared to a king's daughter who smelled a whiff of mincemeat [which is a tasty but undignified sweet]. Should she say [that she wants it]? It would be a disgrace. Should she not say anything? She will suffer. Her servants took initiative and brought it to her quietly.[17]

There are two ways to explain this *Chazal*. The first is that of R. Chaim Volozhiner:

> Hashem's Oneness as expressed by "*Shema Yisrael... Hashem echad*" is that Hashem is the Master and He is one and alone in all the worlds. All the creatures are completely and literally one. Everything is considered as nothingness, and there is absolutely nothing else besides Him.
>
> But in order that we should not ponder this matter, *chas v'shalom*, and try to understand its nature and how it could be, we thus say afterward: *Baruch shem kevod malchuso le'olam va'ed*, which relates to the existence of free choice — for as we perceive things, there is a reality of worlds and creatures created by Hashem and in need of His blessing, and He rules over them.[18]

In other words, *Shema Yisrael* expresses the real truth: that Hashem and His Will is all that exists. There is nothing else. *Baruch shem kevod*, on the other hand, expresses that Hashem rules over the world which is known to us. The world does not function on its own. Hashem is involved in everything that happens. And the more Hashem is involved, the more perfection and joy there is in the world.

R. Chaim Volozhiner says further that *Shema Yisrael* is a

17. *Yalkut Shimoni, Vayechi*, chap. 157.

18. *Nefesh HaChaim* 3:6.

much greater praise of Hashem than is *Baruch shem kevod*. This is because *Shema Yisrael* conveys that Hashem's ineffable Oneness makes everything into nothingness. Accordingly, it is not such a great praise to say that He rules over our world, as conveyed by *Baruch shem kevod,* for it is like praising a great and lofty king by saying that he rules over a hundred million ants.

In spite of this, the praise of *Baruch shem kevod* is beloved to Hashem and greatly desired by Him. This is because Hashem wants people to understand His closeness to them; to recognize His rulership over every detail in the world. Thus we recite *Baruch shem kevod.* But we do so in a whisper, because compared to *Shema Yisrael* it is not such a great praise.

The Maharal explains the matter completely differently:

> In truth, only for Yaakov is it fitting to recite *Baruch shem kevod*. This is because Yaakov is the holy one of Hashem, as it says, *"They will sanctify the holy Yaakov."*[19] And *Baruch shem kevod* may be recited only in holiness. This is why it is fitting for the angels, who are separated and sanctified from materiality, to recite the praise of *Baruch shem kevod*. Only he who is separated and disconnected from the material can bless Hashem's Name [i.e., to recite *baruch shem*], since His Name expresses His nature. Therefore, this blessing of *Baruch shem kevod* is fitting for the angels, who are sanctified from material physicality.
>
> The only time we recite *Baruch shem kevod* out loud — as the angels do — is on Yom Kippur, the day when man is separated from the material. On Yom Kippur, man is forbidden to eat and drink and is separated from other physical matters, to the point that he is holy and is on the specific level of the angels.[20]

19. *Yeshayahu* 29:23.
20. *Netzach Yisrael*, chap. 44.

In other words, we say *Baruch shem kevod* in a whisper because it is a much loftier praise than is *Shema Yisrael*. *Baruch shem kevod* is so profound that we cannot say it out loud in this world. We have to whisper it, except on Yom Kippur.

This seems to be quite an extreme disagreement. R. Chaim Volozhiner says it is unbecoming for the great King to be praised for ruling over this lowly world, and the Maharal says just the opposite: *Baruch shem kevod* is such a great praise that it can only be recited in a whisper.

Furthermore, the Zohar that R. Chaim Volozhiner quotes from seems to disprove the Maharal: It says that *Shema Yisrael* is a high-level unification of Hashem, and *Baruch shem kevod* is a low-level unification of Hashem. Doesn't this contradict the Maharal?

In truth, R. Chaim Volozhiner and the Maharal are in agreement. It just depends from which perspective we look at it. Let us ask a question: Which is a greater expression of Hashem's greatness — *Shema Yisrael* or *Baruch shem kevod*? Surely, *Shema Yisrael* expresses a much more superior praise of Hashem. It conveys the real truth, that Hashem is so magnificent that He makes everything else into nothingness, as R. Chaim Volozhiner explained.

But when it comes to our connection to Hashem, it is not enough to just praise Him without mentioning how we fit into the picture. And which is a greater expression of our connection to Hashem: *Shema Yisrael* or *Baruch shem kevod*? Surely, it is *Baruch shem kevod*. This is why the Maharal says that *Baruch shem kevod* is greater.

Although *Shema Yisrael* expresses the absolute truth that Hashem is One, and nothing else exists besides Him, we cannot live on the level of this truth. It pertains to a reality beyond our level of comprehension. It is something we can relate to as a principle of faith; we can perhaps have a faint notion of it, but it does not impact our daily life so strongly. This is why we close our eyes when we say *Shema Yisrael*. It is above and beyond the world we live in.

Thus the Maharal says that *Baruch shem kevod* is greater than *Shema Yisrael*. Entertaining deep thoughts about the true nature of God does not grant a Jew his special greatness. Only *Baruch shem kevod* makes a Jew great.

According to this, we might think that *Shema Yisrael* is a deep philosophical declaration about the Oneness of Hashem, while the actual acceptance of His Kingship upon ourselves is through *Baruch shem kevod*. Yet, *Chazal* teach us that this is not so! They say that *Shema Yisrael* is where we accept upon ourselves Hashem's Kingship. *Shema Yisrael* is our *kabbalas ol malchus Shamayim*! We can understand this as follows.

When we received the Torah at Mount Sinai, certain conditions were made. One of them was:

> *And you will be a kingdom of nobles and a holy nation for Me.*[21]

This verse teaches that we are required to live a true Jewish life; a life of a *ben Torah*. What does that mean?

There are people who say, "I accept the obligations of Torah and mitzvos and I will do my best to keep them. Within the context of living a normal life (after all, we are only human) I will try to aspire to what the Torah asks of me. But I want to make something clear: Torah and mitzvos has to fit me, or it just won't work." This approach is not Judaism. It is putting one's personality in the center, where Hashem and His Torah should be.

Judaism is *kabbalas ol malchus Shamayim*. This means that I am not the center of everything; Hashem is the center of everything. When the Jewish people stood at Mount Sinai they said *Na'aseh v'nishma*. They built their whole life according to Hashem's will.

21. *Shemos* 19:6.

There is only one way we can have true *kabbalas ol malchus Shamayim*: we have to close our eyes and say something we do not truly understand, something that expresses a level beyond us and our personalities. At the same time, the greatness of a Jew lies in *Baruch shem kevod*. This means to put Hashem in the center of our lives, to actually live with *kabbalas ol malchus Shamayim*.

Before *Yetzias Mitzrayim,* Moshe Rabbeinu said: "They will not believe me." And what's worse, they might not even want to go out. These points remain the biggest problem until today. We are willing to hear all sorts of inspirational talks, to learn all the *Mussar sefarim,* yet we feel that it should be rendered to fit us. It has to suit our lives and our personalities. And if it does not fit so well, we start to cut off a little here and a little there...

Indeed, we need to bring Torah and mitzvos into our real, everyday lives. We live on the level of *Baruch shem kevod,* not on that of *Shema Yisrael.* Nevertheless, Judaism begins with *Shema Yisrael*. We must know that there is a level of greatness that is beyond us, and be willing to search it out. We must be willing to give up ourselves and our personalities in order to find it. And should we ask, "How can I achieve something that is above my level of comprehension?" the answer is: we can achieve it through the involvement of Hashem Himself, just as it was with *Yetzias Mitzrayim.*

But this will happen only if we want it to. It requires our *ratzon.*

Greatness in Our Generation

Throughout the *galus,* every European town had one Jewish street — the local ghetto. The ghetto was closed up at night; the Jews could not leave. What did they do back then, when they couldn't go anywhere and their lives were so limited? They met Hashem. This was the aspiration that burned in every Jew's heart. Although their street was an unattractive ghetto, in fact, the Jews

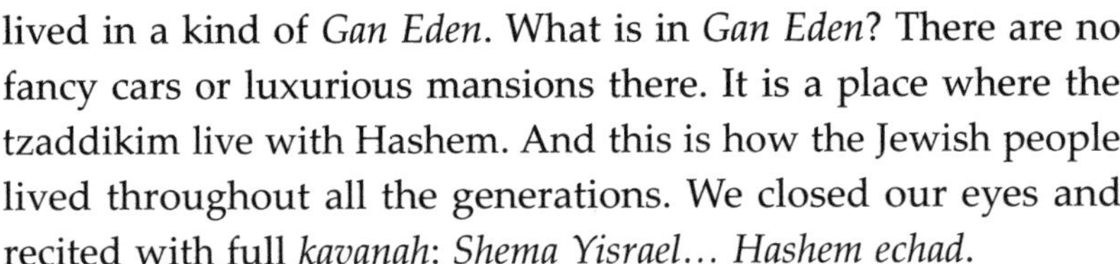

lived in a kind of *Gan Eden*. What is in *Gan Eden*? There are no fancy cars or luxurious mansions there. It is a place where the tzaddikim live with Hashem. And this is how the Jewish people lived throughout all the generations. We closed our eyes and recited with full *kavanah*: *Shema Yisrael… Hashem echad*.

In the last hundred years or so, things have changed. The culture of the world at large has seeped into our society as well. Although we are *bnei Torah,* we live in contact with the world. We take interest in what happens. We follow the news. We have hundreds of pleasures that come from the world at large: the kosher snacks and treats, the Jewish pop music, etc. If we stop for a moment to consider our clothing, our home conveniences, the food we eat, the places we visit — we will see that our lives contain a great many enjoyments that come from the world at large.

And we want to take the Torah, with all its *kedushah* and *mesirus nefesh,* and place it on top of our worldly involvement! What's more, we think it has to fit. If it doesn't, we start cutting.

A Jew needs to close his eyes and say *Shema Yisrael* — I want to live in the world of Hashem! And I believe that there is nothing more pleasurable than this. I will lack nothing. And I don't have to give up living my daily life. I just need to do things as a Jew does, with *kedushah* and *taharah*. I want to be a true Jew as Hashem wants me to be. I will change my life.

If a person does not aspire to this greatness, if he does not aspire to leave *Mitzrayim*, to make a drastic change in his life, then he is missing the basics of being a Jew.

This world is not an easy place. We did not come here to play. "Words of Torah endure only for he who kills himself over them."[22]

The Torah does not change, what is expected of us does not

22. *Gittin* 57b.

change, and *Shema Yisrael* does not change. There are no effortless alternatives. Indeed, it is not easy to close one's eyes, forget about the world and say *Shema Yisrael*, especially in our generation. But when we have *ratzon* and *emunah*, when we desire it and believe it possible, we are guaranteed to experience what our forefathers did: *"I will bring you out… I will save you… I will take you to be My people… You will recognize that it is I, Hashem, your God, Who is freeing you from the burdens of Egypt."*[23]

23. *Shemos* 6:6–7.

"כי א-ל חי בקרבכם"

6

The More Real Hashem Is to Us, the Greater We Are

What Makes One Generation Different from the Next?

We are all familiar with the concept of *yeridas ha-doros*, that each generation is spiritually lower than the one that preceded it. This has been going on for a long time: there was the generation that left Egypt, the Prophets, the Tannaim, the Amoraim, the Geonim, the Rishonim, the Acharonim, up to our own generation.

One of the basic rules in Torah study is that if an Amora makes an assertion that is found to be against a Tannaic teaching, he is thereby disproved. This is because the Tannaim were greater than the Amoraim. Similarly, if the Rashba says something that seems to go against the Gemara, it is a *kushya* on the Rashba. And if R. Akiva Eiger contradicts the Rashba, it is a *kushya* on R. Akiva Eiger.

In our generation, if a Rav is asked for his ruling and is about to state his opinion but discovers that the *Mishnah Berurah* says otherwise, he will surely change his ruling accordingly. This is because everyone knows that our generation is on a lower level than the preceding one. We are not equal to the sages of the past generation, and certainly not to those several generations back.

This *yeridas ha-doros* is not just in Torah learning. It is also in *emunah*. Just as a vast difference in Torah learning separates our generation from that of the Chafetz Chaim, so is there a vast difference regarding our *emunah* in Hashem.

Just as our Torah learning cannot be compared to that of the Chafetz Chaim, so the Chafetz Chaim felt about himself in comparison to the sages of the generation before him. And so on back to the Amoraim, the Tannaim, the Prophets, all the way back to the holy *Avos* whose depth of understanding in Torah was well beyond anything we can even conceive.

This *yeridas ha-doros* applies to women as well. We cannot compare a *tzaddekes* of today to a *tzaddekes* of a hundred years ago, nor her to a *tzaddekes* of five hundred years ago. And so on, until we get back to the holy *Imahos* whose spiritual level was well beyond anything we can even begin to comprehend.

When we talk about men it is easier to quantify the difference between the generations. When we say that R. Akiva Eiger was greater than us, the difference can be seen in his vastly greater knowledge and understanding in Torah. The Tanna R. Eliezer HaGadol describes this as follows:

> I learned a lot of Torah. But I did not absorb from my masters even as much as a dog absorbs by licking the sea.[1]

How would we quantify the difference between the generations as far as women are concerned? Let's imagine we are now entering the home of the Vilna Gaon. We find the Gaon sitting and learning Torah, which he did uninterruptedly almost twenty hours a day. Even the window shutters are closed, lest distractions disturb his utterly intense absorption in the depths of Torah.

After quietly gazing upon the Gaon sitting and learning, we tiptoe into the kitchen to visit the Rebbetzin. What do we find?

1. *Sanhedrin* 68a.

It is Erev Shabbos and she is preparing a kugel. What tremendous greatness do we see here? Did her kugel taste thousands of times better than ours? Was she thinking in Torah twenty-four hours a day? Were her stockings incredibly more modest than ours? No, that is not where we find the basic difference between her and us. She did all the same tasks that women of our generation regularly do: cooking, cleaning, etc. Nevertheless, she was incomparably greater than any woman today. Where does this greatness lie?

Hashem Is as Real as Can Be

To understand the answer we must know that the foundation of a Jew is his *emunah*. This is where we find the basic difference between the generations, both for men and for women. With women, however, it is more apparent. What does it mean to have stronger *emunah*? It does not mean that the Vilna Gaon's wife was more convinced of the existence of Hashem than we are. We all believe fully in Hashem. The point rather is: how real and alive is Hashem for us? Here lies the fundamental difference between us and the previous generations.

As we mentioned earlier, R. Yochanan ben Zakkai blessed his disciples before his death as follows:

> May it be His will that you should fear Heaven the way you fear people.[2]

People are real to us. If we know there are people around we feel embarrassed and uncomfortable to do something wrong. When the presence of Hashem is just as real to us as is the presence of people, we have reached a high level of *emunah*.

Let's take a chair, for instance. Our knowledge that a chair is real is not something we acquired through study of philosophy.

2. *Berachos* 28b.

Neither is it taught in yeshivah or Bais Yaakov. Nevertheless, we know very well that chairs are real. We will not test it out by trying to walk through a chair because we know that we will bang our shins. How real is our Judaism? When we pray, how clear and obvious is it to us that we are talking to Hashem?

Alongside of *yeridas ha-doros* there is an interesting phenomenon: things are constantly progressing and advancing. This is not just in technological matters. We are more advanced than our predecessors in other ways as well. For instance, many of our great-grandmothers back in Europe did not even know how to read. Most girls did not go to school back then. Nowadays, little girls start to learn the alphabet before they even get to kindergarten.

So what are we missing nowadays? It is the heart. We do things out of habit like a robot programmed to perform certain actions. In truth, it is a major accomplishment for someone to stand in front of the wall and daven *Minchah* from the depths of his heart with a real sense that he is standing before Hashem. But what happens nowadays? It is as if someone took a machine and programmed it to stand up every day at four o'clock and daven *Minchah*. For us, davening *Minchah* is very easy!

We have many wonderful holidays. We have the Seder night, we have Sukkos, Shavuos, Chanukah, Purim… but there is one precious holiday it seems we have lost touch with: Tishah b'Av. Can we find people today who are truly moved to tears just by the fact that Tishah b'Av has commenced? Why is this missing?

The answer is simple. You can program a machine to bake matzos with all the *chumros*, and on the Seder night you can exert yourself to swallow the requisite amount of matzah within three minutes. But you can't program a machine to cry. Tishah b'Av is a day of emotion. It reveals to what extent we experience Hashem as a reality, to what extent we feel He is an actual personality that we speak to, to what extent we miss Him since He left us. So what happens? People go to shul, sit down

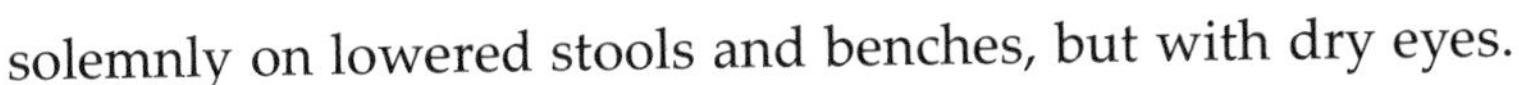

solemnly on lowered stools and benches, but with dry eyes.

The wife of the Vilna Gaon had true, tangible *emunah*. For her, Hashem was as real as can be.

This type of *emunah* is the message of *Matan Torah*. Before the Torah was given, Hashem told Moshe Rabbeinu that He was coming *"so that the people may hear when I speak with you."*[3] Moshe relayed this message to the people, and they were not satisfied with the arrangement. Their response was: "We want to see our King!"[4] They wanted to meet Hashem themselves, not just stand by while Hashem spoke to Moshe. Hashem granted their request, and Mount Sinai became the place where Hashem revealed Himself directly to the Jewish people. We saw Hashem ourselves, and this is the basis of our *emunah*. With our own eyes we saw the Shechinah come down on Mount Sinai; with our own ears we heard Hashem speak directly to us. In other words, we experienced that Hashem is as real as can be. This is the meaning of *emunah*.

The sense that Hashem is real grows fainter as the generations pass, and this is what *yeridas ha-doros* means. We mention Hashem hundreds of times a day. We say *baruch Hashem* and *b'ezras Hashem*. We daven *Shacharis*, *Minchah*, and *Ma'ariv*. But the moment we encounter a *nisayon* of some sort, for instance, a situation involving our self-respect comes up…

Matan Torah comes to teach us that Hashem is real. He is the "living God."

One Hundred Berachos a Day

Let us discuss a wonderful way to get in touch with the living God. First a little background: There are 620 mitzvos, the numerical equivalent of כתר, "crown." This number is made up of the 613

3. *Shemos* 19:9.
4. *Rashi* ad loc.

Torah-ordained mitzvos and the seven Rabbinically ordained mitzvos (Chanukah lights, Megillas Esther, washing hands before bread, etc.). One of the Rabbinic mitzvos is to recite one hundred *berachos* a day.

This mitzvah was instituted by David HaMelech:

> Every day, one hundred Jews were dying. David came and instituted for them to recite one hundred *berachos*. When he instituted this, the plague stopped.[5]

Due to this severe plague, David HaMelech established this mitzvah for all generations — every Jew must recite one hundred *berachos* a day.

On an ordinary day we do not have trouble reaching the sum of one hundred *berachos* if we pray the *Shemoneh Esrei* three times and recite the normal blessings over food. But on Shabbos, the regular prayers contain less *berachos,* so we need to make up for it by eating various treats and snacks, and reciting *berachos* over them, in order to reach the required one hundred blessings.

The number one hundred symbolizes the peak of *shleimus,* of completion and perfection. Ten is a number of *shleimus*: The world was created through ten Divine utterances,[6] and the Torah is contained within the Ten Commandments. The number one hundred comprises ten times ten. It signifies the *shleimus* of ten also in depth, as is explained in early Torah sources. This is why one hundred is *shleimus.*

When David HaMelech saw a terrible plague that caused such mortality, he understood that the Jewish people lacked connection to the Source of vitality. The mitzvah of one hundred *berachos* rectified the situation.

5. *Bemidbar Rabbah* 18:21.

6. *Pirkei Avos* 5:1.

Why was one hundred *berachos* the solution?

To understand the answer, we must know that the more people love one another, the more fire there is when an angry rift develops between them. This is true between father and son, and between two brothers. The following incident illustrates this:

People traveled great distances to participate in a very prominent wedding that took place in the time of R. Akiva Eiger. A few minutes before the chuppah, two witnesses appeared and came up to the rabbi who was to officiate at the wedding. They testified before him that the bridegroom was halachically unfit for this marriage. The chuppah was cancelled, and the question was sent to the leading rabbis of the generation, including the Chasam Sofer. The Chasam Sofer tried to clarify whether the witnesses were perhaps relatives of the bridegroom in some way. This would disqualify their testimony. Indeed, it turned out that they were related.

R. Akiva Eiger was very moved by this and wrote, "My son-in-law [the Chasam Sofer] was inspired by *ruach ha-kodesh!*"[7] Afterwards they asked the Chasam Sofer what made him suspect that the witnesses were relatives. He answered: "This was a wedding that was publicized many months beforehand. Why couldn't these witnesses have come to the rabbi earlier and quietly tell him what they had to say? Why did they wait until the chuppah was about to begin, when all the invited people had already arrived, and only then come and say what they said? Only relatives are capable of such wickedness!" concluded the Chasam Sofer.

When people who are close become alienated from one another, the fire is fierce.

The greatest closeness is between husband and wife. For this reason, an unbelievable amount of anger and cruelty can break

7. See *Teshuvos R. Akiva Eiger*, Responsum 198.

out when a husband and wife who were once close become separated. In such situations, the greatest tzaddik is liable to turn into a wild animal.

And the husband-wife relationship is a common metaphor for the relationship between Hashem and the Jewish people. All of *Shir HaShirim* describes in these terms the closeness between Hashem and the Jewish people.

So when anger and alienation develop between them, the necessary result is terrible troubles. The Chmielnicki massacres, the Holocaust, the Inquisition, and on and on. The fire is awesome.

In such situations, the first step is to come to a hasty cease-fire. The hostilities must be brought to a halt. And the outstanding symptom of hostility between two people is the fact that they do not talk to one another. They are not on speaking terms. In order for the fire to die down a little, the first step is for them to start talking.

What is *shalom bayis?* It is good communication between the couple in all areas of life. Let's imagine a couple that loves each other very much but cannot say a good word to one another. He cannot manage to say "thank you" nicely, and she is incapable of saying "good morning" to him. Is this called *shalom bayis*?

When there was a terrible anger in the world and one hundred Jews were dying of the plague daily, something had to be done fast in order to quiet down the anger a little bit. Thus David HaMelech instituted that every person should recite one hundred *berachos* a day, for this promotes the relationship between the Jewish people and Hashem. They started talking to Hashem again, so to speak.

And these one hundred *berachos* are scattered throughout all areas of life, promoting a positive relationship in all areas. Hashem gives you an apple? Say "thank you," and recite *Baruch Atah Hashem… borei pri ha-eitz.* Hashem gives you eyes? Say "thank you," and recite *Baruch Atah Hashem… poke'ach ivrim.*

Did you ever receive an expensive camera as a gift? Each one of us has an incredibly expensive and sophisticated camera. It is called our eyes. If you want to appreciate your eyes, next time you are walking down the sidewalk, stop and close your eyes for ten seconds. When you open your eyes again and look around you will realize how wonderful your eyes are.

Did you ever think about how marvelous it is to have air to breathe? Try putting your head under water and counting to fifteen. When you take your first breath afterwards you will realize what a sweet feeling it is to have air to breathe. There are people in hospitals who are attached to artificial respirators, fighting for each breath. But we breathe in fresh air without any problem. This is a wonderful gift from Hashem. And what does Hashem ask from us in return? Just recite *Elokai, neshamah shenasata bi… v'Atah m'shamrah b'kirbi…*

We have all kinds of good foods. What does Hashem ask of us? Just to say "thank you" to Him. Can't we speak nicely to Hashem?

Relating to Hashem

You might object: There is no reason to make a big deal out of one hundred *berachos* a day, as it is the least of our problems. All Torah-observant Jews pray three times a day anyway and recite *berachos* when they eat. Isn't this mitzvah automatically taken care of?

Not really. Many of us have not recited a true *berachah* since we graduated kindergarten. We are programmed like robots to automatically "make a *berachah*" when it is called for, but we have stopped talking to Hashem. This is because Hashem is not so real for us.

We are polite people. If something is served to us we will not forget to say "thank you." This is because a real, live person served it to us, and we naturally feel an inclination to thank them. But Hashem is not real and live enough for us.

Once a person sitting next to the Chafetz Chaim recited

birkas ha-mazon, rattling off the passage of *Hu heitiv, Hu meitiv… le'olam al yichasreinu*. The Chafetz Chaim said to him, "Do you know that you just asked for fifteen things?" The person was surprised, and the Chafetz Chaim counted the things for him.

We ask Hashem for (1) *chein,* "grace," that we should find favor in people's eyes and not seem ridiculous to them. Then we ask for (2) *chesed* and (3) *rachamim*. Then for (4) *revach,* "space;" we ask to have enough space and not to be cramped. Then we ask for (5) *hatzalah,* "to be saved." How many times a day do our children cross the street? Then we ask for (6) *hatzlachah,* "success." When we go to learn today, please give us success in our learning. Then we ask for (7) *berachah,* (8) *yeshuah,* (9) *nechamah,* (10) *parnasah,* (11) *chalkalah,* (12) *rachamim,* (13) *chaim,* (14) *shalom,* (15) *kol tov*.

Imagine your children would come to you and say at breakneck speed: "Daddy, I need this and that and the other thing and…" Is that a way to ask for things?

We need to get in the habit of speaking to Hashem in a way that is communication. This does not require greatness on our part. It is a simple habit that anyone who wants to can acquire. And we are promised success, for, "He who seeks to purify himself is assisted by Heaven."[8]

8. *Shabbos* 104a.

"וצדיק באמונתו יחיה"

7

Emunah Includes All 613 Mitzvos

"Chavakuk Came and Brought Them Down to One"

WE KNOW THAT THE Torah consists of 613 mitzvos. Where are they today?

> R. Simlai taught: 613 mitzvos were stated to Moshe... David came and brought them down to eleven... Yeshayahu came and brought them down to six... Michah came and brought them down to three... Chavakuk came and brought them down to one. As it says (*Chavakuk* 2:4), *"A tzaddik will live through his faith."*[1]

This seems strange. In the beginning there were 613 mitzvos, and their number dwindled to eleven, and then to six, to three, and eventually to one. How can this be? Even after Chavakuk came, we continue to fulfill all the Torah's mitzvos (with the exception of those mitzvos which require the *Beis HaMikdash*). If so, what does it mean that he "brought them down to one"? And when Chavakuk brought the whole Torah down to one mitzvah, why did he choose *emunah*?

The following story helps us understand the answer. I once

1. *Makkos* 23b.

heard from Rav Yosef Liss *zt"l* that the Brisker Rav was more disturbed by the desecration of graves in Eretz Yisrael than he was by anything else. It affected him to the point that he cried out in pain in his sleep, and that it caused him to cough up blood. He was terribly anguished over this matter.

One day, Rav Yosef Liss heard the news that graves were once again being dug up in a certain place. He approached Rav Yosef Dov, the Brisker Rav's son, and told him about it. Rav Yosef Dov said, "We have no choice; we must tell my father about this. But I just cannot do it. You do it." When Rav Yosef Liss went in to the Brisker Rav and told him the news, he was afraid the Rav might pass out.

To his surprise, the Brisker Rav responded, "What can I do? I have already done all I can." And then the Rav said an amazing thing. He started by quoting a Midrash[2]:

> There were four kings. That which one asked for, the other did not ask for. They are: David, Asa, Yehoshafat and Chizkiyahu.
>
> David said, *"I will pursue my enemies and I will overtake them."*[3] *HaKadosh Baruch Hu* said to him, "I will fulfill it." As it says, *"David smote them from evening until the next evening..."*[4]
>
> Asa stood up and said, "I don't have the strength to kill them. Rather, I will pursue them, and You do it." *HaKadosh Baruch Hu* said to him, "I will fulfill it." As it says, *"Asa pursued them..."*[5]
>
> Yehoshafat stood up and said, "I don't have the strength either to kill or to pursue. Rather, I will sing in praise, and

2. *Eichah Rabbah* 4:15
3. *Tehillim,* psalm 18.
4. *I Shmuel,* chap. 30.
5. *II Divrei HaYamim,* chap. 14.

You do it." *HaKadosh Baruch Hu* said to him, "I will fulfill it." As it says, "*As soon as they began their singing and praising…*"[6]

Chizkiyahu stood up and said, "I don't have the strength either to kill, or to pursue, or to sing in praise. Rather, I will sleep on my bed, and You do it." *HaKadosh Baruch Hu* said to him, "I will fulfill it." As it says, "*And that night, the angel of Hashem went out and smote the Assyrian camp.*"[7]

Then the Rav asked a *kushya* on the Midrash: If Hashem was willing to help Chizkiyahu to the point that he did not need to do anything at all, why didn't the other kings who preceded him ask for this? Why did David have to fight, Asa to pursue, and Yehoshafat to sing praise? Clearly, Chizkiyahu was not greater than those who preceded him. He was not greater than David HaMelech.

The Rav answered: Each person is obligated to do all that he has the strength to do, and no more. David HaMelech, since he had the strength to fight, was obligated to do so. But when the generations gradually lessened, and the kings no longer had David's strength to fight, each king asked Hashem for help according to his strength — until Chizkiyahu eventually said, "I don't have the strength either to kill, or to pursue, or to sing in praise. Rather, I will sleep on my bed, and You do it."

Concluded the Brisker Rav: "And so it is with me. What I can do, I already did. I no longer have an obligation to take action in this matter."

(By the way, we learn from this story that when the Brisker Rav became sick over the desecration of graves, it was not so much because of the actual desecration as it was because of, "What am I obligated to do about this matter?")

This story helps us understand what it means that Chavakuk

6. Ibid., chap. 20.

7. *II Melachim,* chap. 19.

came and brought the whole Torah down to one mitzvah. In the beginning, when the Torah was given, the Jewish people were spiritually great and were capable of handling all 613 mitzvos, with the many trials and difficulties this entailed. Since they were capable of it, they were obligated to keep all the mitzvos. And so they did.

With the spiritual decline over the generations, David HaMelech came and said: We can handle only eleven mitzvos. What about the rest? If we will handle the eleven, Hashem will give us *siyatta d'Shemaya* and we will be able to keep the others as well. Later came Yeshayahu and said that we cannot handle more than six mitzvos. And so the generations declined one after another until "Chavakuk came and brought them down to one: *'A tzaddik will live through his faith.'*"

Only With Emunah Can We Receive the Mitzvos

Let's make sure we understand this right. Now that Chavakuk came and brought them down to one, it does not mean that we actually have the ability to handle that one mitzvah. In truth we cannot handle anything — not even one mitzvah, the mitzvah of *emunah*. As *Chazal* say, "From the day the *Beis HaMikdash* was destroyed… we have no one to rely on other than our Father in Heaven."[8] We cannot rely on ourselves and our own spiritual ability. Whatever we achieve is only because of *siyatta d'Shemaya*. But we need a "receptacle" in which to receive this *siyatta d'Shemaya*, and the "receptacle" is *emunah*.

This is the meaning of *"A tzaddik will live through his faith."* By means of *emunah*, a person is capable of fulfilling all 613 mitzvos, an ability which he receives as a gift from Hashem.

8. *Sotah* 42b.

"The Bread of Healing"

Let us apply this idea to the mitzvah of matzah. We all know that matzah is a special mitzvah. It is very holy and is supposed to affect us spiritually. *Chazal* call the matzah we eat on Pesach, "the bread of healing."[9] Just as a person goes to the doctor and receives medicine for his illness, so does Hashem, the Healer of All Flesh, give us matzah as medicine for all our spiritual illnesses.

In the Gemara,[10] *Chazal* describe Hashem's remedies:

> Said R. Yehudah son of R. Chiya: Come and see how Hashem's ways are different from the ways of people. The medicine that a person gives to his fellow is beneficial for one part of the body, but injurious to a different part. But Hashem is not so. Hashem gave Torah to the Jewish people, and it is a life-giving medicine for all of a person's body, as it says,[11] "*It is a healing for all one's flesh.*"

The nature of most medicines prescribed by a human being is that they are beneficial for one thing and injurious for another thing. A medicine might be good for eye infections but bad for the heart. That is the way of medications. (The Brisker Rav once commented that a medicine that doesn't hurt, doesn't help.)

The Torah, on the other hand, the medicine Hashem gave us, is different: "*It is a healing for all one's flesh.*" Indeed, *Chazal* say that whatever ails a person — whether it be his head, his throat, his stomach, his bones, or everything all at once — the remedy is to engage in Torah learning.[12]

This is speaking specifically about the Torah. But in truth,

9. *II Zohar* 183b.
10. *Eiruvin* 54a.
11. *Mishlei* 4:22.
12. Ibid.

the teaching of *Chazal* that we quoted before is speaking generally about the ways of Hashem. He is called the "Healer of All Flesh."[13] When Hashem gives a medicine, "*It is a healing for all one's flesh.*" And the same is true when it comes to matzah. Since it is called "the bread of healing," it is a special medicine given by Hashem and has the power to heal all our spiritual illnesses.

Yet, after eating the "bread of healing" for the whole week of Pesach, we look in the mirror afterwards and discover that everything is the same as before. Anger, pride, lust, laziness… all the same old "illnesses" still seem to be there.

Why didn't the medicine work, if it was given by He Who is called *Keil Melech Rofei ne'eman v'rachaman*?[14]

The answer is that when the "bread of healing" is eaten on Pesach, all the illnesses are indeed healed. Everything goes away: anger, pride, lust, laziness, and the rest. But this gift can be received only by means of *emunah*.

If we had real *emunah*, if we truly believed that after Pesach, everything is different because we are now healed of all our spiritual illnesses, then when we looked in the mirror we would not see someone who is lazy, stuck-up, or unrefined, because we were healed by Hashem. From now on things would have to be different. We would have to be careful not to get our newfound *kedushah* all dirtied up.

This may be compared to a little child whose mother dressed him in a new, white shirt on Erev Yom Tov. He must be especially careful not to soil it. His mother will not allow him to romp and play as usual. She will not let him even touch his bicycle. Now, a whole new kind of cleanliness is called for.

But if the child will behave in his usual rambunctious way,

13. *Asher yatzar* blessing.

14. *Shemoneh Esrei* prayer.

five minutes after he gets out the door he will look just like he always does.

That is the simple answer. There is another, deeper reason why we don't recognize the fact that we were healed. The following allegory illustrates it.

A man suffering from a painful skin condition goes to the doctor. The doctor prescribes certain creams and ointments to put on his sores. But it doesn't help. He then goes to a specialist who examines his skin thoroughly, pores over all the test results, and announces: "Your condition is not treatable by creams and ointments. I will prescribe an oral medication for you. You must take one tablet, three times a day, for ten days. That should do it."

The man happily goes home. He swallows a tablet and runs to the mirror to take a look at himself. He is disappointed to see that the sores still look just the same as before. He does not see them disappearing in front of his eyes. But he girds himself with patience and keeps taking the tablets three times a day for ten days. Each day he checks to see if there is any improvement. Nothing.

He goes back to the doctor and expresses his disappointment in the treatment.

The doctor says, "Allow me to explain to you how the medicine works. You came to me with a blood infection. You did not see the infection; you did not even know about it. You saw only the skin lesions it caused. Now, I see from your latest test results that the blood infection was indeed cured by the tablets you took. In a little while, the sores on your skin will start to heal. It takes time for the body to grow new skin over deep, entrenched sores like these. But you should know that you are already healthy. Your infection is completely gone!"

The doctor continued: "Now take care of yourself; don't be foolish. Believe that you are cured. Don't start eating that tainted food again, which made you sick in the first place. Because if you do, your blood infection will come right back before your sores have a chance to heal. Then you will never even see the effect of the medication."

On Yom Kippur we recite again and again, *Baruch Atah Hashem, Melech mochel v'sole'ach la'avonoseinu.* After we have finished praying and the day is over, a Heavenly voice declares, "*Go, eat your bread in joy.*"[15] Jews feel different at that moment when Yom Kippur concludes. They feel the *kedushah.* The Heavenly voice is telling us: You are cured now. You are not the same person!

But if you don't believe it, and let yourself slip right back into your old ways, you won't see the difference.

And so it is when Pesach is over. After a week of eating the "bread of healing" we are like new people. We are completely healthy! So what do we do? We run to the mirror to see what we look like. We are disappointed to discover the same old sores, which are really just vestiges of our former illness. We find we have the same laziness, pride, and lust. And we are not burning with desire to learn a *daf* of Gemara as if we were R. Akiva Eiger. We seem to be just the same person as before.

This leads us to think we never were healed. And before the sores even have a chance to disappear, we go back to our old behavior. Thus we never realize that we became healthy again, and we tend not to believe in the spiritual power of matzah as "the bread of healing." We complain that we don't see results.

The bottom line is that we need to have *emunah.* We must remember that we ate matzah, and that Pesach is *z'man cheiruseinu.* Otherwise, we are like a prisoner, locked in chains, who hears someone whisper in his ear: "We just cut through your chains. Run. This is your chance to get out of jail!" But he refuses to budge, not believing that his chains are really broken,

15. See *Koheles Rabbah* 9:1.

not believing that he has freedom of movement.

Pesach is the time of our freedom. This means freedom from the *yetzer hara,* freedom from *avodah zarah,* freedom from laziness. It is total freedom! But you have to act on it. You have to move, to go forward.

"A tzaddik will live through his faith." A person needs faith in Hashem that Pesach really affords freedom, that it truly is *z'man cheiruseinu.* He must believe that this is not merely theoretical, this is reality.

And so it is with the Torah's other mitzvos. Let's say, for instance, a person puts on tefillin. Is he aware that he has just tied *Hashem echad* to his heart and mind? Does he think about this? Inherent in tefillin is a wondrous spiritual effect, a gift we receive when we wear tefillin. But we receive this gift only if we believe in the power of tefillin.

And so it is with every mitzvah: We receive its gifts only by means of *emunah.* "Chavakuk came and brought them down to one: '*A tzaddik will live through his faith.*'"

"אמת ואמונה"

8

*The Novhardok Approach**

Novhardok — the Way That Once Was, and Is No More

WE WILL SPEAK OF the Novhardok approach[1] to *avodas Hashem*. We will try to explain a little bit of what this approach is and what it stands for. Sad to say, Novhardok is something that hardly exists anymore. What is the reason for this?

There are a number of possible explanations but the following seems to me the truest. It is known that R. Zelme'leh of Volozhin, brother of the famous R. Chaim of Volozhin, died at a very young age. The Vilna Gaon is reported to have said about R. Zelme'leh that he was like a shooting-star in the sky — it leaves behind a little light, but it does not belong to our world at all.

In my opinion, Novhardok is not so different from this. It is a light that needs to be remembered. But in truth it did not belong to us, rather to exceptional individuals who lived in a

* This chapter is based on a talk delivered in the Beis Hillel yeshiva in Bnei Brak, on the yahrzeit of R. Yosef Yoizel Horowitz *zt"l*, the Alter of Novhardok.

1. This refers to the school of Mussar promulgated by R. Yosef Yoizel Horowitz *zt"l*, founder of the chain of Novhardok yeshivos in Lithuania/Russia.

higher and more elevated world. The public as a whole cannot live according to the Novhardok approach because the greatness it stands for is too sublime for us. Since Novhardok represents something that is beyond us, it is hard to properly define it and understand it. Nevertheless, it is much too important to be ignored, so we will make an attempt.

To understand Novhardok we need to understand the trait of *emes*, "truthfulness."

The Truthfulness and the Deceptiveness of Yaakov Avinu

Parashas Vayeitzei is all about Yaakov Avinu. Anyone who pays attention to what is going on in these *parshiyos* sees right away that there is a sort of contradiction. Yaakov represents the trait of *emes*, as it says, "*Emes l'Yaakov* — Truth to Yaakov."[2] However, we see numerous instances in which he seems to act with deceptiveness.

First of all, Yaakov's very name connotes deceptiveness. The Prophet Yirmeyahu says, "*Let each man beware of his friend; do not trust any relatives! For every relative acts deceptively* (עקוב יעקב)*, and every friend spreads evil gossip.*"[3] We might argue that Yaakov acted deceptively with Eisav and Lavan only because that is the proper and straight way to deal with such people. As it says: "*With the crooked, act deviously.*"[4] But this does not solve the problem. If his deceptiveness was not part of his nature, why was he named "Yaakov"?

This was, in fact, Eisav's claim. After Yaakov took the blessings, Eisav exclaimed: "*Is that why he was named Yaakov, for he has ensnared me twice?!*"[5] Eisav claimed that Yaakov's name fit him

2. *Michah* 7:20.
3. *Yirmeyahu* 9:3.
4. *Tehillim* 18:27.
5. *Bereishis* 27:36.

well: he was indeed an untruthful and deceitful person. How do we answer Eisav's claim? And why wasn't Yaakov given a name that connotes truthfulness and honesty, if that is his trait?

The difficulties do not stop with Yaakov's name; they involve his deeds as well. After all is said and done, he received the blessings from his father Yitzchak in a way that seems patently dishonest. We all know Rashi's explanation of Yaakov's famous words, *"I am Eisav your firstborn."*[6] Yaakov meant: "*I am* bringing you the food. *Eisav* is *your firstborn.*" Now, how would you explain that to a child?

The same questions may be raised regarding how Yaakov handled Lavan. In fact, Yaakov himself says to Rachel, "I am Lavan's brother in deception."[7] In other words, Yaakov says about himself that he is exceptionally skilled in trickery: he is Lavan's equal! It seems that Yaakov expressed a novel idea at this point, as his wife-to-be, Rachel Imeinu, did not think that tzaddikim are allowed to be deceptive in any circumstances.[8] This shows it is not so simple to say that the straight thing to do is to treat crooked people deceptively. The holy Rachel Imeinu was puzzled: how could it be permitted to act in such a way?

All this needs to be explained.

Emes V'Yatziv versus Emes V'Emunah

In the morning after *Keri'as Shema* we recite the blessing of *emes v'yatziv.* At night, the blessing is *emes v'emunah*. The reason for this difference comes from the verse, *"To proclaim Your kindness in the morning, and Your faithfulness in the nights."*[9] In the morning, i.e., when there is light, we see the truth. We see

6. Ibid., 27:19.
7. Ibid., 29:12; *Rashi* ad loc.
8. See *Megillah* 13b.
9. *Tehillim* 92:3.

Hashem's kindness and speak about it. There will come a time when all the people of the world will live with the truth. But at night when there is darkness, we do not see the truth. Then we live with the truth of *emunah,* faith. This is *emes v'emunah.* On its simplest level, *emunah* refers to something we cannot see clearly with our eyes, but we nevertheless believe it exists.

The Brisker Rav was once asked about the mitzvah of *emunah,* of believing in Hashem. The question was: when *Mashiach* comes, and *"the land will be filled with knowledge of Hashem, just as water covers the sea,"*[10] and everyone will know the truth and recognize Hashem, how will we then fulfill the mitzvah of *emunah*?

He answered: There will always be room for *emunah.* This is because Hashem is infinite. As much as we will understand and perceive Him, there will always be aspects that we do not understand and perceive. Regarding this we will have the mitzvah of *emunah.* (This can also explain how the Bnei Yisrael were able to fulfill the mitzvah of *emunah* after the giving of the Torah — after all, Hashem declared (*Shemos* 20:19), *"You have seen that I have spoken with you from Heaven,"* so what was left to believe? The answer is as we just stated: there is always a hidden part to Hashem that requires belief.)

It comes out that there are two "truths," so to speak. There is *emes v'yatziv,* the truth that stands out (*nitzav*) in front of us, truth that is capable of being perceived. This represents the world of light in which we see the truth with our own eyes. And then there is *emes v'emunah.* This is the truth of faith. We don't see the truth but we believe it is there.

> *"You bring on darkness and it becomes night"*[11] — This refers to this world, which resembles night.[12]

10. *Yeshayahu* 11:9.
11. *Tehillim* 104:20.
12. *Bava Metzia* 83b.

Here, *Chazal* tell us the true nature of this world: it is darkness. In this world, which is completely dark, we go around with our eyes opened and "see" very many things. A person goes through 120 years of life and sees millions upon millions of things. But *Chazal* tell us: Know that you are living in darkness! Whatever you "see," that is not the truth. The truth can be attained only by *emunah*. Whatever we know to be true through *emunah*, that is the truth about the world. Therefore, a person lacking *emunah* sees absolutely nothing true.

The Rambam says as follows:

> The foundation of all foundations, and the pillar of all wisdoms, is to know that there is a first Being Who brought all of reality into existence. And all of reality — from Heaven to earth and whatever is in between — came into existence only by means of His true reality.[13]

The Rambam is speaking here about believing in Hashem's existence. He says that this *emunah* is not just "the foundation of all foundations," but also "the pillar of all wisdoms." This means that a person who does not live with the realization that Hashem "brought all of reality into existence" is a person lacking all wisdom and understanding. He does not understand things even a little. He has no sense at all!

Hashem is the soul of the world, so to speak. He grants existence to everything, and He is everything. In other words, if the world is real — if there is a ceiling and a floor, there is light, there is time, there is you and me, there is oxygen in the air, etc. — it all comes from Hashem. He is the Source of reality.

Since Hashem is the Source of all reality, He also is the Source of all truth. This is because Hashem creates and defines reality. Let's say a person asks himself, "Do I truly exist? Am I

13. *Mishneh Torah, Hilchos Yesodei HaTorah* 1:10.

real?" The answer is that he exists only as much, and only as long, as Hashem wills him to exist. A person has no independent existence and reality. Only Hashem does.

Now, truth is something that is valued by all of humanity. Everyone recognizes that truth is a virtue. Let's say Reuven is driving his car through an unfamiliar neighborhood, trying to find a certain street. He rolls down his window, sees a scary-looking guy walking around and asks him cautiously, "How do I get to such-and-such street?"

The man answers, "Go straight and take the second right."

What does Reuven do? He goes straight and takes the second right, just like he was told. But why? Maybe the man was lying? Isn't it obvious that he is of questionable character?

The answer is that by nature, human beings have respect for truth. They will not lie for no reason. This adherence to truth is because a person's soul comes from Hashem. His very life comes from Hashem. And Hashem is Truth; there is nothing else true and real besides Him.

This brings us to the conclusion that whatever Hashem wills, that is truth — in the simplest sense of the word. And whatever is against Hashem's will is falsehood. But we live in a world of darkness and we "see" things differently. For this reason, it is necessary to give truth a special name: *emes v'emunah.* This is the truth that is based on *emunah*. The truth based on *emunah* is true, and whatever is not based on *emunah* is false.

A Puzzling Sight

People look at what happens in the world and are often puzzled by it. The way Hashem runs things doesn't always seem to make sense. Why are there evil people living it up and driving around in fancy cars while there are righteous people who can't afford bare minimums? Where is the justice in this?

The following well-known allegory from the Chafetz Chaim helps to answer this question:

A king had a good friend. The king relied on him heavily and gave him control over many matters of the kingdom. One day, it became known that the friend was a traitor. The king wished to punish him severely. He decided to imprison him in a glass cage and place it in the center of town, so that everyone would see him starving to death.

And so he did. A large glass cubicle, sealed on all sides, was placed in the town square, and the traitor was put inside.

The first day it was not yet apparent that the traitor was hungry because before he went in he ate to his heart's delight. Curious onlookers saw him sitting and relaxedly reading a book.

On the second day the onlookers saw that his expression had changed and he looked distraught. On the third day his hands started to tremble and he could not stand up. When he saw someone outside walking by with food, he would make unintelligible sounds.

On the fourth day he broke down. He pulled off his shoe and started chewing on it, a sign that he was now in a serious stage of starvation. At that moment a stranger arrived. He had heard that a traitor had been caught and publicly imprisoned in a glass cage so everyone would see him die of starvation. But when the stranger looked through the glass doors, what did he see? A man sitting there with his mouth full.

He asked the people next to him: "Is this the man who betrayed the king? I thought he was punished to die of starvation. But here he is, munching away in front of everybody!"

"You fool," they answered him; "he is chewing on his own shoe. He is so starved that he is losing his sanity."

We can apply this allegory to our topic. A person looks at what happens in the world and says, "I see with my own eyes that evil people are happily munching away. They are living it up and driving around in fancy cars. Don't tell me stories about

'this world' and 'the next world.' I see what's going on."

But what this person "sees" is false. Was the man in the cage happily munching on a steak? On the contrary, he was not someone to be envied. He was so starved that he was chewing on his own shoe.

We go around in the world with our eyes opened, but we don't know what we are seeing.

Chazal recount:[14]

> R. Yosef son of R. Yehoshua ben Levi fell ill, and expired. When he regained consciousness, his father asked him, "What did you see there?" He answered, "I saw an upside-down world. The prominent people were on the bottom, and the lowly people were on the top." His father replied, "My son, you saw a clear world."

What we see in this world is upside-down; far from the true reality. Truth has only one name: *emunah*. Someone who lives with *emunah*, lives with the truth.

This is the kind of person that Yaakov Avinu was. He lived with the truth. He lived with *emes v'emunah*. And this is why he is called *"Ish tam — A man of wholesomeness."*[15] What was his *temimus?* It was *"Yosheiv ohalim — He dwelled in tents."*[16] In other words, he was in the *beis midrash*.[17] His entire outlook, all his thoughts, came from the *Chumash*. There will be a day when Yaakov Avinu will live the truth of *emes v'yatziv*. But here in this world, he lived the truth of *emes v'emunah*, which indeed is the truth.

14. *Pesachim* 50a.
15. *Bereishis* 25:27.
16. Ibid.
17. *Rashi* ad loc.

Yaakov Avinu — Man of Truth

Getting back to the question: why does Yaakov Avinu bear a name that connotes deception and falsehood?

The key to the answer lies in the *melaveh malkah* meal held on Motza'ei Shabbos. The Rishonim tell us[18] that we have a tiny, indestructible bone in our body, called *luz*, which does not derive benefit from any of the food we eat, other than that of *melaveh malkah*. Through this bone we will come alive again in the time of *techiyas ha-meisim*. In the *Zohar*, this bone is called *rama'ah*, "the deceptive one." It is compared to *Lavan Ha'arami*, "Lavan the deceptive one."[19] This is what the *Zohar* says about it:

> R. Shimon said: Out of all the bones, why does this bone remain intact? Because it is the deceptive one. Unlike the other bones, it cannot tolerate the taste of people's food. For this reason it is stronger than all the bones. This is the main bone, since the body will be built from it. As it says, *"Lavan Ha'arami."*[20]

We see that eating does not necessarily bring strength. The Rambam tells us that eating a lot of healthy food does not make us healthy and strong: "Most of the illnesses that come upon a person are only because he fills his stomach and overeats, even if it is healthy food."[21]

A family member once recounted to me that the doctor put him on a very strict diet. He complained to the doctor that a person could die from eating so little food. The doctor responded,

18. See *Taz, Shulchan Aruch Orach Chaim* 300:1; *Pri Megadim* ad loc.

19. Lit., "Lavan the Aramaean." The word "Lavan" also means "white," the color of bone.

20. *Midrash HaNe'elam I, Toldos* 137a.

21. *Mishneh Torah, Hilchos De'os* 4:15.

"You should know that none of my patients have yet died from eating too little, only from eating too much."

This little bone called *luz* does not take sustenance from what a person eats all week long, it is sustained only from the *melaveh malkah* meal. We would think that it should be the first to decompose, because it hardly eats. It fasts from Shabbos to Shabbos; it must be weak and puny! But in truth this is not so. It is the only bone that stays intact forever, and the person's body will be built from it at *techiyas ha-meisim*.

This little bone manages to fool everyone. That is why it is called "the deceptive one," and is compared to Lavan Ha'arami. The *luz* bone maintains that eating makes one weak, while fasting makes one strong, contrary to what everyone else says.

This sheds light on the meaning of deceptiveness. You are deceptive if your life is such that you consider true what others consider false, and you consider false what others consider true.

What is Yaakov Avinu's name in this world? "Yaakov" — the deceptive one. Why? Because he fools everyone. He deceives the whole world because his truth is different from the "truth" that everyone is accustomed to. He does not live according to what the eye "sees" in this world of darkness. He lives in a completely different world. He lives with *emes v'emunah*.

To Yaakov, two plus two makes four only as long as Hashem so wills it. This is because Hashem's will creates and defines reality. This is *emes v'emunah*.

To Yaakov, it makes no difference whether he says, "I am Yaakov," or he says, "I am Eisav." It all depends on which statement is in accordance with Hashem's will: If my words are in accordance with Hashem's will, they are true. If my words are contrary to Hashem's will, they are false and deceptive.

Since Yaakov's values are different from other people's values, he is called "Yaakov" in this world. This is because he is the biggest "liar" around. What all the other people in this

world say is true, Yaakov says is false. What everyone else says is false, Yaakov says is true. He lives according to a completely different truth and sees all of reality from a completely different outlook.

The following allegory illustrates how superficial is the outlook that many people have on the world.

Farmer Joe has all sorts of livestock on his farm. He feeds his geese a tremendous amount of food to fatten them up. His horse and ox, however, hardly get anything to eat. A goose proudly struts over to the horse and says, "Hey, who is better off here? I have plenty of food to eat, while you guys are almost passing out from hunger. Admit that geese are better than horses!"

Silly goose. This is the outlook of someone who lives in the dark and is unaware of reality.

There is only one truth. On the farm there are no rich animals and no poor ones. There are no "successful" ones and no "schleppers." Geese are not inherently better off, even in the short run. This is because everything depends on one thing alone: The man who runs the farm. He decides according to his judgment what to do with his animals. He has decided to raise the geese for slaughter, so he feeds them generously in order to fatten them up. He sees no need to fatten his horse and ox, so he gives them only a small amount of food. Yet, they will outlive the geese by many years.

There was a man of truth in the world: Yaakov Avinu. His whole life was *emunah*. He saw nothing other than *emunah* because that is the truth, and there is no other truth. The following hypothetical dialogue illustrates the point.

You go up to someone and ask him, "Excuse me, what is your name?"

"Ben," he answers.

"And why do you think your name is Ben?" you ask.

"Everyone calls me Ben, and has been doing so since I was born — so that's my name!" he replies.

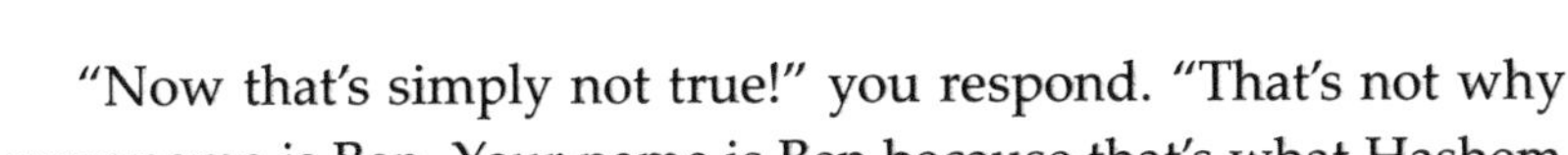

"Now that's simply not true!" you respond. "That's not why your name is Ben. Your name is Ben because that's what Hashem wants you to be called, and that's the only reason."

Yaakov Avinu was a man of truth. Which truth? *Emes v'emunah*. This is the truth which is attained only by means of faith.

Who's Crazy?

In my opinion, this was the Novhardok approach: simply to live in a different world. The people around them sometimes thought they were crazy. This is because the Novhardokers saw a different world, a world whose soul is *HaKadosh Baruch Hu*, and they saw nothing else.

The Chanukah miracle illustrates this point. Let's try to imagine what happened: Thirteen men decide to declare war on the Greek empire. They did not go out on a suicide mission. They went to wage war.

Now, this is very strange. Can a man wage war with his bare hands against a solid concrete wall? When he pounds his fists and bangs his head against the wall, is this called "war"? Yet, thirteen weak men go out to war against the vast Greek army. How could this be?

The answer is: When we calculate the chances of success in war, we base ourselves on "facts" that belong to the world of falsehood. We think that a million people are stronger than thirteen people. This outlook belongs to the world of darkness.

"But of course a million well-trained and equipped soldiers are stronger than thirteen weak civilians. It's crazy to think otherwise!" the Greek commander would surely exclaim. Yet, the thirteen men were not crazy at all. This is because in truth, it makes no difference how many soldiers each army has. The only important factor is Hashem's will, and nothing else. And so the thirteen men went out to war.

The Novhardok approach is not a matter of exceptional piousness. It is not being extremely *frum*. It is simply a different outlook on the world. It is looking at the world from the perspective of pure, unadulterated truth. The truth of *emunah*.

I knew certain great people who actually lived this way. One of them went to a certain shul in Russia and hung a handwritten sign on the door: "Novhardok yeshivah." When he was asked, "Where are the students?" he answered with calm confidence, "What do you mean? If this will be a yeshivah, there will be students, too!"

Upon hearing such an answer, many people would question the man's sanity.

Indeed, in the world of darkness this is not considered sensible behavior. But in the world of *emunah* it is quite normal and reasonable. This man's line of thinking went something like this: I am in the world in order to sanctify the Name of Heaven. There are Jewish children in Russia whose souls are thirsty for Hashem's word, and I have something to offer them. Hashem wants me to do this. And the Torah obligates me not to be deterred from going forward with it. So why shouldn't I? Because the communists will give me trouble? *Nu*, that doesn't bother me.

It is all a matter of perspective.

Novhardok and Bitachon

Everything we have said up to now is the easy part. But in Novhardok they took it a step further. They held that the truth of *emunah* is the truth of this world as well. They did not suffice with relating to *emes v'emunah* as the hidden but true reality. In Novhardok, even reality on its simplest level — even the reality of this world — is the truth of *emunah*.

To them, the proper approach to this world is: "He Who decreed that oil should burn, will decree that vinegar should burn."[22]

22. *Taanis* 25a.

Why does oil burn? Because it obeys Hashem. Thus it makes no difference whether it is oil or vinegar. If Hashem so wills it, vinegar can burn as well.

Hashem created a world that is not limited by any law of nature. Even the most basic laws of nature simply do not exist. The fact that oil burns, and vinegar does not, is only because when we look at oil, we think it will burn. And when we look at vinegar we think it will not. That is why vinegar does not burn. But what would happen if we would look at oil and understand the true reason why it burns? What if we would realize that oil has no inherent ability to burn, and therefore is no different from vinegar? Then vinegar would burn for us just as well as oil does.

In the language of Novhardok, such an outlook on reality is called *bitachon*. In other words, *bitachon* does not mean that I rely on Hashem to change the world's nature for me. It means I believe that the world has no inherent nature. Hashem's will is all that exists! This belief is what *Chazal* call *emunah*, "faith."

> Said R. Ami: Come and see how great it is to have faith. From where do we see this? From the weasel and the pit. If it is so with someone who places his faith in a weasel and a pit, someone who places his faith in *HaKadosh Baruch Hu* — how much more so![23]

Rashi explains what this is all about:

> There is a story in the Aggadah about a young man who said to a young woman that he would marry her, and promised her so, in all faith. She said, "Who will be the witnesses [that you so promised me in all faith]?" There was a pit there, and a weasel, and the young man said: "The pit and the weasel are witnesses for this."

23. *Taanis* 8a.

Some time passed by and he broke his faith. He married a different woman, and fathered two children from her. One of them fell into a pit and died, and the other was bitten by a weasel and died. His wife said to him, "What is happening? Why are our children dying in unusual ways?" He told her the story.

The weasel and the pit are Hashem's creations, and thus express the truth of Hashem. In essence, they are a reflection of their Creator. If a person relies on them, it means he relies on Hashem Who created them. And that is why Hashem assists him.

This is what *Chazal* mean by, "Someone who places his faith in *HaKadosh Baruch Hu* — how much more so [does he merit Hashem's assistance]!" This expresses the meaning of *bitachon*.

The Alter of Novhardok *zt"l* was an indescribably great man. He was an *ish tam* like Yaakov Avinu. He simply saw a different world, a world of *emunah*. He knew clearly that there is a Creator, "Who brought all of reality into existence. And all of reality — from Heaven to earth and whatever is in between — came into existence only by means of His true reality."[24] Aside from Hashem and His will, there is absolutely nothing.

What an outlook! What illumination!

And he did not allow this greatness to remain locked up inside him. He built a world. He raised many disciples who followed in his ways. Although the world of Novhardok does not really exist today, its brilliant light is something for us to long for. We cannot live on such an exalted and uplifted level but we can know it exists. We can bring into our lives the awareness that the truth of *emunah* is the real truth. We can know that this is what the world is really all about.

The day will come when Yaakov will be called "Yisrael."

24. Rambam, cited above.

This represents a more elevated world, a world of *emes v'yatziv* in which the real truth will be perceived by all. But simply speaking, the world we live in today is a world of *emes v'emunah.* We see the truth only by means of *emunah.*

True News — Only from the Torah

What does all this mean for us, practically speaking?

Our society used to be quite different. People lived within the confines of their own immediate surroundings, with a few neighbors, and mainly in the *beis midrash.*

Nowadays we live our lives with the whole world. A man goes to the *mikveh* and hears talk of the news. He picks up a newspaper and fills his head with an enormous amount of facts and information, forecasts and analysis, etc. In this way he injects himself with thousands and thousands of drops of falsehood.

Let's say he reads in the paper, "Our forces returned fire." This doesn't sound so bad. Ostensibly it's just news, that's all. But we should know that these are words that penetrate our heart and wreak damage. They blind us and warp our whole outlook on the world. Such darkness! Words such as these have no basis in reality. They do not express the real truth; they express what is "seen" in the world of darkness.

These words from the news that filter into our minds are not innocuous at all. If we pay attention we can see the effect they have. We often hear people saying things like, "I think that if so and so would be prime minister, he would save the day…" Or, "It seems he doesn't stand a chance…" These and other such statements are at best nonsense, and at worst reflect a denial that Hashem runs the world. They run counter to a true outlook on the world.

Day after day, our minds absorb hundreds of lies from the news.

Yaakov Avinu was an *ish tam*. He had *temimus*, wholeness and perfection. He had a perfected worldview. Not only that, "*He dwelled in the tents of Torah.*" He derived everything from the *Chumash*.

It is true that everyone enjoys hearing about current events. The question is: where do we find the true news?

If you want to know what is happening in the world, look for instance in *Chumash Devarim* or in *Sefer Yeshayahu*. Or take a look at what it says in *Parashas Ha'azinu*: "*Remember days of yore; contemplate the years of one generation and another.*"[25] This is literally where the true news is written. This is where the holy Torah tells us what happened, what is happening, and what will happen. This is where we find the *emes v'emunah* of the world.

She Doesn't Have Eyes

The halachah states that we should pray *Shemoneh Esrei* with closed eyes:

> A person should close his eyes, or pray from the siddur and not look out, so that he will not lose his concentration due to something intervening in front of him.[26]
>
> The Acharonim wrote that he who does not close his eyes during *Shemoneh Esrei* will not merit seeing the Shechinah when his soul departs.[27]

It says in the Torah that Leah had eyes. She had "soft" eyes, which means she had tearful eyes of attachment to Hashem. Rachel, on the other hand, is described as "a beautiful maiden who has no eyes."[28] This matter is explained in early Torah sources.

When a person prays the *Shemoneh Esrei,* he should be like a

25. *Devarim* 32:7.
26. *Mishnah Berurah* 90:63.
27. Ibid., 95:5.
28. *II Zohar, Mishpatim* 95a.

"beautiful maiden who has no eyes." In other words, he should shut his eyes. He who does so will merit seeing the Shechinah when he leaves the world. It says, *"No man can see Me and live"*[29] — but at the moment of death, a person can see the Shechinah. However, if a person opens his eyes while he davens *Shemoneh Esrei,* then instead of seeing the holy Shechinah when he dies, he will see the angel of death.

These are deep matters. We will explain them briefly, according to the simplest understanding of the *inyan;* just to give us some sort of idea of what they mean.

The Jewish people have two *Imahos*: Rachel and Leah. Rachel reflects the simple Jew. She is the mother of every single Jew: *"Efraim, My precious son."*[30] And a simple, ordinary Jew should be like "a beautiful maiden who has no eyes." This does not mean that he literally has no eyes; it means he knows how to close his eyes. A person who goes around in the world with his eyes wide open, looking at all sorts of things and thinking to himself that they are true and real, is not living as a Jew should. He has lost touch with *emes v'emunah*. Rachel Imeinu teaches us that to be a "beautiful maiden," and to recognize Hashem's truths, we have to behave like someone "who has no eyes." We cannot live our life according to what we see in the world.

You might ask, "If so, why did Hashem give us eyes?"

That is why we have another Matriarch, Leah. She was the elder and more prominent sister, and her descendants are Kohanim, Leviim, kings, heads of the Sanhedrin. This represents a different, more exalted type of Jew. Leah has eyes. We were given eyes in order to know what the *Kehunah* is, what the *Leviyah* is, and generally what *avodas Hashem* is. We were given eyes

29. *Shemos* 33:20.

30. *Yirmeyahu* 31:19. The Jewish people are called "Efrayim," who was a grandson of Rachel.

in order to behold spirituality. It does not say that Leah was a "beautiful maiden," but it does say she had eyes: she saw the shining truth. Seeing the truth with one's eyes is a higher level than shutting one's eyes.

On the other hand, Rachel was a "beautiful maiden." What does this mean? A Jew lives in a beautiful world. Hashem says to him, so to speak: Yes, you can use this beautiful world. But I am giving it to you on one condition: You must be like someone "who has no eyes." You must shut your eyes to this world and know that what you see is not the real truth. The real truth is only *emes v'emunah*.

The *Shemoneh Esrei* prayer is when a person lives with the real truth, the truth of Hashem. He is with Hashem in private. And this is also when the true reality of man's self emerges. At other times man lives in the world, using his eyes, but this kind of seeing is not correct vision. Throughout the day he saw trees, cars, all sorts of things; but it was all perceived through the physical eye. But we should know that the beautiful world we see is not the real truth. We are called "a beautiful maiden who has no eyes."

When a person starts davening *Shemoneh Esrei,* then he has eyes! Only when he closes his physical eyes can he see things as they really are. And if he has the true perspective on life, then when he leaves this world he will see the holy Shechinah.

And what happens if a person keeps his physical eyes open during these exalted moments of prayer, and continues to relate to this world? Then the day will come when everything will die. The day will come when he will see the angel of death in front of his eyes.

When it is time for *Minchah* and a person stands up to daven the *Shemoneh Esrei,* closing his eyes, he is saying the following, so to speak: "Soon the sun will set. Let me take a moment to 'open my eyes,' that is, to close my physical eyes and relate to Hashem. To speak to Him, and to live *emunah*. To see the truth

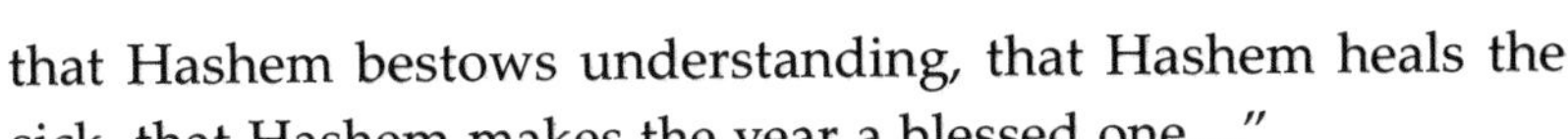

that Hashem bestows understanding, that Hashem heals the sick, that Hashem makes the year a blessed one…"

This is a moment of having eyes!

Yaakov Avinu was a man of truth who dwelled in the tents of Torah. And we, too, can come to recognize the truth through our Torah learning.

Hashem's Existence Is Very Easy to Discern

"The Whole World Is Full of His Glory"

Hashem our Lord, how mighty is Your Name over all the earth, [You] Who have set Your majesty upon the Heavens.[31]

Hashem placed His majesty on the Heavens — i.e., from there He works great and wondrous things, and His Name thereby becomes known throughout the world.

Hashem's Name is literally right in front of everyone's faces. There is nothing more out in the open, nothing more clear and obvious than the existence of Hashem. People fail to recognize this for one simple reason: they do not use the right tools in their search for Hashem.

This may be compared to someone who is informed that certain household devices are producing sound waves in his home. But he doesn't see the sound waves.

What does he do? He buys glasses. But he still doesn't see the sound waves. So he goes and buys a microscope, and that doesn't help either. He borrows a large telescope, and he still

31. *Tehillim* 8:2.

can't discern any sound waves. He brings a very fine, silk-mesh net which can catch even the tiniest particles, sifts the air in every room, and aside from a little dust, he turns up absolutely nothing. He is puzzled: where are these mysterious sound waves?

The answer is that he needs to use the proper tools to detect them.

In fact, if we want to make sure that this person will never detect the sound waves, we will let him look at things through a top-quality microscope. Then he will discover new and fascinating worlds: Bacteria, amoebas, etc., and become so excited that he will start to feel that anything that cannot be seen through a microscope simply does not exist! This way, he is guaranteed never to find the sound waves no matter how long and hard he looks.

Chazal say:

> *"You bring on darkness and it becomes night"*[32] — This refers to this world, which resembles night.[33]

At night, everything you saw during the day is still there. You just can't see it. Hashem is the same. He is right here in this world, but He placed Himself under a thick cover of darkness. He is here but cannot be seen.

> *Indeed, You are a Hiding God.*[34]

Someone who is hiding is here. You just can't see him because the hiding place obstructs your view. Hashem is the same. He is here, but is hiding from us, so to speak.

Hashem puts us in the world, and says to us, so to speak:

32. *Tehillim* 104:20.
33. *Bava Metzia* 83b.
34. *Yeshayahu* 45:15.

"Go and take a look around." Man sees the whole wide world and looks around for God. He puts on his glasses, but he doesn't find Him; he takes a flashlight and checks under the couch, but nothing. He gets on a rocket and flies to the moon; he goes into a submarine to explore the depths of the sea, but still doesn't find Him.

After searching with all these tools he is "forced" to the conclusion that God does not exist. If He was there, He would have turned up by now!

This conclusion is laughable. You don't find God by looking for Him with flashlights and submarines and radar telescopes. But if you take the right tool, you will see Him right away. Not only that, you will find yourself pointing with your finger and saying, *"This is my God, and I will glorify Him"*[35] — here He is!

The tools that enable us to see God are: a healthy mind, honesty and good character traits. If a person with a healthy mind contemplates the capabilities of the human eye, or the functioning of the kidney and the heart, he surely will recognize their enormous complexity. And if he is honest, he will admit that they are truly astounding and could not possibly have come into existence on their own. And if he is possessed of good character traits, so that he can bear the thought that God actually exists, he will be willing to fulfill everything God commands him.

Once this simple truth dawns on him, he will start to see God everywhere. He sees a flower, and thinks, *"This is my God, and I will glorify Him."* His child comes home, and he thinks, *"This is my God, and I will glorify Him."* God's existence spreads out everywhere the eye can see. *"The whole world is full of His glory."*[36] All we have to do is use the right tools.

35. *Shemos* 15:2. See *Rashi ad loc.*

36. *Yeshayahu* 6:3.

This is the simple meaning of, *Hashem our Lord, how mighty is Your Name over all the earth!"* It means that Hashem is found everywhere. When we drink a glass of water, we recognize Hashem and recite the blessing of *shehakol*. After performing a bodily function, we recognize Hashem and recite the blessing of *asher yatzar*. We can see Hashem everywhere if we just want to. He does not really hide from us. He is *"a Hiding God"* only for someone who looks for Him with a flashlight and a microscope.

Indeed, if we equip ourselves with the wrong tools then this whole world is nothing but darkness which hides Hashem's presence. Everything we see with our physical eyes just drives us farther and farther from Hashem. But in actuality, Hashem is not hidden from our perception — He is right in front of everyone's faces. The entire creation cries out, *"How mighty is Your Name over all the earth!"*

Believing in the Unlikely

The mitzvah of *emunah* is to believe in things that are against the ways of nature and against what your intellect tells you is true. For instance, to believe that you could be a millionaire tomorrow without even buying a lottery ticket. Now, how is that supposed to happen? Let's say your father is not wealthy and neither are any of your relatives. It takes *emunah* to believe that you could wake up tomorrow a millionaire if Hashem so wills it. Similarly, it takes *emunah* to believe that Hashem has the ability to take the whole world and slip it into a matchbox. These are things that our natural senses protest against.

But believing that God exists does not require *emunah*. It is self-evident. Yet, many people fail to recognize this obvious truth. Why? Because the world throws a thick cover over Hashem. All day long, we are in the habit of relying on our physical senses and judging reality according to what they tell us. When we want to find something we put on our glasses and go looking for it. Then, when we look under the couch and don't see what we are looking for, we conclude that it simply isn't there.

This is why we must fight against the great lie of this world. The world tries to convince us that what we see with our physical eyes is real, and is the *only* reality. There is nothing else, period! Although this false claim runs against common sense, although it contradicts the dictates of our intellect, we must put up a fight in order not to be swayed by it.

Some people are of the opinion that simple faith in Hashem means to believe because so they were told. To believe simply and innocently, without thinking about it on their own. But I am of the opinion that this approach is mistaken.

Someone who believes only because so he was told is *"A fool believes everything."*[37] This is not how intelligent people approach things. Rather, simple faith in Hashem means to believe that what we see and perceive is in fact the simple truth. Not to look for devious explanations. Let's say, for instance, we look up and see the ceiling. We could entertain doubts, and say, "Maybe I am dreaming. Maybe there is no ceiling here at all and what I see is just a refraction of light coming in from the window. Maybe…" But this way of thinking is foolish. There is no valid reason to say that the things we see are not really there.

We see Hashem everywhere. Who created everything? Who supports us? Who gives us strength? Hashem gives us everything. Simple faith means to live with the conviction that what we see and know to be true is in fact true. Not to be foolish and devious.

The world is composed of three main religions: Christianity, Islam, and — *lehavdil* — Judaism. All agree that God is One. It is just that the Christians think that so-and-so was God's prophet,

37. *Mishlei* 14:15.

and the Muslims think that so-and-so was God's prophet. The world was not born yesterday; it has existed for thousands of years. And the entire world sings praise to Hashem: *"For from where the sun rises until where it sets, My Name is great among the nations."*[38]

Except that recently, some foolish voices started piping up: "Maybe God doesn't exist, after all?" But this is nonsense. The whole world cries out and testifies to God's existence. Nothing is more simple and obvious.

This is what David HaMelech meant by, *"Hashem our Lord, how mighty is Your Name over all the earth!"* Hashem's existence is revealed and right in front of everyone's faces wherever they go and wherever they look. Its truth is inescapable. There is no corner of the world that does not proclaim God's existence.

It is recounted that the Baal HaTanya once asked his son, "What do you see there?" His son answered, "The ceiling." The Baal HaTanya responded, "And don't you see Godliness?!"

You don't have to be the Baal HaTanya to grasp this point. Anyone who uses his mind even a little can see Godliness in every detail in the world. Who could fathom the amazing wisdom contained within the sun or the moon? Who can describe the wonders of one flower? Every grain of sand reveals Godliness.

Today's scientists have discovered that each molecule is composed of atoms and subatomic particles whose intricate patterns and orbits resemble those of the vast solar systems and galaxies that make up the universe at large. In one grain of sand there are millions of atoms, in each of which is the imprint of the entire universe. This is not hard to understand, because the very same Creator left His imprint on each of these things. Hashem, Who created the entire world, created the grain of sand as well. Every grain of sand contains the entire celestial system!

38. *Malachi* 1:11.

The King's Clothes All this sounds very convincing, right? So why is it difficult for people to grasp the idea that God exists?

Early Torah sources employ the metaphor of man's stature. Man is comprised of head and body. The head is revealed, while the body is covered. And Hashem created the world in a similar way. The head, which is the more powerful part, is revealed, while the body is covered: it is enclothed.

If we meet someone and want to get to know them, the first step is to take note of their clothes. But are the clothes really the person? Surely not. So what expresses the real truth about the person? The real truth is out in the open. It cannot be hidden by clothing. If I would ask you whether a person's face or his clothing better expresses his nature, what would you say? The face expresses the person's true inner nature—who he really is. On the other hand, it is not so easy to interpret someone's facial expressions. There is something elusive about the face. It is easier to take note of the clothes, even though this is much more superficial. A person's clothing gives us some easy clues about who he is and what he does. For instance, if we see someone dressed in a police uniform we may assume that he is a policeman.

Hashem's existence is the most openly revealed thing in the world: "*Hashem our Lord, how mighty is Your Name over all the earth!*" Nothing is more revealed than Hashem. Paradoxically, this is why it is so easy to miss Him. Because Hashem's existence is not "enclothed," it is elusive to our physical senses; we don't have the tools to identify Him.

Another way to explain this point is by employing a certain well-known children's game as a metaphor. The outline of a shoe is drawn on a piece of paper, and around it are drawn all sorts of other objects which conceal the shoe's outline. A child might study the paper intently and declare: "There is no shoe here." But after he is shown where the shoe is hidden in the drawing, he exclaims, "Here it is!"

A person can go around in the world for a long time and not manage to see Hashem. But the moment his eyes are opened and he succeeds in perceiving Hashem, he points and says, *"This is my God, and I will glorify Him"* — here He is!

If we were to speak of the ABCs of being a *ben Torah,* then the 'A' would be to grasp this point of, *"This is my God, and I will glorify Him."* Someone who grasps this point no longer has to study the Rambam's *Moreh Nevuchim* or the *Sha'ar HaYichud* section of *Chovos HaLevavos.* These philosophical works are intended only for those who are still searching for God. But if someone already discerns God's existence, if he can look up at the Heavens and the sun, and see that Hashem created them, then he doesn't need anything else. He doesn't need elegant logical proofs to persuade him of the truth. He has already penetrated the darkness and seen the truth with his own eyes.

NEFESH SHIMSHON

Thirteen Principles of Faith

מבוא לי"ג עיקרי האמונה

1

Believing in the Thirteen Principles

"All Israel Have a Portion in Olam HaBa"

The Rambam, author of the Thirteen Principles of Faith, actually formulated them in the context of his commentary on the Mishnayos. The following Mishnah prompted the Rambam to state the Principles of Faith:

> All Israel have a portion in *Olam HaBa* ... And these are the people who do not have a portion in *Olam HaBa* ...[1]

Let us say a few words about this Mishnah before we go into the Thirteen Principles themselves. This Mishnah seems to contradict itself. First it says that everyone has a portion in *Olam HaBa,* and then it starts talking about the people who do not have a portion in *Olam HaBa*. What is the Mishnah telling us? In order to understand the Mishnah, first we will talk about what *Olam HaBa* is.

Some people would say that *Olam HaBa,* the World to Come, is life after death. There is a lot of truth to this but on its own this is not a complete answer.

1. *Sanhedrin* 10:1.

The idea of life after death is not unique to Judaism. It is something self-evident, and is based in the simple reality of this world. Anyone possessing natural intelligence can see that there is no reason why one's personality and being should disappear when one's heart stops beating. Basically, all of humanity is aware of this fact, and knows that when one's heart stops beating — which is called "death" — one's person continues to live. The only difference is that until now, one's personality was connected to the body, whereas now it is severed from the body.

The only question is: where does this personality go?

This is where Judaism comes into the picture. Judaism teaches us that one's personality and being, what is known as one's "soul," is drawn to the place that it longed for all one's life. It goes to the place that it was always attracted to. If a person longed for closeness to Hashem all his life, then when he dies and is severed from his body, he returns to Hashem. He is drawn to Hashem like a magnet. But if he sought physical pleasure his whole life, then even when he dies, he remains the same. His personality and being, which is his "soul," is naturally drawn in that direction. This is a most unfortunate fate.

That is what *Olam HaBa* means: returning to Hashem. In this world a person is connected to natural reality. He is connected to the sky, to the sun and the moon. He is connected to the people around him. And he is connected to his own physical self. But the day will come when he will leave his body and go to the place that his personality and being had a natural longing for. He will go where he wanted to be all along.

The Mishnah says, "All Israel have a portion in *Olam HaBa*." This conveys the idea that every Jew is naturally connected to Hashem and longs for Him. A Jewish infant who is only one day old is already connected to Hashem. Even if he would die a few hours after his birth, *chas v'shalom*, his soul will always be connected to Hashem and will return to Him. *Chazal* say that Hashem Himself sets aside a special time every day to learn

Torah with these little children who did not have a chance to learn Torah during their lifetime.

However, the Mishnah goes on to say: "And these are the people who do not have a portion in *Olam HaBa*." A Jew is capable of disconnecting himself from Hashem. He is given free choice and may cut his connection if he so wishes. The Mishnah goes on to detail a list of sins that indeed sever a Jew's connection to Hashem.

The Thirteen Principles and Our Natural Connection with Hashem

What criteria determine whether a person is connected to Hashem or cut off from Him?

Here we come to the Rambam's thirteen principles of *emunah*. They are the basic foundations of Judaism. When a Jew believes in them he is considered a member of the Jewish people not just physically but also spiritually.

And what if a Jew fails to believe in one of these principles? Then even if he fulfills all the mitzvos of the Torah, he has ceased in a spiritual sense to be a member of the Jewish people. The Rambam describes this in no uncertain terms:

> He has ceased to be a member of the community; he has denied that which is fundamental; he is called a Sadducee and an apostate and "one who cuts the plants" [in the garden of faith]. It is a mitzvah to hate him.[2]

Such a person severs himself from the Jewish people. He is cut off from Hashem, and will have no portion in *Olam HaBa*.

On the other hand, what if a Jew believes in the thirteen principles of *emunah*? Then even if he eats pork, even if he commits the gravest sins, Heaven forbid, he will be duly punished — but

2. *Rambam's Commentary on Mishnayos, Sanhedrin* 10:1.

will remain a member of the Jewish people even in the spiritual sense. He is still connected to Hashem and he will have a portion in *Olam HaBa*.

Ignorance of the Thirteen Principles

Rav Chaim of Brisk discusses the concept of "principles of *emunah*" and asks how the Torah could have such a set of principles.[3] Someone who denies any of the Torah's mitzvos, even if he denies one single word in the Torah, is already considered an apostate and has forfeited his portion in *Olam HaBa*. If so, what is special about the "principles of *emunah*"? In what way are they more fundamental than any other part of the Torah?

He answers by citing the Rambam's third principle of *emunah* and the Raavad's commentary on it. First, the Rambam:

> The Creator, may He be blessed, has no body… and He has no likeness at all.[4]
>
> There are five types of heretics… [among them is] he who believes there is one Master, but He has a body and image.[5]

This sounds like a pretty basic point. Everyone knows that Hashem has no body. Surprisingly enough, the Raavad questions the Rambam's ruling:

> Why does the Rambam call such a person a heretic? Many people who were greater and better than him followed this [mistaken] way of thought. They did so because of what they saw in Scripture. [For instance: "*Under His feet*," "*Hashem's eyes*," "*Hashem's hand*" — see Rambam, *Hilchos Yesodei HaTorah* 1:10.] And even more so because of what they saw in certain Aggados which tend to confuse a person's outlook.[6]

3. Cited in *Kovetz Maamarim*, p. 19.
4. *Thirteen Principles*.
5. *Rambam, Mishneh Torah, Hilchos Teshuvah* 3:7.
6. *Hasagos HaRaavad* ad loc.

The Raavad is saying that the Torah itself gave rise to this erroneous idea that Hashem has a body. This is because the matter is not stated clearly and unequivocally in the Torah. So someone who interprets certain verses in an overly literal way and thus falls into this error should not be called a heretic. He wants to believe everything the Torah says. He does not deny a single word; he just misunderstood something.

And what does the Rambam say about this? Such a person is a heretic nevertheless. It doesn't matter *why* the person doesn't believe; the fact of the matter is that he doesn't believe. He is lacking one of the principles of *emunah*. If a person fails to observe one of the Torah's mitzvos, he is not cut off from the Jewish people and from Hashem. But the thirteen principles of *emunah* are the basic foundation stones on which a Jew is built. Only by knowing them and believing them can he go to *Olam HaBa*.

If someone misses one of these principles, even by mistake and even due to no fault of his own, he still is lacking a fundamental part of a Jew's spiritual nature. Therefore he loses his portion in *Olam HaBa*. As Rav Chaim of Brisk put it, "*Der vos iz nebich apikorus iz oich ahn apikorus*" — Someone who is not to blame for being an apostate is still an apostate.[7]

There are those who hold that these words of Rav Chaim were not meant completely literally. A Jew who never heard about a certain principle of *emunah* cannot be considered an apostate, for he never denied or rejected anything. Only someone who denies a principle of *emunah* is considered an apostate, even if his denial is innocent and he is not to be blamed for it.

However, in the school of Brisk it is said that Rav Chaim meant it quite literally. A Jew who lacks knowledge of the principles of *emunah* is not connected to the Jewish faith. It is as

7. Cited in *Kovetz Maamarim*, p. 19.

simple as that. And this holds true even if he never learned them or heard of them. Since he lacks that which connects him to the spiritual eternity, his very being is cut off from this reality, and he has no portion in *Olam HaBa*.

The Thirteen Principles — Based on Two Basic Principles

The Rambam was the first to enumerate the thirteen principles. He writes that he did not find them listed anywhere, but gathered them from various important Torah works, and thereby formulated the thirteen principles.[8] He emphasizes: "I did not write them down as I happened upon them, rather after great thought and deliberation."[9]

How did the Rambam decide what should be considered a "principle"?

Not all the Rishonim readily accepted the Rambam's list of thirteen principles. One of the *kushyos* of the Abarbanel is that while the Rambam enumerated thirteen principles in his commentary on the Mishnayos, he did not actually include all of them when he stated the halachah, in *Hilchos Yesodei HaTorah* of the *Mishneh Torah*. The Rambam stated a few of them there, and stated another few in *Hilchos Melachim.* On the other hand, there are fundamental points such as loving Hashem and fearing Hashem which the Rambam did not list among the thirteen principles, yet he did state them in *Hilchos Yesodei HaTorah.*[10]

In light of this, what was the Rambam's purpose in formulating these principles? And what is a "principle"?

The Rambam indeed intended that the thirteen principles of *emunah* be taken as halachah. And it seems that we have

8. *Commentary of Rambam on Sanhedrin* 10:1.

9. Ibid.

10. *Rosh Amanah*, chap. 5.

accepted his ruling, because the thirteen principles are printed in our siddurim. Furthermore, we sing *Yigdal*, which is built on the thirteen principles. As Rav Chaim of Brisk explained, these principles form the very foundation of the Jewish soul.

It seems that the thirteen principles are built on one central and fundamental point. And this point then divides into two. The primary point is Hashem. This is what it all stands on, as the Rambam writes in the beginning of his work:

> The foundation of all foundations, and the pillar of all wisdoms, is to know that there is a first Being Who brought all of reality into existence.[11]

All the thirteen principles, which the 613 mitzvos are the details of, stand on one fundamental point: Hashem exists.

And the second fundamental point is: myself. Indeed, there was once a very great revelation on Mount Sinai. We, the Jewish people, saw Hashem. But after all is said and done, we recognize Hashem by means of our own intellect, our own eyes and our own understanding. If we would not exist, we also would not recognize Hashem. Since Hashem exists, and I exist, I must know in what way I relate to Hashem. This is the second point.

These are the two fundamentals on which the thirteen principles stand. The first is: What is Hashem? Hashem came before me. He is "prior"; He preceded everything. He is not dependent on anyone and does not need anyone. This is the subject of the first few principles.

The second fundamental is: Every member of the Jewish people must know in what way he relates to Hashem. This is the subject of the rest of the principles. By knowing this we acquire the basis for all of Judaism. However, if a person merely recognizes the existence of Hashem and doesn't understand that

11. *Mishneh Torah, Hilchos Yesodei HaTorah* 1:10.

this fact affects him personally, he is missing the most basic fundamentals of faith.

In my opinion, all the thirteen principles stated by the Rambam are based on this one point, which divides into two.

Knowing the Details

Many people have a mistaken attitude towards this topic. They say: We know that we must keep the Torah's mitzvos, such as tefillin, mezuzah, sukkah, etc. And we recognize the importance of reaching out to non-observant Jews and drawing them to Torah and mitzvos. But why do we have to know the thirteen principles in all their minute details? What is so critically important about this? We know that Hashem exists, that He gave us the Torah, etc. This is already enough for us to be Torah-observant Jews. When we get around to it we will delve into all these theological matters but it does not seem so pressing because it does not really affect our practical observance of mitzvos.

I think this attitude is mistaken, and I will explain why.

In the hymn *Keser Malchus,* authored by R. Shlomo Ibn Gabirol, it says, "Everyone desires to fear Your Name." What does this mean, "*Everyone* desires"? Is there no one without a desire to fear Hashem? There are all sorts of idolaters and nonbelievers in the world!

I once heard this point explained by means of the following parable.

A deceitful man once sent a telegram to an isolated little town with the message that the German Kaiser was coming to the town for a visit. He then dressed up as the Kaiser, bought a regal carriage with six fine white horses, hired some servants, and came to town on the appointed day, as if he were the Kaiser. Of course, he was received royally and showered with gifts. He declared various decrees for the welfare of the town, and then continued on his way to the next town.

When the Kaiser heard of this he ordered his soldiers to

execute all the people of the town. He regarded their behavior as a flagrant rebellion against the kingdom.

The people of the town hurriedly sent a delegation to the Kaiser, bearing the following message: "When we showed honor to that impostor, we really intended to honor His Majesty. Did we honor that faker? Surely not. We thought it was the Kaiser! All the honor and pomp and gifts that we showered upon him were really intended for you, O Highness. Except that he deceived us. He is deceitful, not us. We wanted to honor *you*!"

And so it is with, "Everyone desires to fear Your Name." Even those who bow to the sun and moon, even those who worship idols, really intend to serve the Creator of the World. Everyone desires to fear Hashem. But they don't know Who He is, so they bow to other things. This idea is similarly used to explain the verse, *"From where the sun rises until where it sets, My Name is great among the nations."*[12]

In my opinion, the message of this parable is not right. To illustrate why, I will tell the same parable, with some slight changes.

There was once a deceitful man who wanted to receive a lot of gifts. He had it announced that the German Kaiser would be coming to visit a certain little town, and on the appointed day he bought a regal carriage pulled by six powerful horses. In addition, he bought a donkey with long ears, dressed it in royal robes, placed a gold crown on its head and put it into the carriage. Then he sent the carriage into the town.

When the carriage with the "Kaiser" arrived, all the people of the town came to greet it. They cheered in honor of the donkey as the carriage made its way down Main Street. They praised and lauded the donkey, and showered it with gifts.

Some time later an order arrived to execute all the people

12. *Malachi* 1:11.

of the town on account of rebellion against the kingdom. The people of the town hurriedly sent a delegation to the Kaiser to explain that their sole intention was only to honor the Kaiser, not the donkey!

The Kaiser replied: "That is exactly why you deserve to be put to death. If you thought that the donkey with long ears was me, this is the most severe form of rebellion imaginable!"

And so it is with our subject. Does "Everyone desires to fear Your Name" mean that the idolaters think the sun or the moon is Hashem? This is not acceptable. The ABCs of serving Hashem is to know what He is. Someone who does not know what Hashem is, and goes around with a mistaken concept of Him, is not honoring Hashem. He is honoring something else, and serving something else. This applies not just to someone who bows down to a wooden statue. If someone worships the sun and the moon, it is the same type of rebellion. It is like cheering in honor of the donkey with long ears.

Details of the Second Fundamental

The second fundamental on which the thirteen principles stand is the way in which we relate to Hashem.

A person gets the wrong idea about things if he does not know what the "Jewish people" really is, if he does not understand how we connect to Hashem. Even if he knows that Hashem gave us the Torah, and that he must keep 613 mitzvos in all their minute details, he still is missing a critically fundamental point if he does not how Hashem relates to the Jewish people.

As we said before, someone who does not know Hashem's basic characteristics is worshiping something other than Hashem, even if he believes that there is a Supreme Being that runs things. And this holds true with the second fundamental as well. If a person does not know how we relate to Hashem and Hashem to us, he has missed the boat altogether.

This second fundamental is critical because after all is said and done we see Hashem through our own eyes, feel Him through our own heart and grasp His greatness with our own intellect. So if we do not recognize the true nature of a Jew, and his greatness, we will not recognize Hashem either.

If a person does not know what his self looks like, then he has a false image of himself. Even if he keeps the entire Torah, it is not the same. He is missing a fundamental. He is like the people of the town who thought the donkey was the Kaiser. They were out of touch with reality, and so is he.

But someone who has these two fundamentals has everything. The principle that Hashem gave us the Torah is part of our relationship with Hashem. And the principle of reward and punishment is part of our relationship with Hashem. Someone who does not believe in reward and punishment does not believe that Hashem cares about each and every move we make. This is a matter of relationship.

These two fundamentals are the measuring stick by which the Rambam determined what is considered a principle of *emunah*. All the other principles define and give the details of these two fundamentals.

There is a class of things that are essential to the Torah but are not called "principles." They are called *yesodei haTorah*, "basic concepts." These basic concepts pertain to the Torah's mitzvos. But with the thirteen principles we are not dealing with concepts in mitzvah observance. The thirteen principles touch on only two points: Hashem, and myself. Everything else is beyond the realm of the principles. The *yesodei haTorah* are a different subject.

Thus as we begin to explain the thirteen principles, everything will center on one of two points: 1) to know Who Hashem is, and 2) to know how Hashem and His people relate to one another.

"אני מאמין באמונה שלמה"

2

Defining Emunah Sheleimah

What Is Faith? EACH OF THE THIRTEEN principles, as printed in the siddur, begins with the words *Ani maamin be'emunah sheleimah* — "I believe with perfect faith."

What does "perfect faith" mean? It means something whose truth is totally clear, not something that was heard second-hand and is merely "assumed" to be true. *Emunah* denotes clarity and knowledge. Hashem says, "*You are My witnesses.*"[1] We are witnesses to the truth; it is a matter of one hundred percent certainty.

The Rambam writes:[2]

> Based on what did they believe in Hashem at Mount Sinai? [On the fact] that our own eyes, and not a stranger's, saw, and our own ears, and not someone else's, heard, the fire and the thunder and the torches. Moshe approached the thick cloud, the Voice spoke to him, and we heard, "Moshe, Moshe, go tell them such-and-such." And so it says, "*Hashem spoke to you face to face.*"[3]

1. *Yeshayahu* 43:10.
2. *Mishneh Torah, Hilchos Yesodei HaTorah* 8:1.
3. *Devarim* 5:4.

And it is written:

You have seen what I did to Egypt.[4]

We saw the ten plagues in Egypt, and we saw the Reed Sea split. And we saw even greater than this at Mount Sinai, where we said, "We want to see our King."[5] Indeed, Hashem Himself came down on Mount Sinai to the eyes of all the people.[6]

The Exodus from Egypt was itself a very solid foundation for *emunah*. As the Torah says, we saw these powerful miracles with our own eyes. In other words, there was no more room left for doubt. On a truth scale it measured one hundred percent.

This is basic to Judaism: We know the truth clearly and have no question whether we should believe. Hashem and His Torah is one hundred percent true for us beyond a shadow of a doubt. We saw it with our own eyes!

Faith and Knowledge

When speaking of the thirteen principles we are accustomed to using the term "faith." We "believe" with perfect "faith." But let us not be fooled by the words. What we really mean is "knowledge." In other words, we "know" with perfect "knowledge."

Indeed, there are levels of *emunah* that go beyond knowledge. This is because there are things that are beyond our comprehension; things we cannot even conceptualize. For such matters we have "faith" since we cannot properly know and understand them. But this does not apply to the thirteen principles. To know that the world has a Creator, that God is One, that He runs the world, that He gave the Torah to His people — these

4. *Shemos* 19:4.
5. *Yalkut Shimoni, Shir HaShirim* 981.
6. *Shemos* 19:11.

are all things that we know and recognize as facts. They are not a matter of "faith."

Someone who does not know these things is simply not opening his eyes and using his mind. He is blind to reality. But even after a person recognizes the factuality of these matters, there is still room for higher levels of *emunah*. When a person starts to delve into the thirteen principles and examine their profound underlying concepts he discovers points that human intellect is too limited to grasp. For that which he cannot conceptualize, he needs faith.

However, our relationship with Torah cannot be defined as a matter of "faith." It is a matter of knowledge. It is a cold, hard fact that God gave us the Torah: *"You [yourselves] have seen that I have spoken with you from Heaven."*[7]

We know that God exists, that He created the world, that He runs the world, that He gave us the Torah at Mount Sinai. This is all clear. It does not require any faith. No matter how we look at it, we find it to be true: whether we look at it from the perspective of what our tradition tells us, or from the perspective of philosophical investigation, etc., etc. It is like a physical object that we hold in our hands. Whatever angle we look at it from we come to the same conclusion: it exists, it has such-and-such dimensions, and so on. The truth of these matters is tangible to someone with a balanced mind.

There are many things in the world that we heard about but never saw. Nevertheless, we regard them as facts. Let's say someone has never been to Canada. He never even made it to Niagara Falls. Does he have "faith" that Canada exists, as opposed to someone who once visited Montreal, who "knows" that Canada really exists? Surely not. He has not a shadow of a doubt that Canada is right there, to the north of the United

7. *Shemos* 20:19.

States. Indeed, we are even surer of the existence of Hashem than we are of the existence of Canada. This is the degree of truth we are talking about.

If so, what is "faith"? Let's take the matter of Hashem's omniscience, for instance. Hashem knows, He is that which is known, and He is knowledge itself.[8] Since this idea is beyond human comprehension, since we cannot grasp the nature of Hashem's thought, we have faith in it. We "believe" it is so although we cannot really understand it. On the other hand, the awareness that Hashem created the world, runs it, and commanded us to wear tzitzis and tefillin does not require faith. These are elementary facts, based on cold logic. There is nothing more basic than this!

Faith in Things that Are Beyond Our Comprehension

Things that we know and have no doubts about are called *emunah sheleimah,* "complete faith," which is actually clear knowledge. All the thirteen principles are matters of *emunah sheleimah,* even the last ones. This is because a person who recognizes Hashem, and knows how reliable and trustworthy Hashem is, will rely fully on what Hashem tells him. In this way, even the last principles become clear knowledge, *emunah sheleimah.* We know Who told us these things, and we rely on Him.

Such is the case with *techiyas ha-meisim* and the coming of *Mashiach.* We did not see these things but we have *emunah sheleimah* in them, because we know Who told us that they will eventually happen. We know what these things are based on and we understand that it cannot be otherwise. Thus we have *emunah sheleimah,* clear knowledge.

The following illustrates this point. I have a good friend who

8. *Rambam, Mishneh Torah, Hilchos Yesodei HaTorah* 2:10.

learns with me every day and knows me well. If I tell him that I was just in America, and in America there are such-and-such cars, he knows that what I told him is correct. This is because he knows me well, and he knows I would not lie to him or tell him utter nonsense.

So it is, *lehavdil,* when a person gets to know Hashem. He recognizes just how reliable and trustworthy Hashem is. He then regards whatever Hashem tells him as the simple truth.

However, if we start to examine more deeply the principle that Hashem has no body, even though we know the actual principle is a fact, we will see that we are incapable of comprehending the full depth of this principle. (When we think of Hashem as not having a body, in our minds we are merely substituting a gross, physical body for a subtler and more metaphysical one. But this is also a "body"! In truth, we are incapable of having any true concept of Hashem. This point will be discussed more fully when we come to the third principle.)

As the Rambam writes about this, "Man's mind does not understand the real truth of this matter, and is incapable of comprehending and investigating it."[9] Here we leave knowledge and come to *emunah,* because "Man's mind does not understand." However, *emunah* of this type does not detract from our basic knowledge that Hashem has no body. This remains as a clear fact to us.

There Is a Limit to Everything in the World

As we said, Judaism is built on things that we know one hundred percent. To know something with such surety is unique.

Let's say a person needs an operation. After the anesthesia takes effect, the surgeon performs the operation. This person relies on the medical staff. He puts his life in

9. *Hilchos Yesodei HaTorah* 1:9.

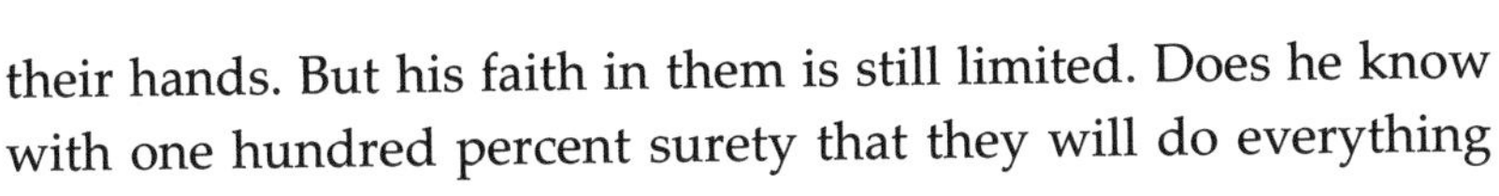

their hands. But his faith in them is still limited. Does he know with one hundred percent surety that they will do everything right?

Our knowledge of Hashem, however, is one hundred percent. How do we attain such a degree of surety?

Everything in the world has a certain limited nature. Everything has its parameters. There is nothing that is infinite, that transcends all limits, except for Hashem.

Let's take man's imagination, for instance. As R. Yisrael Salanter said, "Man is free in his imagination."[10] A person is capable of having a wild imagination and reaching far-flung dimensions. He can imagine very strange things indeed. But even the power of imagination is not infinite. A person cannot imagine that five million people are walking through his front door at once. He cannot imagine that three trains fit into one train of equal size. Imagination has to stop at a certain point.

Or let's take falsehood, for instance. Falsehood is a tremendous power. It has millions of shapes and directions. But even falsehood has its limits. Anything that is true is off-limits for falsehood. As soon as it approaches the truth, it has to stop there. This is quite limiting.

Everything in the world has certain parameters and characteristics that limit it. Science concerns itself with defining the world's phenomena. It searches for formulas, it maps out structures and it categorizes everything it deals with. It tries to figure out the qualities of every substance: what it can and cannot do. This is because everything that exists has limits.

Even the word "maybe" has its limits. Maybe I am adopted? Maybe I see as blue what everyone else sees as red? Maybe, maybe, maybe… There are millions of maybes. But even "maybe" has its limits. Anything that surely is, or surely isn't, is off-limits

10. *Iggeres HaMussar.*

for maybe. It cannot touch an established fact nor can it challenge sound reasoning. So Hashem made this world: *everything* has limits. To illustrate this point, we have chosen as examples some of the wildest, most uncontrollable things that exist. And even they have limits.

"Hashem descended upon Mount Sinai."[11] There were three million people who came and testified that they saw Hashem. As we will explain, at Mount Sinai they actually saw all of reality, including all the maybes and all the falsehoods and all the wild flights of imagination. They saw everything that man is capable of conceiving.

Let's say we draw a big, big circle and put everything inside. The whole world, including space, time, and everything else. Now we expand the circle a little and put all the maybes inside it. "Maybe" there is another universe, "maybe" there is another god, maybe… But there is a limit to all these maybes — they all must stay contained within the circle. Did we think of more maybes? No problem: we expand the circle again, and again. We can expand the circle as much as we like, but everything is still *inside*. It is limited.

The idea of this circle appears in the writings of the Arizal. On the first page of *Sefer Eitz Chaim* there is a drawing of a circle. The Arizal explains that the world began with *chalal,* emptiness. He says that all the possibilities and all the flights of imagination and all the falsehoods were enfolded within this void. All the maybes that could possibly be thought of.

And all this was seen at Mount Sinai when Hashem gave the Torah to the Jewish people. All the *kushyos* that anyone would ever consider, maybe this and maybe that, all the wildest possibilities; the Jewish people saw them all at Mount Sinai. This is because reality in its full sense encompasses all of reality's

11. *Shemos* 19:20.

possibilities and variations. Put whatever you wish inside this expanded circle of reality. All the various forms of heresy, all the atheism and agnosticism, all the idols and deities, all the erroneous philosophies and ideologies… Although there are billions of possibilities, they are still limited. They will all ultimately be enclosed within our circle.

And the Jewish people saw all this at Mount Sinai. This is the simple meaning of the verse:

> *You have been shown, so you will know that Hashem is God. There is nothing besides Him!*[12]

Rashi on this verse, citing *Chazal*, explains as follows:

> On the day the Torah was given… Hashem opened the seven firmaments for them. Just as He tore open the upper ones, so did He tear open the lower ones… He said to them, "See that there is no one else with Me." As it says, "*You have been shown, so you will know.*"

Hashem opened up the "upper ones" and the "lower ones." What is this telling us? The seven firmaments include all the true philosophies. And the "lower ones" include all the falsehoods: all the wickedness, all the atheism, all the idolatry, all the imaginary things which are not. They are all limited, and are all included within the boundaries of the circle of reality.

We saw reality in all its possibilities at Mount Sinai. And we also saw the One Who controls the circle of reality. The seven firmaments were opened up, down to the depths. In other words, all of reality was opened up for us to see.

What is "reality"? It is the sum total of all that is. Thus, "reality" is the simple translation of *Havayah,* Hashem's four-letter Name. This is because *Havayah* means "existence." It

12. *Devarim* 4:35.

conveys the idea that Hashem brings all of reality into existence. *"Hashem (Havayah) descended upon Mount Sinai."* We saw all of reality, and we saw that Hashem is the One Who makes it all exist.

It is written, *"You have seen that I have spoken with you from Heaven."* How did we see this? A person has five senses: sight, hearing, touch, taste and smell. With which of them did we perceive Hashem at Mount Sinai? There are people who lack the sense of sight. A person born blind does not even know what it means to see. On the other end of the spectrum, there are people with enhanced senses. There is regular seeing, and there is prophetic seeing.

The Rambam describes prophecy as the type of seeing which is not subject to doubt. It leaves no room for mistake. Sometimes we don't see things quite right when we use our ordinary sense of sight, which is limited like everything else in this world. Prophetic seeing, on the other hand, is by nature infallible. When we saw Hashem at Mount Sinai, it was an enhanced type of seeing. It was a seeing that affords one hundred percent surety.

The Formula

Everything has a formula or equation of some sort that governs it. If I speak at a certain volume, there is a formula to calculate the chances that what I say will be audible to you if you are standing ten feet away. We can create conditions in which I will have one hundred percent success in transmitting verbal messages to others. This is because distortion and unclarity have limits. They exist only within certain parameters. For example, we can set up a system of perfect transmission: the one who receives a message must repeat it many times and is threatened with terrible consequences if he does not give over the message exactly as he received it.

Hashem created such a formula to guarantee success in the transmission of His messages. This is the structure by which the Torah is passed down from generation to generation. Let's take *keri'as haTorah* as an example. All over the world, when the Torah is read in shul, people listen and follow along. If they hear a mistake in the reading they immediately correct the reader, forcing him to go back and read the word again, even if the mistake was an insignificant one. Furthermore, countless people all over the world read *shnayim mikra v'echad targum* every week. All this is part of the formula that guarantees the successful transmission of the Torah.

Another part of this is the holidays which we celebrate. The festival of Shavuos is such a powerful force. The four year olds come home from nursery school with "crowns" for Shavuos, because each Jew received two crowns from Hashem at Mount Sinai. The four year olds know this, and so do the five year olds and the six year olds. This way Jews grow up with the feeling that the two crowns of Shavuos, which represent *na'aseh v'nishma,* are an essential part of their life. They wouldn't give them up for anything. The same is true with Pesach, a holiday overflowing with various customs whose sole purpose is to save us from the remote possibility of eating a tiny particle of chametz. And we train our children and grandchildren not to make the slightest change in these customs. In this way we pass on to them the Exodus from Egypt and our coming to Mount Sinai to receive the Torah.

The *Maharshal* writes[13] that a Jew may not make a change in any halachah, causing the halachah to be different from what the Torah actually says, even if he is threatened by death. The Gemara recounts an incident in which the Roman government sent two officers to the Sages with an order to teach them the Torah. The Sages in fact taught these officers the Torah. Later on, shortly before these officers passed away, they confessed to the Sages: "We examined your entire Torah, and it is true, except

13. *Yam shel Shlomo, Bava Kamma* 4:9.

for one thing: When the ox of a Jew gores the ox of a non-Jew, the Jewish owner is exempt from payment. But when the ox of a non-Jew gores the ox of a Jew, the non-Jewish owner must make full payment to the Jew, even if the ox had not gored previously."

The *Maharshal* asks: Why didn't the Sages change that particular halachah when they taught it to the officers? Weren't they concerned that it would bring the Romans to persecute the Torah and the Jews? The *Maharshal* answers that the Sages put their very lives on the line, risking persecution and execution, in order not to change a single law in the Torah. He writes: "One statement of the Torah is like the entire Torah." To say about a single halachah that it is incorrect is no less serious than saying about all of *Maseches Shabbos* that it is incorrect.

A Jew must give up his life rather than tamper with the Torah. Indeed, countless Jews have been slaughtered throughout the generations over one word of the Torah.

Another point: Torah learning is transmitted through a very rigorous tradition. When we study the Torah we do not just peruse a digest of the Torah's message, translated into the vernacular by anonymous scribes. On the contrary: We insist on seeing the original text! We study what the Tannaim said, what the Amoraim said, what the Rishonim said. We have a tradition starting from when the Torah was given, which lists the leading Sages of every generation. It states who was the son, who was the grandson and who was the grandson's grandson.

The "Foolproof" Program

There is a certain program that has been used with much success in Arachim's outreach seminars. The participants are told to imagine that they are Holocaust survivors facing the ludicrous claims of Holocaust deniers. The participants, as Holocaust survivors, want to make sure that the Holocaust will never be forgotten. How should they go about guaranteeing that the memory of this event will be preserved? People suggest various methods: make a "Holocaust Association"; have the members wear special clothing; every year, on the date that Auschwitz was built, hold gatherings and speak about the Holocaust, etc. The moderator lists all the ideas and then asks the participants: Are you sure that these suggestions will be effective? And everyone agrees that it would be impossible to forget the Holocaust if these suggestions were followed. At that point, the participants are shown that these suggestions are already written in the Torah. We gather on the Seder night in family groups to speak about the event of the Exodus, we wear special garments: tzitzis and tefillin, etc.

There is another exercise used in such seminars. The participants are asked to imagine that they are deep inside enemy territory and they need to smuggle out a detailed message. How will they make sure that their message arrives intact and accurate? People suggest various methods: the message should be encrypted in a code known only to a few; it should be sent multiple times along different routes; a copy of the original should be kept, etc. After the various suggestions are collected, it is pointed out that these, too, are part of the tradition which guarantees that the Torah is faithfully and accurately passed down from generation to generation.

In short, we see that the Torah tradition has been transmitted to us in a foolproof manner. The bearers of the message have absolute dedication to maintaining its integrity, there are unforgettable reminders, codes are employed, there are records, backup systems are created, quality checks are utilized — there is everything needed to make it scientifically sure that the message will arrive intact until the last generation. If we take a look at this formula we will see that it is simply impossible that there was a break in the middle.

When could a break have taken place? In the time of Yehoshua? In the time of R. Akiva? In the time of the Rambam? We are only a hundred generations since the Torah was given, and every generation is documented. In the time of the *Beis HaMikdash*, the entire Jewish nation would gather there three times a year. Moshe Rabbeinu instituted the public reading of the Torah, and since then it has been read every Monday, Thursday, Shabbos and Yom Tov. Even today in our lowly generation the children sit and study the Torah. Young and old, men, women, and children talk about Mount Sinai and the Exodus from Egypt. The formula of the Torah tradition is built in a way that guarantees one hundred percent success in transmission. And at the center of this well-preserved tradition lies the clear message: *"You have seen that I have spoken with you from Heaven."*

All the above is just one of the many thousands of proofs and explanations for the truth of the Torah. We spoke at length about how our tradition has been transmitted in a foolproof manner. But there are many other proofs as well. For instance there is the very structure of the Torah. There are many, many other proofs, each a whole subject on its own.

We spoke of the transmission of our tradition because it is something that everything is built upon.

> The tradition passed down from father to son can never be false. This is because no man would choose to bequeath a lie to his son.[14]

Our tradition is so strong that it keeps the key events of the Jewish people vibrantly alive even today. Just take a walk on Pesach or Erev Sukkos in areas where observant Jews live. It feels like, *"This day you went out of Egypt."*[15] It is fresh and exciting. People are intensely involved with all the intricate details of the mitzvos. The matzos have to be baked just so, the esrog has

14. *Sefer HaIkkarim* 4:44; see *Ramban, Devarim* 4:9.
15. *Shemos* 13:3.

to look just so, etc. When the children grow up they will never forget the experience of going to bake matzos.

It all comes to underscore the fact that we stood at Mount Sinai. And what did we see there? An all-encompassing reality. This is the simple meaning of the Name *Havayah*. It means that Hashem brings everything into existence, and encompasses all of reality. *"Havayah descended on Mount Sinai."*

The Torah Stands Up Under Critical Examination

Another remarkable thing about the Torah is that we approach it with a critical mind. We ask, we challenge, we raise contradictions, we scrutinize... Let's take for example how Rashi begins his commentary on the Torah. The first thing he writes is a *kushya*: "Said R. Yitzchak: 'The Torah should rather have begun with, *"This month shall be to you ..."*'" Now, if we would write a commentary on the Torah we would start with something like, "Blessed is He Who gave the Torah to His people Israel..." Even if we would have chosen to begin with a question, we would have phrased it differently: "Why doesn't the Torah begin with, '*This month shall be to you...*'?" But Rashi begins with a challenge: "The Torah should rather have begun..."

A certain person who went on to become an outstanding Torah scholar told me how he first returned to Judaism: "There was a lecture about 'what is a page of Gemara?' They showed us the structure of the Mishnah, and then the Gemara. They went through the Gemara's *kushya* on the Mishnah, and its *terutz*. They explained to us Rashi's commentary, and the difficulty that Tosafos finds with Rashi. The Maharsha objects, R. Akiva Eiger answers, R. Chaim of Brisk explains... I said to myself: 'For goodness sakes! Information that goes through this kind of critical examination has got to be true. Each scholar questions what the other one said.'"

There is no chance to slip by something shoddy. Anyone who tries will immediately be called on the floor.

We enjoy *kushyos* more than we do *terutzim.* And what do we gain from all the *kushyos?* We see more and more how true the Torah is. We take the Torah apart and put it back together again. We study and examine each part to understand where it fits and what its function is. If we would take a book written by a famous author and rip it apart the way we do the Torah, after thirty days we would come to the conclusion that the author is not as great as people claim, and we'd throw the book away. We'd say, "Why should we waste our time on this; let's write a better book!" But then what would happen with the "better" book if we'd dissect it? Would we be able to read a mere storybook day after day, year after year, *shnayim mikra v'echad targum*? Certainly not!

Let's take the story of Yosef and his brothers, for instance. How many times have we heard this story? Yet, when a little child comes home from *cheder* and tells it to us, it interests us anew. This is a clear proof that the "book" was written by God. If it was not Godly and infinite, then children and adults would not be reading the same book. There is no book that is taught both in university and in first grade. There is no way that such a book could be examined back and forth, again and again, yet still be found interesting. If we would take the most fascinating storybook in the world and try to read it *shnayim mikra v'echad targum,* year after year, we would grow quite tired of it. We would not want to hear it again. Yet, how many times have we heard the story of Adam and Chavah?

Emunah Peshutah

Now we come to the issue of *emunah peshutah,* "simple faith." Much has been said about the greatness of *emunah peshutah.* But what is it?

We are often told that our grandmothers from the old country, and all the simple people back then, had *emunah peshutah.* We usually think this means that they believed what they were taught. They were taught that Hashem created the world, and

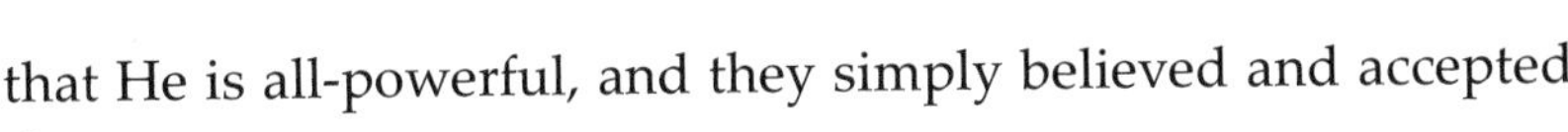

that He is all-powerful, and they simply believed and accepted this as true.

But this point always bothered me. What is so great about simply believing what one is taught? Why is it praiseworthy not to examine and investigate?

Then I realized that this point is misunderstood. I will illustrate what I mean. Let's say both of us walk into a certain house and I say, "Did you notice how they put the door over here on the side? They should have put it in the middle." Then you say to me, "Who told you that someone built this house?" Now, what is the answer to your question? Indeed, who told me that someone built this house? The answer is that I have *emunah peshutah* that someone built the house. It is something that I know implicitly without having to be told so.

This is how Jews of old believed in Hashem. It was not so much faith in what they were taught. It was more a faith in what they saw for themselves. They saw with their own eyes, and understood that which is implicitly true. This is *emunah peshutah*. If there is an amazingly complex and beautiful world, it must have been created by Someone. This is called "simple faith" because it requires no sophistication or study of any kind. Anyone with a mind must immediately recognize it to be true, it is so simple!

"Deep faith" is when we examine and investigate how we know it to be true. There is philosophical investigation, there is tradition, there are many ways to arrive at the truth. We could sit for a couple hours and bring proofs to the fact that someone built the house. But a sensible person will realize without need for any proofs that someone obviously built it. *Emunah peshutah* does not mean that Jews of old just believed what they were told. It means they believed what they saw and knew to be obviously true.

העיקר הראשון

3

The First Principle

אֲנִי מַאֲמִין בֶּאֱמוּנָה שְׁלֵמָה, שֶׁהַבּוֹרֵא יִתְבָּרַךְ שְׁמוֹ הוּא בּוֹרֵא וּמַנְהִיג לְכָל הַבְּרוּאִים, וְהוּא לְבַדּוֹ עָשָׂה וְעוֹשֶׂה וְיַעֲשֶׂה לְכָל הַמַּעֲשִׂים.

I believe with perfect faith that the Creator — may His Name be blessed — creates and directs all created beings, and that only He did, does, and will do all that is done.

"I Believe with Perfect Faith"

"PERFECT FAITH" MEANS SOMETHING known to be perfectly true, not something that is merely assumed to be true because it was heard second-hand. "Faith," *emunah,* denotes something known to be true. (This was explained at length in the previous chapter.)

"The Creator"

The first principle of our belief is that Hashem is the "Creator." A "creator" is one who makes things *yeish mei'ayin,* out of utter nothingness. We believe that Hashem created everything out of utter nothingness. This belief is actually the first word of the Torah: *"Bereishis."* In other words, the world has a beginning.

It is hard for us to conceptualize what it means to create out of utter nothingness. If we see someone pull a rabbit out of a hat, we know that the rabbit must have been there before. You can't just "create" a rabbit out of thin air! It boggles the human mind to relate to such a thing. Yet, Hashem created the entire world out of utter nothingness. His abilities are unlimited. His deeds are not bound by what we can visualize.

What does "utter nothingness" mean? This, too, is beyond our powers of comprehension. *Chazal* say that if someone thinks about what was before the world, he would be better off had he never been born.[1] It is a subject we are not even allowed to think about.

The following allegory explains this prohibition: A child is climbing up a ladder and wants to reach the moon. His father says, "No, I don't let!" The father means to say: If you climb up the ladder you will never reach the moon. Instead, you will just fall on your head.

This is what *Chazal* mean when they tell us we are not allowed to think about what was before the world. It does not mean that if we were allowed to, we would be able understand it. Rather, it means that it is totally beyond our reach. The only thing we will achieve is to damage ourselves.

"All Created Beings"

"All created beings" means more than just the physical things that we see: people, animals, earth, water, etc. And it is more than celestial beings, like angels, *seraphim, ofanim,* and *chayos ha-kodesh.* It includes even matters such as time and space. They, too, are creations of Hashem. We cannot conceptualize what was before time and space existed. Yet, they were created by Hashem out of utter nothingness. Before Creation there was no darkness and no light, no distance and no closeness, no up and no down. This is something we accept on faith because we cannot understand

1. *Chagigah* 11b, *Rashi* and *Tosafos ad loc.*

it. That Hashem exists is obvious and self-evident. But to believe that all the concepts which are fundamental to human comprehension, such as up and down, and right and left, are merely "creations" of Hashem? This is something we accept on faith because we are incapable of conceptualizing it.

Simply speaking, time and space were created on the first day of Creation. Early Torah sources discuss at length what exactly Hashem created on the first day, what is "space," etc. But this properly belongs to the subject of *Ma'aseh Bereishis*, about which *Chazal* said in *Chagigah* 11b that it is among the Torah's esoteric secrets. It is not our topic. We are discussing the thirteen principles, which are for everybody.

When we say that Hashem is the "Creator," we mean that He created absolutely everything that is known to us. Today, science recognizes that the entity called "space" is not a constant. It does not have a fixed, independent existence; it is relative and interacts with other factors such as time and velocity. In other words, "space" is a created being with its limitations, just like everything else.

This is the first point: Hashem has the quality of being the "Creator," and He created "all created beings" — all of reality.

"Directs"

In addition to believing that Hashem "creates," we also believe that He "directs."

Belief in Creation alone is not enough. We need the belief that Hashem leads and directs everything. Nothing happens, big or small, that does not come straight from Hashem. What about the entire complex system of angels and celestial beings? What about the influence of the planets and stars? They may be compared to a glove. Hashem covers His hands with gloves, so to speak, when He acts upon the world. These "gloves" are the stars and angels. But Hashem is doing everything Himself.

It is not comparable to a person using a stick. When a person hits with a stick, he is assisted by the weight and shape of the stick. His mere hands would not achieve the same effect. But when someone uses gloves, he is doing it all with his own power. The gloves merely hide the direct contact. You don't see the hand that did it, but you know it is there.

"Creating" and "directing" is really one and the same. If we think about it we will realize that if Hashem created everything, He must lead and direct everything, too. This is due to the second principle: Hashem is One. This principle is described in the hymn of *Yigdal,* "There is no end to His Oneness." Hashem is the sole Creator and there is no limit to His Oneness. Everything is from Hashem. He personally directs everything that happens in the world.

To illustrate this point, let's say we walk down the street and notice a house with a certain number of windows. Each window has its particular qualities: size, shape, color, etc. Hashem alone is responsible for all these details. This is the meaning of "There is no end to His Oneness." There is no end or limitation to the fact that everything is from Hashem.

Now let's imagine that one of these windows would change its shape by a micro-millimeter from that which Hashem willed. What would happen? The entire universe would crumble. All the worlds would cease to exist. Why? Because everything is part of Hashem's Oneness. If any entity is removed from Hashem's sole control, then there are now two independent forces, *chas v'shalom.* This unravels the oneness and unity of all reality. It undoes the basis of all of existence, since everything is based on Hashem's unlimited Oneness.

Let's take another example. Sitting in front of us is a fine strainer with five thousand holes. If we would claim that Hashem has no reason for the strainer to have exactly this number of holes, and by chance it happened to come out this way, then we are claiming that Hashem is not One. We are saying that the number of holes was determined by the strainer, not by Hashem. We have removed part of reality from Hashem's sole control.

The nature of Hashem's actions is that He has sole control over all. This idea is expressed by the fact that Hashem created the world in the shape of a circle. The Heavens, the earth's globe, the sun, the moon, all of nature is in the shape of a circle. This is very significant. If you slice off any part of a circle, this changes its entire shape: it is no longer round. It is not a circle anymore. But an object with rectangular sides is different. If you shorten one side, this does not necessitate a change on the opposite side. The object's shape remains essentially the same. A circle, on the other hand, is completely dependent on every one of its points.

This is comparable to the Torah, which, like Hashem, is one inseparable unit. We believe that if a single letter of the Torah would cease to exist, the entire world would revert to nothingness. This is because the Torah and Hashem are one. Similarly, it is unthinkable that anything should cease to be under the rule of Hashem's will. If the strainer has five thousand holes, then we must make up our minds: either Hashem willed that it should have exactly this number of holes, or there is another reason for it. And if there is a different reason for it, then His Oneness has an end, *chas v'shalom*. We believe that "There is no end to His Oneness."

Hashem's plan for reality is that it should constitute one inseparable unit. If there is anything that stands independently, the whole plan is thereby cancelled and collapses.

Hashem Directs the World Personally

We need to understand that Hashem leads and directs the world in a very personal way. He sees to every matter Himself. To an astounding degree, He involves Himself in every detail from the depths below to the highest Heavens above. There is nothing that He is not directly involved with. The angels and all the celestial beings are like inanimate objects. Hashem did not endow them with independent thought or the ability to make a decision. They act, but not on the basis of free choice. In other words, they are not "in charge" of anything. This is the meaning of, "He directs all created beings."

This is what "There is no end to His Oneness" means. If we would claim that there is some point, some grain of sand, some star, some spark of light, that is beyond the realm of Hashem's personal involvement, then we would be saying that there, Hashem is not One. We would be saying that there is a limit and boundary to His Oneness, whereas we believe the opposite to be true: "There is *no* end to His Oneness." Every ant crawling on the sidewalk, every light fixture hanging from the ceiling, every far-flung galaxy in outer space — it all is created and directed by Hashem Himself. "Only He did, does, and will do all that is done."

The Great Importance of Nothingness

Getting back to the point that Hashem created everything *yeish mei'ayin,* out of utter nothingness: we should know that this is actually one of the world's most hotly disputed issues. It is a critical point, and the whole Torah stands on it. This is what all the big debates, all the philosophical battles against Judaism were about. It is the main issue that divides people who believe in Torah from those who deny it.

We should know that the idea of Creation *yeish mei'ayin* is unique to the Torah. Pure philosophy does not lead to this conclusion. The Rambam writes that the Greek philosopher Aristotle reached the greatest heights attainable by the human mind. When the human mind meditates upon the natural world, it indeed discovers the existence of God. It recognizes God's greatness and glory. But without the Torah, it does not realize that God created the world *yeish mei'ayin*. This is why the classical philosophers did not recognize this principle, and denied its truth. Yet, if someone does not believe that Hashem created the world *yeish mei'ayin,* he also does not believe that Hashem is One.

There are a lot of profound things to say on this subject. In my Hebrew *kuntres* called *Breichos B'cheshbon,* I went into it a little more in depth (the discussion starts on p. 11), but here we are keeping it simple. There is one very sensitive point, though, that we cannot skip over. I feel it necessary to speak about this point because if I don't, you may hear about it from other sources. And if you misunderstand it, you are erring in the very fundamentals of *emunah*. Therefore, since there is much confusion over this issue, I will state what I was taught by my *rebbeim* about it:

The world does not have an aspect of Divinity and Godliness to it. It is no more than a creation of Hashem. If it had a Divine, Godly aspect, it would not be "created," for it would possess an aspect that always existed, just like God always existed. But this cannot be so, because it contradicts the fundamentals of *emunah*. We believe that the world did *not* always exist. The world and everything it contains was created out of utter nothingness. Hashem alone always existed. This has been our faith since Moshe Rabbeinu took us out of Egypt. We will now get to the crux of the matter: Even the *neshamos* of the Jewish people were created by Hashem out of utter nothingness. In other words, Jewish *neshamos* did not always exist.

"A Part of God from Above"

It is oft quoted from Torah sources that a Jew's soul is "A part of God from above."[2] What does this mean? Is a Jew's soul Divine and Godly? If so, what separates man from God?

I was taught by my *rebbeim* that the matter is as follows. Hashem created a being that possesses all the same qualities that He has, down to the tiniest details. This being is man. In other words, man is a carbon copy of Hashem, but with one difference: the former is the Creator, and the latter is a created

2. See *Reishis Chochmah, Sha'arei HaKedushah*, chap. 14.

being. This is an enormous difference. It may be compared to a man standing in front of a mirror. The real man looks just the same as his reflection. The same eyes, the same ears — everything is identical. But there is one difference. The former is a man, and the latter is nothing. The former is real, and the latter is an illusion.

So it is with God and man. Man is a created being just like everything else in the world. However, he resembles the form of his Creator. He has all the same qualities, and possesses tremendous power. In this way, God and man are so close that we could say one is a "part" of the other. Their resemblance is so striking that the Torah describes man as being in the image of God above. *B'tzelem Elokim.* This is the meaning of "A part of God from above."

But a created being has no independent existence. It exists only as long as Hashem so wills it, and possesses only the qualities that Hashem desires it to have. On its own, a created being is a total non-entity. Hashem willed that man should possess the same qualities that He does. Man, as a created being, was bestowed with tremendous power. But none of this is his own. Man resembles Hashem in a striking way, but ultimately, man is nothing. Just as an ant is zero as compared to Hashem, so a Jew is zero as compared to Hashem.

The idea that Hashem created everything *yeish mei'ayin* is indeed a profound one. When the Rambam remarked that man's mind is incapable of conceptualizing it, he was not speaking just of Aristotle. He was speaking even of the greatest Kabbalist. We cannot grasp the meaning of *yeish mei'ayin* in its true depth. But we are taught that the world and everything in it — including the *neshamos* of the Jewish people — was created by God out of utter nothingness. Before then, nothing existed other than God Himself.

The Torah, too, was created by Hashem out of utter nothingness. If so, what is the meaning of, "*Yisrael, Oraisa, veKudsha*

Brich Hu chad hu" (The Jewish people, the Torah, and Hashem are one)? It means that they are so powerfully unified that they look and seem to be "one."

It means that when Hashem created the Torah, He endowed it with tremendous power, to the point that it is unified with Him, with His qualities, with His infiniteness. But even the Torah is no more than a created entity. It is not Hashem. Hashem is One and Only. There is nothing other than Him.

This is something that we must know clearly: Hashem is One and Only. There is nothing other than Him, and we are created beings. In the beginning, Hashem created everything — *yeish mei'ayin*! *Bereishis bara Elokim.*

Don't Get Confused

The Rambam wrote to his son:[3]

> Sometimes you will come upon a deep verse or a perplexing statement in the Torah or the Prophets, or in the writings of the Sages, and you will not understand it. You will not know how to unravel its secret. And it will seem to contradict the principles of Torah or of common talk [i.e., classical philosophy]. Do not move from your beliefs, and do not allow your mind to become confused. Stay with what you have established, and attribute the lack of understanding to yourself. *"For it [the Torah] is not an empty thing, [unless it is] from you."*[4] Put the statement on the side and do not contaminate all your beliefs because of a certain wise teaching that you failed to understand.

The Rambam is saying that if you know of a certain Torah principle, and then you hear something that seems to conflict, put that something on the side and don't worry about it. The

3. *Rambam, Iggeres HaMussar* (written to his son R. Avraham).
4. *Devarim* 32:47; see *Bereishis Rabbah* 1:14.

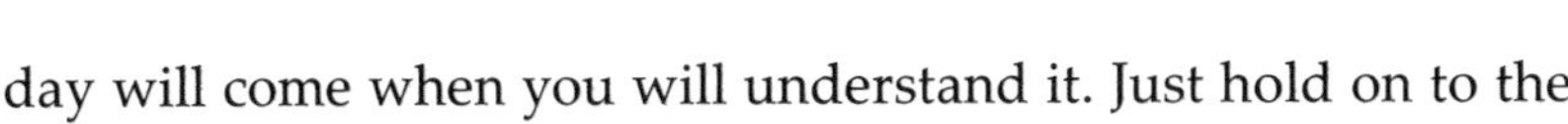

day will come when you will understand it. Just hold on to the principles that you were taught!

There is no lack of misleading statements. There are plenty of confusing approaches. And there is no end to the nonsense that people speak. We need to hold onto the principles of *emunah* that we were taught and that we know to be true.

It says in the Zohar, "If a person goes in and does not come out, he would be better off if he had never been created."[5] In other words, if you can't get back out, don't go in. You can go to whatever depths you wish. But there is a condition: that you can come back out again. "Come out" means to return to the point from which you started.

This is what it says in *Sefer Yetzirah*: "If your mouth is running to speak, and your heart to contemplate, return to *HaMakom*."[6] One explanation of this is to return to your "place." Get back to where you started from, to your original understanding. *Sefer Yetzirah* is saying that you are allowed to run, but in the end you must return to your original place. If you can't, don't run.

A person should think as follows: How did I understand matters before I started to run? I understood that Hashem is the One and Only Creator of everything. He created us all. If you can get back to this *emunah* after your deep investigations, then you may run. But if not, don't even start.

If you are concerned that perhaps you might not be able to get out again, you should not go in. How can you know this before you start? It is like entering a steaming hot bath. First you stick in the tip of your toe to check how hot the water is. If you can stand it, then you put in your whole foot, and then both feet, and so on. But if you can't take the heat, you pull your foot out right away.

5. *Idra Rabbah, Naso* 141a.

6. *Sefer HaYetzirah,* 1:7.

Some people have the type of mind that does not feel comfortable with questions that don't have answers. They feel perturbed when they just leave things up in the air, unexplained. If this type of person has a *kushya* that was not resolved by the end of the learning session, he is plagued by it during davening.

When issues in *emunah* are the subject under study, the situation starts to become more serious. People like this can start to have unsettling doubts when they hear certain things. And each explanation offered them is unsatisfying. It just leads to another question, and they feel that their basic religious beliefs are coming under question. People like this must be careful. Someone who needs every question to have a conclusive and satisfying answer would be better off not opening any *sefer* that deeply investigates matters of *emunah*. If a person is not in the habit of approaching touchy issues with equanimity, with simple faith in the principles that our tradition teaches us, then he might have a hard time getting back to the point he started from.

Personally, I don't have to have all the answers. If I hear an interesting explanation regarding something that relates to principles of faith, that's fine; it's another building block in my understanding. I don't care if someone can raise a problem with it. The bedrock of my *emunah*, which I received already in *cheder*, remains — that the Torah is the only truth. Someone who feels that he must understand completely, without any questions, shouldn't delve into these subjects.

In our times, the air is full of spiritual and moral corruption of the worst kind. We are surrounded by temptations of all types. There is a general atmosphere of denial and disbelief. Therefore, we need to exercise special caution when we deal with issues of *emunah*.

We should rather take the approach of simple *emunah*, as we have been taught by our unbroken tradition which goes back to Moshe Rabbeinu. The *Mishnah Berurah*, citing *Maharshal*, says something most appropriate about this: "Do we know anyone greater than R. Shimshon of Chinon? Yet, after he learned the secrets of the Kabbalah, he prayed [with utter simplicity] like a little child."[7]

"I believe with perfect faith that the Creator — may His Name be blessed — creates and directs all created beings." This is the simple truth.

7. *Mishnah Berurah* 25:42.

הָעִיקָר הַשֵּׁנִי

4

The Second Principle

אֲנִי מַאֲמִין בֶּאֱמוּנָה שְׁלֵמָה, שֶׁהַבּוֹרֵא יִתְבָּרַךְ שְׁמוֹ הוּא יָחִיד וְאֵין יְחִידוּת כָּמוֹהוּ בְּשׁוּם פָּנִים, וְהוּא לְבַדּוֹ אֱלֹקֵינוּ, הָיָה הֹוֶה וְיִהְיֶה.

I believe with perfect faith that the Creator — may His Name be blessed — is One, and that there is no oneness at all like His, and that He alone is our God; He was, is, and will be.

Simple Oneness and True Oneness

THE SECOND PRINCIPLE IS Hashem's Oneness. What does it mean that Hashem is "one"? Simply speaking, it means that Hashem is the one and only Creator, and He is the one and only Director. There is no one else besides Him.

However, there is more to the topic of Hashem's Oneness than this idea. All the Rishonim — including the Rambam — do not spend much time on this simple meaning when they speak of Hashem's Oneness. Instead of focusing on the fact that Hashem is the sole Creator and Director, the Rambam emphasizes that "There is no oneness at all like His." This means that Hashem's unity is absolute. Hashem is not dividable into parts. By contrast, a table is composed of parts. A human being, as well, is composed of parts. But Hashem does not have "parts"; His unity is absolute.

Hashem's Oneness is a topic that contains many details and principles.[1] It is not clear how many of these points are considered basic requirements for believing that Hashem is One. (We will discuss this issue in a separate chapter, after the thirteenth principle.) Our aim here is to cover only the basic points of *emunah,* not to delve into finer philosophical issues. However, Hashem's absolute unity is one of those basic points. The Rambam, the *Chovos HaLevavos*[2] and other early Torah sources seem to consider Hashem's absolute unity to be the main point in the topic of Hashem's Oneness. This is called the *yichud ha-amiti,* "the true Oneness."

At the same time, we should not lose sight of the simple meaning of Hashem's Oneness: He is the one and only Creator and Director. There is no end to His Oneness. In other words, everything is from His will and under His control, to an endless degree. We elaborated on this in the previous chapter.

We can understand the idea of Hashem's absolute unity, what is called *yichud ha-amiti,* by contrasting it with ourselves. Let's say a person knows that bananas are yellow and apples are red. Is this knowledge "him"? If he would forget this knowledge for a moment, would there be something missing from his essential being? Would he be less of a person for not knowing that bananas are yellow? Certainly not. There is one thing called what he "is," and there is something else called what he "knows." In other words, we are composed of various parts: our essential being and our knowledge. But with Hashem this is not so.

The Rambam writes:[3]

> *HaKadosh Baruch Hu* recognizes the truth, and knows it as it is. He does not know it with a knowledge that is external to

1. See the end of *Chovos HaLevavos,* in the "*bakashah*" section, s.v. "*Binosi.*"
2. *Sha'ar HaYichud.*
3. *Mishneh Torah, Hilchos Yesodei HaTorah* 2:10.

> Him, like we know things. We and what we know are not one. But with the Creator, may He be blessed, it is different: He and His knowledge and His life are one. This is true from every side and from every point and from every way of unity.

What Hashem is, and what He knows, and what He wills, are all the very same thing. It is all one.

A person has various parts and elements. We can speak of a person's *da'as,* as apart from his *binah,* and as apart from his *chesed*. But there is no such thing as Hashem's *"chesed"* as a separate element. Hashem is a total and absolute unity that includes everything. As the Rambam puts it:[4]

> It comes out that Hashem knows, He is that which is known, and He is knowledge itself — it is all one. This is something that the mouth cannot speak, nor the ear hear, nor man's faculty of understanding properly grasp.

This is a very important aspect of Hashem's Oneness. We must know that Hashem is one, indivisible reality. On this reality depends our reality and everything we have.

Examples There are certain concepts that are hard to say in words, but examples help a lot. For instance, there is a well-known Gemara concept called *yi'ush shelo mi-da'as*. This refers to a lost object, regarding which the owner has "unknowing despair" that he will ever retrieve his object. This concept is disputed at length between Abaye and Rava.[5] When this *sugya* of the Gemara is taught, regardless whether it is in the fifth grade, in *beis midrash* or in *kollel,* the same problem always arises: how do you define "unknowing despair"? The more you

4. Ibid.
5. *Bava Metzia* 21b.

talk about it, the less you understand it. Usually what is done is to briefly state the concept and then jump into the Gemara's discussion. The first proof for *yi'ush shelo mi-da'as* is presented, and rejected. And then the second. And then the third. There is a flow of *kushyos* and *terutzim* that involve various examples. It is seen how *yi'ush shelo mi-da'as* applies to *terumah,* to *shlichus,* to *pe'ah,* etc. The students gain a picture of *yi'ush shelo mi-da'as* and grasp how it works.

The same is true with the concept of Hashem's unity. Talking about it and trying to define it will not get us there. The Rambam has already informed us that it is impossible to describe Hashem's true unity in words. But if we will apply this concept practically, in various areas, we will start to grasp what it is and how it works.

Can You Hear without Ears?

Everything that Hashem created is composed of two basic elements: form and matter. But with Hashem Himself, this is not so. He is one, indivisible reality. He is not composed of form and matter.

Although we cannot conceptualize such a thing, we can know that Hashem is a very powerful reality. He is perfect in every way. He has every positive quality and every capability. His superiority is absolute. Nothing can hold Him back, and He carries out His will above and below.

Why am I stressing such an obvious point? What does it even have to do with our topic? The answer is we are liable to think that since Hashem is not built like us, therefore He does not have the same abilities that we do. How do we hear? We are endowed with 248 various organs and limbs, and among them are our ears, which are physical organs composed of form and matter. Without them we cannot hear. But Hashem doesn't have ears. Does this mean He can't hear? To answer this, it says: "*He*

Who creates the ear, can He not hear?"[6] The verse is telling us that Hashem's perfection does not deprive Him of any capability, lofty or lowly. The fact that His unity is absolute, that He is not composed of form and matter, that He does not have 248 various limbs and organs, does not stop Him from doing anything. He can even roll in the dust, so to speak, if He so wishes. And it is written that in fact He does so. Since we have sinned, and because He loves us, His great kindness brings Him to wallow in the dust for our sake.[7]

This is an expression of Hashem's absolute unity. He is indivisible, and He encompasses all of reality.

Having It All

It says in *Tanna D'vei Eliyahu*:

> Perhaps you will say that he who learned much of the Written and Oral Torah, and he who learned little of the Written and Oral Torah, will have equally shining faces in the World to Come? It is not so. Blessed is Hashem; blessed is He. He shows no favoritism… rather, each person receives according to his way.[8]

This *Chazal* addresses the question whether someone who learned a lot of Torah has an advantage over someone who learned a little Torah. But why is this even a question? Why would we think that the Vilna Gaon, who learned Torah nonstop in great depth his whole life, might not look any different in the World to Come from someone who once wandered into a *daf yomi shiur* and learned a few lines of Gemara? Why should their faces be equally shining?

The answer is that learning Torah connects and attaches us

6. *Tehillim* 94:9.

7. See *Ma'amar Tikkunei Teshuvah, Rema MiPano*, chap. 14.

8. *Tanna D'vei Eliyahu Zuta*, chap. 12.

to Hashem. If a person learns a little bit of Torah, he has a little point of connection with Hashem. And once a person is connected to Hashem, he has everything. This is because Hashem's unity is absolute. There is no "more" and "less" when it comes to Hashem. He is One. Someone who learns Torah for a few minutes has already acquired a hold on the infinity of Hashem. And there is nothing that can be added to infinity.

That was *Chazal*'s question. And what was their answer?

"He shows no favoritism." For each additional moment that a person learns Torah, he receives anew an entire infinite connection to Hashem. How can a person receive more, if he already has it all? We don't understand. Nevertheless, it is so — whether we understand it or not. This is something that is beyond us.

Thinking in this way about Hashem's absolute unity is the greatest *mussar sefer* that could possibly be. It enables us to understand the loss incurred by one moment of *bittul Torah*.

Here is another *Chazal* that illustrates the point.

> Did you ever hear of a kind of merchandise that the seller is sold along with it? *HaKadosh Baruch Hu* said to the Jewish people: "I sold you My Torah, and I was sold along with it, so to speak."[9]

If we grab hold of Torah, we grab hold of *HaKadosh Baruch Hu* too. He "comes along with it," so to speak. Let us understand this point. What happens when we hold on to a person? We can grasp his hand, his foot, his *chesed*… but not his *chochmah*. A person's intellect is not something we can grasp and hold. With Hashem, however, it is not so. His unity is absolute. If we have a hold on one word in *Chumash*, we have Hashem Himself, so to speak, in all His infinity. Just think what is contained within each word of Torah that we learn!

9. *Shemos Rabbah* 33:1.

This is only because of Hashem's absolute unity. Otherwise we would have just what we actually grasped. But Hashem is One, and because of this, one word of Torah contains a treasure trove that is absolutely indescribable.

Doing It All

As we know, the Torah's mitzvos are numerous. This is expressed in the well-known teaching of *Chazal*:[10]

> R. Chananya ben Akashya says: "*HaKadosh Baruch Hu* wanted to bestow merit on the Jewish people. Therefore, He gave them a lot of Torah and mitzvos."

The Rambam comments on this as follows:[11]

> It is a principle of our Torah faith that when a person properly and correctly fulfills one of the 613 mitzvos, he thereby acquires life in the World to Come. This is when he does the mitzvah for its own sake, out of love, as explained above, and does not have in mind any worldly goal at all. Regarding this, R. Chananya said that the mitzvos are many, and therefore it is impossible for a person to go through life without doing one of them in a right and complete way. And when he does that mitzvah, his soul will live because of that act.

Every Jew will end up doing at least one mitzvah properly during his lifetime. And that one mitzvah will give him an infinite and eternal connection with Hashem. If so, why does he need to do more than one mitzvah? And why should we think that he will receive more reward if he does, when the first mitzvah already gave him eternity?

The answer is: "Blessed is Hashem; blessed is He. He shows no favoritism… each person receives according to his way."

10. *Makkos* 3:16.

11. *Rambam's Commentary on Mishnayos* ad loc.

Every mitzvah that we do bestows upon us infinity and eternity all over again, even though we cannot comprehend this.

A mitzvah that is done *lishmah,* "for its own sake," is a mitzvah that is done in a complete and perfect way. I hesitate to say this but when a person wakes up late and quickly jumps out of bed to recite the Shema before it is too late, this is a mitzvah done in a complete and perfect way. Why? Because there are no ulterior motives involved; it was done solely because Hashem said a Jew must recite the Shema. (But I don't recommend acting this way!)

That is why the Rambam says it is virtually impossible for a Jew to go through life without fulfilling at least one mitzvah *lishmah,* i.e., in a complete and perfect way. Life has so many opportunities for this! And when a person merits doing this perfect mitzvah he has thereby attached himself to Hashem's Oneness. And when he has even the smallest attachment to Oneness, he is attached to everything. This is because Hashem's Oneness does not divide into various parts. It is absolute.

Echad, Yachid, and Meyuchad

As we mentioned at the beginning of this chapter, the topic of Hashem's Oneness contains many principles. One of them is the simple meaning of Oneness (there is only one God). Another is *yichud ha-amiti* (absolute unity). And there are yet others. Early Torah sources sum it all up by saying that Hashem is *echad, yachid, u'meyuchad* — "One, only, and unique."

Echad means that Hashem's unity is one and indivisible.

Yachid means that Hashem is the one and only. There are not two creators. It is recounted that when R. Yehoshua Leib Diskin was a child, his father taught him that there is only one God. R. Yehoshua Leib replied, "But that is obvious. It says, '*The whole world is full of His glory.'*[12] If so, there obviously is no room for another one!"[13] This way of understanding it is quite true, and quite deep.

Meyuchad means that Hashem directs everything, and that there is nothing else besides Him and His will. While *echad* and *yachid* refer to Hashem, *meyuchad* expresses what takes place in the world. It means that everything is from Him.

Echad conveys that Hashem is an absolute unity in every way.

Yachid conveys that Hashem is alone; there is no other besides Him.

Meyuchad conveys that everything is unique to Him. In other words, everything that we see, whether it is a table, a star, or anything else, is all from Hashem.

12. *Yeshayahu* 6:3.

13. Cited in *Amud Eish*, p. 17.

הָעִיקָר הַשְּׁלִישִׁי

5

The Third Principle

אֲנִי מַאֲמִין בֶּאֱמוּנָה שְׁלֵמָה, שֶׁהַבּוֹרֵא יִתְבָּרַךְ שְׁמוֹ אֵינוֹ גוּף, וְלֹא יַשִּׂיגוּהוּ מַשִּׂיגֵי הַגּוּף, וְאֵין לוֹ שׁוּם דִּמְיוֹן כְּלָל.

I believe with perfect faith that the Creator — may His Name be blessed — is not physical, and cannot be perceived by physical means, and there is nothing at all to which He can be compared.

"Not Physical" Means Not Limited

AFTER HAVING EXPLAINED THE previous principle of Hashem's Oneness, this principle of Hashem's non-physicality is actually quite simple. "Not physical" means that Hashem is not limited to anything that can be conceptualized. He is not limited to anything material.

When we speak of "material," we mean it in the broader sense of the word. Angels are often described as form without matter. In other words, they are non-material beings. But in the broader sense, angels too have matter, although it is a much finer matter than what we are composed of. Matter in its broader sense means anything that can be conceptualized; anything that is related to substance.

When we say that Hashem "is not physical," we mean that He has no materiality at all in any sense of the word. We cannot illustrate this point by comparison to the angels, but we can illustrate it by comparison to the *neshamah*. As far as we can perceive, the *neshamah* has no material aspect. Yet, it exists. When we say, "*I* see," or "*I* hear," what is this "I" that we are speaking of? It is something without any materiality.

Yet, Hashem is beyond this as well. He "has no physicality," meaning that we have no way at all to conceptualize what He is. "There is nothing at all to which He can be compared."

Even our *neshamah,* which is the greatest example of "form without matter" in our lives, has a certain type of matter to it. We cannot see this matter, but it exists. The very fact that we can say that the *neshamah* is a soul, and not a table, shows that we can define it. We have a conceptual hold on it. But with Hashem, "There is nothing at all to which He can be compared." If we want to define Hashem, we have only one way of doing it: "Hashem." The *neshamah*, on the other hand, can be defined in various ways: the "soul," the "I," "the inner self that sees," etc.

With Hashem, "There is nothing at all to which He can be compared." This means that no created being in the entire universe has any concept of what Hashem is. Even the angel Metatron, who is called by the name of Hashem,[1] has no idea what Hashem really is. All we know is that He exists, and that He is Hashem. We don't know anything about His nature.

"If I Knew Him, I Would Be Him"

If someone thinks he understands what Hashem is, he is denying the Jewish faith. This is because we human beings are able to conceptualize only things that our physical senses give us a connection to. We understand abstract, "spiritual" concepts only if we are able to relate them in some way to the reality that we perceive. The concept must be connected at least

1. *Sanhedrin* 38b.

indirectly to something real and physical. This is because something completely detached from our senses is beyond our ability to understand.

The word *da'as*, "knowledge," connotes connection, as in: "*And Adam knew...*" (*Bereishis* 4:1). If we have no connection to something's actual existence, we will never be able to comprehend it! If we say that a thing is definable, that we can comprehend its nature and significance, then we are saying that we have some type of connection with it. But if someone says this about Hashem, he is denying the Jewish faith.

Why? What basic point is he contradicting? Someone who claims that he has a connection with Hashem's very being is denying that Hashem created him out of utter nothingness. He is denying that Hashem is One, only and unique. He is denying that Hashem's unity is absolute. (These concepts were explained in previous chapters.)

Early Torah sources express this point as follows:

> If I knew Him, I would be Him.[2]

Why is this so? The Rambam states:

> Hashem knows, He is that which is known, and He is knowledge itself.[3]

Since Hashem is knowledge itself, if we would have an understanding of Hashem, we would be Hashem! But we don't have to understand Hashem's true nature. We accept these matters as they are, even without understanding them.

Let's say a person says, "I agree that we can't really understand Hashem's true nature, but at least we can understand *a little bit* about Him!" This, too, is denying the Jewish faith. It

2. *Derashos HaRan* 4; *Sefer HaIkkarim* 2:30.
3. *Rambam, Mishneh Torah, Hilchos Yesodei HaTorah* 2:10.

is denying Hashem's absolute unity. This is because Hashem is one indivisible whole. We cannot say that this part we understand and that part we don't, because Hashem doesn't have parts. Thus we cannot understand Him even a little.

In this way, the third principle flows naturally from the second principle. The fact that Hashem's unity is absolute brings us to the conclusion that, "There is nothing at all to which He can be compared."

We have absolutely no concept of Hashem's essence. Like we mentioned above, the third principle flows naturally from the second principle. Since Hashem and His *da'as* — that is, knowledge of Essence — are one, Hashem's knowledge of Himself is not separated from His self. He and what He knows is one. Therefore, "If I would know Him, I would be Him." It is that simple. It is so simple and logical that it does not even need an illustration.

All we can know about Hashem is that He is Hashem. When we say that He is Hashem, we mean: "There is nothing at all to which He can be compared."

What He is, we don't know. But *that* He is, we know. Hashem exists!

Knowing Hashem's Deeds

We can understand how Hashem acts. Hashem is all-powerful and therefore can do whatever He wills. He can bestow kindness. He can exact judgement and vengeance. He can do whatever He wills, in the way He wills it.

If we ask what Hashem is, we can only answer that He is. But if we ask what He can *do*, this is what the whole Torah is about. He made the world. He created us. He brings down the rain, etc, etc. We see and know the things He does.

All of the qualities that we ascribe to Hashem mean something different from what they mean ordinarily. For instance, about Hashem it is said, "You are wise, but not with a wisdom that is known."[4] Hashem's way of knowing is different from our way of knowing. He knows with a knowledge that is He Himself. And with this perfect knowledge, He can do anything that He wills.

The classical philosophers did not challenge the idea that God is non-physical. Neither did they challenge the idea that God is above human comprehension, and that God is one. Why? Because these ideas do not intrude on a person's practical life! The philosophers challenged only the principle that God can do anything He wills. This is an idea that Judaism introduced to the world.

We believe that Hashem can act in all sorts of ways. He can act in a limited way, and also in an unlimited way, and it is not a contradiction. He knows everything we do and He can punish us; and at the very same time, in His infinite kindness, He causes the blood to flow in our veins.

Everything that Hashem does, He does it Himself. "Not by an angel and not by a *seraph* and not by an emissary but *HaKadosh Baruch Hu* Himself."[5] It is said that Hashem has angels that He uses to carry out His will. But in truth, He does everything by His own hands. This is because only He grants existence and life to the angel. It is true that *Chazal's* statement of, "I, and not an angel,"[6] applies specifically to *Yetzias Mitzrayim*. But this is because *Yetzias Mitzrayim* was the place where Hashem's personal involvement became openly revealed. There was a *gilui Shechinah* there. But in fact, He does everything Himself, all the time. It is usually said that angels carry out His will because Hashem's personal involvement is usually concealed from our perception. We know He is doing it, but we don't see it.

4. *Tikunei Zohar* 17b.
5. *Haggadah shel Pesach.*
6. *Yalkut Shimoni, Bo* 199.

He does it all Himself because, "There is no end to His Oneness," as we say in the hymn of *Yigdal*. There is no limit to how far His Oneness reaches. He does everything Himself, to an infinite degree.

Closer than Anything

This idea enables us to understand how the great people of the past lived their lives. For them, these ideas were as real as can be. They were part of their practical lives, not abstract concepts as they are for us today. When they would daven to Hashem their hearts would overflow with feeling. When they would say the words *Baruch she'amar vehayah ha'olam,* it was not just words. It was an expression of, "There is no end to His Oneness." And it was also an expression of, "There is no understanding His greatness." For them, Hashem's greatness is not divorced from His closeness and personal involvement in our lives. On the one hand He is infinite and unlimited, and on the other hand He personally does the things that are closest to us. It is all unified.

These ideas are not meant to be philosophical concepts. They are meant to be translated into *avodas Hashem*. They are meant to move us and excite us. Jews of old were indeed moved. And even more moved than them were the *Avos,* and Moshe Rabbeinu, for whom all this was a very tangible reality. Their awareness of this did not waver even for a moment — even when they ate, even when they slept. It filled every moment of their lives. Let us follow in their ways.

הָעִיקָר הָרְבִיעִי

6

The Fourth Principle

אֲנִי מַאֲמִין בֶּאֱמוּנָה שְׁלֵמָה, שֶׁהַבּוֹרֵא יִתְבָּרַךְ שְׁמוֹ הוּא רִאשׁוֹן וְהוּא אַחֲרוֹן.

I believe with perfect faith that the Creator — may His Name be blessed — is the first and the last.

Something Must Exist

THE PRINCIPLE THAT HASHEM "is the first and the last" expresses the idea the Rishonim state, that Hashem's existence is necessary and absolute. Let us understand this idea.

Everything else in the world does not have to exist. It did not have to be, and it did not have to be the way it is. But Hashem's existence is different. It is something that absolutely must be. The Rambam puts it like this:

> The foundation of all foundations, and the pillar of all wisdom, is to know that there is a first Being Who brought all of reality into existence. And all of reality — from Heaven to earth and whatever is in between — came into existence only by means of His true reality. If we would entertain the possibility that He does not exist, then nothing else would exist.[1]

1. *Mishneh Torah, Hilchos Yesodei HaTorah* 1:10.

The Rambam is saying that Hashem's existence is the basis of everything else that exists. If we exist, then, perforce, Hashem exists. But it is a one-way equation: Hashem could exist without us, although we could not exist without Hashem, and neither could anything else in the world. This being so, we are led to the conclusion that Hashem must have always been, before everything else came into being. This idea is very simple and self-evident.

There are examples for this idea. They do not express its full truth, but they at least serve as allegories. The best allegory for this is the concept of space. By space, we mean three-dimensional reality, as in the expression, "time and space." Thanks to space we have basic concepts such as up and down, right and left, in and out. Without space, none of these would exist. Nothing would take up any space, because there would be no space! We have no way to imagine this kind of a reality. It makes no sense to us. Yet, before the world existed, there was no space.

According to our natural way of thinking, what would we say if we were asked, "Who created space"? We would say that the concept of space must have always existed. We would say about space that it is "the first and the last." Since it encompasses everything, it must have been before everything, and will be after everything. If there would be no space, reality simply could not exist. There would be absolutely nothing.

This in fact is why Hashem is called *HaMakom*, "Space." It is because space is an allegory for Hashem.

> Why do we give *HaKadosh Baruch Hu* another name and call Him *HaMakom?* Because He is the space of the world, and the world is not the space of Him.[2]

Space encompasses and bears everything. Without space, nothing could be. Everything would just disappear. In the same

2. *Bereishis Rabbah* 68:9.

way, *HaKadosh Baruch Hu* is called the "space" of the world. This is because He encompasses even space.

He encompasses space, rather than space encompassing Him. *HaKadosh Baruch Hu* is called "Space" because it is a most appropriate allegory to Him. This illustrates the idea that Hashem's existence is necessary and absolute, an idea that is basic to our faith. But we cannot contemplate on it too deeply. As it says in *Sefer Yetzirah*, "If your heart runs, return to *HaMakom*." Return to this allegory, and go no farther.

We have now explained the principle that Hashem "is the first and the last": Hashem's existence is necessary and absolute. There is nothing that has to be, except for Him. Therefore, He is the One Who brought everything else into existence. As the *Chovos HaLevavos* says, "Everything that has an end, has a beginning."[3] But Hashem never comes to an end, just as He has no beginning. If so, He must always be.

"Judging" the Truth

How do we know that God exists? It is written, *"You shall know this day, and bring it into your heart, that Hashem is God."*[4] According to the *Chovos HaLevavos*, this verse teaches us that we must investigate the matter of Hashem's existence. We should understand how we know this to be true.[5] We are allowed to investigate this because we need to know Hashem.

People follow various approaches, but before everything, we must understand what it means to judge the truth of a matter. We will illustrate this point by comparing it to a court case, in which there is the role of lawyer and of judge. The lawyer works for the litigant, and devotes all his efforts to promoting

3. *Sha'ar HaYichud*, chap. 5.
4. *Devarim* 4:37.
5. *Sha'ar HaYichud*, chap. 2.

his client's case. His arguments are biased and one-sided. The lawyer is sure that his client is right. On the other hand, the judge treats both sides equally and must decide between them.

This explains why certain people run into difficulty when they try to investigate the issue of God's existence. It is because they turn into "lawyers." If they would allow themselves to be the "judge" and examine the matter in an impartial manner, it would not take them very long to come to a clear conclusion. They would bow flat on the floor and declare, "Hashem is God!" However, taking the role of lawyer, they are likely not to recognize the truth at all. Sometimes a person is such a good "lawyer" that he indefatigably presents one possibility after another, maybe this, and maybe that, and maybe the other thing... there is no end to his maybes. If a person firmly insists on evading the truth, he is likely to succeed.

The *yetzer hara* has many forms and shapes. There is a *yetzer hara* of *avodah zarah*. A person has a vested interest in maintaining that God does not exist. Thus, all his senses and faculties place themselves at the service of his "lawyer" approach. This is why people run into difficulty.

In today's world there is an *avodah zarah* called the theory of evolution. Similarly, there is the "big bang" theory, which maintains that the world was created by a powerful explosion, after which everything developed on its own over the course of millions of years until it became the way it is now. But reality contradicts these theories.

There is a basic problem with these theories: They claim that the world built itself. However, there is nothing we see or know of that builds itself. Nothing in the natural world can serve as a case in point for this supposed process. On the contrary, there is a widely observed phenomenon of entropy. Things tend to fall apart and decompose over time. If we take a cassette recorder and leave it for a hundred years, it will not develop into a computer. It will rather turn into a rusty piece of junk.

There is nothing in the world that builds itself and develops to a higher stage of existence. Not just scientists know this; even children know this.

The same applies to living beings. If we take an animal and place it in conditions that are not life-supporting to its species, it will die. It will not evolve over the course of thousands of years into something higher. Rather, it will decompose and become dust.

How could someone go ahead and present such ridiculous theories to the whole world, young and old, learned and ignorant? How could someone argue that everything we see just happened by chance? The eye, the moon, the grass, etc., etc., all started out as "chance occurrences." And this was followed by an unbroken chain of millions upon millions of "chance occurrences," all going against the trend of nature, until things developed to the way they are today?

The answer is that a lawyer is capable of presenting any and every false claim he can think of. He will persistently fabricate excuses in order to defend his client. The proponents of these theories never sat down and considered the issue impartially, in the role of judge. They rather adopted the role of lawyer.

When we discuss and examine topics such as these, we will have a much harder time recognizing the truth if we act as "lawyers." But if we will be "judges," we will find it a very easy case. We will recognize the truth quite clearly. This is because the arguments of the non-believers are implausible and full of contradictions.

Hidden Right in Front of Your Eyes

R. Moshe Chaim Luzzatto describes, in the introduction to *Mesillas Yesharim,* the nature of his *sefer*'s topic:

> The better that something is known and the more obviously it is true, the more frequently it is ignored and largely forgotten.

We are taught that the *Mesillas Yesharim*, which seemingly has a simple orientation, is actually founded on the deep teachings of Kabbalah. If so, then its introductory statement, too, reflects a deep teaching of Kabbalah. Let us bring out the idea.

Early Torah sources tell us that each spiritual world is enclothed within the world below it. And each spiritual world has a complete structure, from "head" to "foot," similar to the structure of a man. This is because *tzelem Elokim* resembles the form of man. The matter may be compared to a father (the higher world) and son (the lower world). The father is tall, and the son reaches only to the father's neck. The son "enclothes" the father, but the father's head remains revealed and not "enclothed." And so it is with the spiritual worlds, each of which is enclothed within the next.

In this manner, each world expresses itself by way of its "clothing." The "clothing" covers the body and not the head, similar to our clothing. We express ourselves practically by way of our body, which is enclothed. The head does not express itself practically. Nobody can see what is "in your head." Only actions can be seen.

Thus, the head cannot be perceived. At the same time, it is revealed. That which is the deepest and truest is also the simplest and most revealed. The most fundamental matters are at the same time the most revealed, and the most hidden.

The fact that the world has a Creator, and that His greatness is infinite, is the deepest and most hidden thing there is. At the same time, it is the simplest and the most revealed! The reason we do not see it is because the most revealed things are also the most hidden. We can perceive something only by way of its "clothing."

This explains the nature of *emunah*. If a person wants *emunah* and looks for it, if he is not trying to deny it, then for him it will be the simplest and most revealed thing in the world. He will find that it is impossible to think otherwise.

It is written:

> *If your brother... will lead you astray, saying: "Let us go and worship other gods"... from the gods of the peoples around you who are close to you, or who are far from you...*[6]

Chazal say about this as follows:

> What does it matter whether the peoples are close to you or far from you? The verse is rather saying that from the character of the close ones, we can learn the character of the far ones.[7]
>
> He who leads people astray will usually speak of an idol that is far away and unfamiliar to people. He will speak falsely and claim, "It eats this and drinks that," [as if it were a real being]. Therefore, we are told to look at the idols close to us, and see that they are not real. And from them, we can learn the character of the faraway ones.[8]

The Torah is teaching us that if we want to know about faraway idol worship, we should check out the local idol worship. Let's say we hear that in Tibet there are priests who are very special and who practice abstinence from all worldly matters. If we think that they might be achieving some type of spiritual purity, all we have to do is go down to the church over on the next street. Whatever is going on there, it is no different in Tibet.

And if we want to know the nature of idol worship throughout history, we can find out about it by looking at the modern methods of leading people astray. Just as it is full of nonsense today, so it always was.

6. *Devarim* 13:7–8.
7. *Sanhedrin* 61b.
8. *Rashi* ad loc.

According to the theory of evolution, everything developed over the course of millions of years. But if so, we should see some evidence of the stages. There should be a half-developed eye, a quarter-developed eye, etc.

The most advanced camera today cannot do anything close to what the eye of a child can do. Even so, if we would claim that such a camera developed by itself, there would have to be millions of stages of development. Even when a camera is produced in a factory, there are plenty of waste materials left behind to testify to the process. But where do we find evidence of the stages of the eye's development, or of anything else for that matter? A professor goes somewhere in Africa and finds a bone, and says, "Aha! I have found the connection between man and the ape." And the whole world bows down and believes him.

"They say to a piece of wood, 'You are my father.'"[9] Once upon a time they said that a stick and a stone made the world. Now they have found a new god: "No one." They claim that "No one" created the world. Human society never before deteriorated to such a state of non-belief. What is claimed today makes less sense than ever. Yet, from today's idolatry we can learn about the nature of ancient idolatry.

Knowing the truth is very, very simple. There is nothing more revealed than it. Yet, Hashem created man with the ability to not recognize the truth. The author of *Mesillas Yesharim* wrote his introduction about this. He teaches us that the more a matter is revealed, the more it can be missed. Whoever wants to find it will see it standing right in front of him. And whoever wants to miss it, he possesses such a capability. If we want to find Hashem, the first step is to be a judge, not a lawyer.

If a judge sees that the case is 90% versus 10%, he goes with

9. *Yirmeyahu* 2:27.

the 90%. But *emunah* is much surer than this. In practical life, we go according to percentage. If we want to cross the street and the pedestrian light shows green, we start walking. There is always the slight chance that a drunk driver will come barreling down the road and run us over, *chas v'shalom*. But practically speaking we don't worry about it too much since it happens such a small percentage of the time, even though it is a matter of life and death. We rather rely on the overwhelming percentage of pedestrians who have successfully crossed the street on a green light.

Emunah is more than this. It is one hundred percent. We can prove things conclusively.

Someone for whom one hundred percent is not enough will object: "But maybe this, and maybe that, and maybe the other thing…" He will bring up possibilities that are not logical and reasonable. If someone does not wish to believe, we cannot force him to believe. But he should know the reality: he is going against a one hundred percent level of surety! The Torah is not built on 99%.

Anyone who contemplates the world in an impartial manner will readily agree that Hashem "is the first and the last." It is an inexorable conclusion.

הָעִיקָר הַחֲמִישִׁי

7

The Fifth Principle

אֲנִי מַאֲמִין בֶּאֱמוּנָה שְׁלֵמָה, שֶׁהַבּוֹרֵא יִתְבָּרַךְ שְׁמוֹ לוֹ לְבַדּוֹ רָאוּי לְהִתְפַּלֵּל, וְאֵין רָאוּי לְהִתְפַּלֵּל לְזוּלָתוֹ.

I believe with perfect faith that it is fitting to pray only to the Creator – may His Name be blessed – and it is not fitting to pray to another.

Prayer Is Our Relationship with Hashem

A BASIC PART OF THE Jewish faith is that prayer is a reality. It is possible to pray to Hashem and communicate with Him. He hears us, takes interest in us and cares about us. However, Hashem's relationship with man is not like other relationships which develop naturally. That is to say, Hashem's greatness is not limited, *chas v'shalom*, and thus He is naturally able to descend to the level of relating to lowly man. On the contrary: because of His tremendous power and greatness, He is able to relate even to the smallest of creatures.

The *Meshech Chochmah* writes in the very beginning of his commentary on *Chumash* that this is one of the Torah's fundamental principles. Just as there is nothing too big for Hashem, so there is nothing too small for Him.

It is important that we understand this point properly. Our relationship with Hashem is not one of brotherhood; it is not a relationship established on the basis of similarity. "Can there be friendship with Heaven?!"[1] Indeed, in our prayers we express how Hashem relates to our lives: "He supports the living in His kindness, He brings the dead to life in great mercy." But we immediately follow by expressing how Hashem is lofty and separated from us: "You are holy and Your Name is holy..."

Hashem comes to visit us when we are sick[2] but this is not because we have something in common. Hashem is above and beyond anything we can even conceptualize. Hashem's *kedushah* is so great that it extends infinitely. It reaches so far that He cares about the smallest thing. There is nothing outside the realm of His personal involvement. This is one of the most basic ideas in the outlook on prayer.

"He Dwells on High; He Bends Himself Down to See"

It says in the beginning of *Sefer HaKuzari* that the classical philosophers never denied the existence of God. Rather, they considered God to be so great that He cannot have a relationship with the lowly, physical world we live in. He could not possibly be involved with the trivial lives of human beings. They argued as follows: Man can learn any language in the world, but cannot learn the language of the animals and birds. This is because the distance separating man's reality from that of the animals is too great. A relationship of true communication cannot develop between them.

And so it is, said the philosophers, between God and man. This is because God is far above anything the human mind can even imagine. Not only does this lowly world not interest Him, He could not possibly have contact with it.

By way of illustration, the legendary giant Og Melech HaBashan was so great and powerful that he could uproot a

1. *Berachos* 33b.
2. *Sotah* 14a.

mountain the size of three parasangs.[3] But he could not climb into the tiny passages of an ant hill.

In contrast to the classical philosophers' outlook, Judaism believes that Hashem is so great, powerful, and unlimited that He has the ability even to make Himself small, so to speak.

Hashem's greatness is what enables Him to bridge the enormous gap that separates His reality from ours. He can have contact with the lowly, physical world we live in.

This point is illustrated by Shlomo HaMelech. Due to his tremendous wisdom he could bridge the gap separating humans from animals. He understood the language of animals and birds. His very greatness is what enabled him to communicate with beings lower than him. If Og Melech HaBashan had been truly powerful, he would have been able even to climb into the passages of an ant hill.

David Hamelech put it like this:

> *Who is like Hashem, our God, Who dwells on high, [yet] lowers [His eyes] to look into the Heavens and the earth.*[4]

It is only because of Hashem's extraordinary greatness, because He "dwells on high," that He is able "to look into the Heavens *and* the earth." His greatness is what gives Him the ability to relate to the earth.

We can apply this idea to ourselves as well. When a person is truly great, he is capable of descending from his heights and involving himself with little details. A person who can relate only to great things is very limited. A truly great person cares about the personal problems of the people around him. The more their little problems concern him, although they stand in contradiction to his lofty nature, the greater he is.

3. *Berachos* 54b.
4. *Tehillim* 113:5–6.

Hashem Makes Our Problems His Problems

The above-mentioned outlook of the classical philosophers is actually the same mistake made by all the idolaters that ever were. Idol worshipers believe that if you want to get in contact with Divine power, you have no choice but to go through an intermediary. You need to employ the services of a being that is both lowly enough to relate to human beings and lofty enough to relate to God. In other words, idol worshipers deny that we can have any direct contact with God.

In contrast to this, Judaism believes that we can, and should, turn directly to Hashem. This is not only because the supposed "intermediaries" are false and empty. It is also because there is no need for intermediaries at all. Judaism believes that Hashem hears us, understands us, and cares about us. He feels our pain. The simplest and lowliest thing that pains us, pains Him as well, so to speak.

Let's say a man buys a tie and is disappointed because its color is not exactly what he wanted. It doesn't quite fit his suit... Even this pain is felt by Hashem. It hurts Him too, so to speak. This is the Jewish faith. There is no pain felt by a Jew that Hashem does not care about.

This expresses Hashem's tremendous greatness. He is so incredibly great that there is nothing too small for Him. There is no limit on how far His involvement extends, or restriction on what kind of miracles and wonders He can work. Just as He is unlimited in regard to great things, so is He unlimited in regard to little things.

His Mercy Is Inexhaustible

Sefer HaIkkarim writes[5] that even if a person believes in the power of prayer, he still is making a serious mistake if he thinks that due to his

5. 4:16.

sins he is not fitting to stand in prayer before Hashem. Why does he think that other people *are* fitting to stand in prayer before Hashem? Even if a person is perfectly righteous and learns Torah continuously his whole life, even if he is as great as Moshe Rabbeinu, he still is not "fitting" to stand in prayer before Hashem. No human being can ever be Hashem's friend and associate, and be "fitting" to talk to Him! Yet, Judaism believes that whatever condition a person is in, no matter how lowly, Hashem always wants to hear his prayer. Hashem cares about him, no matter what.

Hashem's incredible capacity to relate to His creatures is poignantly expressed by the story of Menasheh, king of Yehudah. The Midrash recounts[6] that Menasheh was exceptionally wicked. The king of Ashur captured him, put him in a copper pot, and lit the fire underneath. Menasheh called out for help to every idol in the world. When he saw that none of his gods came to his aid, he said: "I remember that my father would read me the verse, '*When you are in distress, and all these things happen to you… for Hashem your God is a merciful God.*'[7] I will call out to *HaKadosh Baruch Hu*. If He saves me, it is well. And if not, He is the same as the others."

The Midrash goes on to say, "At that moment the ministering angels went and closed all the windows of Heaven. They said to Hashem: 'Master of the World, will You accept the repentance of a man who set up an idol in the Temple's sanctuary?' Hashem answered them: 'If I do not accept his repentance, I am closing the door to all repenters.' What did *HaKadosh Baruch Hu* do? He dug a tunnel under His glorious Throne, in a place where no angel can reach [thereby enabling Menasheh's prayer to ascend to Him]."

6. *Ruth Rabbah* 5:6.

7. *Devarim* 4:3–31.

Menasheh's reasoning was as follows: It is true that I have been as wicked as can be. I am even worse than the Canaanites who once inhabited the land. And I have led my nation astray with idolatry.[8] However, if You do not accept my repentance, if You do not hear my prayer, it means there is a limit to how far Hashem's mercy reaches. If a person goes beyond that limit, Hashem can no longer help him. This would mean that Hashem is limited!

This is the same point that *Sefer HaIkkarim* was making. Hashem hears the prayer of every person, no matter how low he is. Even the wicked King Menasheh was accepted by Hashem when he repented. Hashem's capability to relate to His creatures is limitless.

The distance separating Hashem from our physical world is infinite. In comparison to infinity, the difference between wicked Menasheh and his righteous father Chizkiyahu is nothing. Hashem is way above the highest Heavens, yet He can hear the prayer of Chizkiyahu. If so, He can also hear the prayer of Menasheh.

"Hashem Is Close to All Who Call Out to Him"

It is one of the principles of *emunah* that prayer is a reality. It calls for *emunah* because there are many situations which, for various reasons, cause us to question the reality of prayer. Nevertheless, we know that there is Someone to pray to. Hashem is personally involved with us. He does not place us under the jurisdiction of any angel or Heavenly being; He rather cares about us and takes personal interest in every detail of our life. God Himself is close to us.

This is because Hashem can "lower His eyes." He sees what happens in the Heavens, and He sees what happens on

8. See *II Melachim* 21:11.

earth. For Him, both entail the same act of "lowering His eyes." Hashem is indescribably far from Heaven, just as He is from earth. Compared to Hashem's infinite greatness, the lofty angel Metatron, the smallest ant, and the simplest Jew are all the same.

Chazal express this as follows:[9]

> *HaKadosh Baruch Hu* seems far but there is nothing closer than Him. Levi said: From the earth to the firmament is the distance it takes to walk 500 years. And from one firmament to another is the distance it takes to walk 500 years. And the thickness of the firmament is the distance it takes to walk 500 years. And so it is with every firmament… The hooves of the *chayos hakodesh* are the distance it takes to walk 500 years…
>
> Thus we see how high Hashem is above His world. Yet, a man goes into the synagogue, stands behind a pillar, and prays in a whisper, and Hashem listens to his prayer... and hears it like someone into whose ear his friend is speaking. Is there a God closer than this? He is as close to His creatures as is a mouth to an ear.

Chazal express this also in the following way:[10]

> *HaKadosh Baruch Hu* is far, yet close. How is this so? From here to the firmament is the distance it takes to walk 500 years. And so with every firmament, and so between every firmament. Thus we see that He is far. Yet, when a man stands and prays, and meditates within his heart, *HaKadosh Baruch Hu* hears his prayer.

The distance separating Hashem's Heavenly Throne from man on earth is millions of years. All these "years" are just metaphors. They convey distance, they describe multitudes

9. *Yerushalmi, Berachos* 9:1.

10. *Yalkut Shimoni, Va'eschanan* 825.

of levels, they express immense power. But in spite of all this tremendous distance, *HaKadosh Baruch Hu* is as close to us as, "Someone into whose ear his friend is speaking… as is a mouth to an ear." And *HaKadosh Baruch Hu* is even closer to us than this: a person who "meditates within his heart, *HaKadosh Baruch Hu* hears his prayer."

We have already explained the main point of this principle: there is Someone to pray to. *"Hashem is close to all who call upon Him, to all who call upon Him in truth."*[11] We will now proceed to explain the details of this principle.

Two Parts

This principle of *emunah* states as follows: "It is fitting to pray only to the Creator — may His Name be blessed — and it is not fitting to pray to another." In the Sefardic siddur, it ends a little differently: "And there is no serving another." Both versions express the same basic idea.

There are actually two parts to this principle, as seen from the Rambam[12] and the Mabit.[13] The first part is to believe in serving Hashem. This means to believe in prayer and *korbanos.* The second part is that we should serve nothing else besides Hashem.

On the basis of the principles of *emunah* discussed earlier, we could think that Hashem created us, that He is One, that He is everlasting, that in His ineffable wisdom He bestows goodness upon His creatures — but nevertheless, we have no contact with Him. He does not ask anything of us, and we cannot communicate with Him, *chas v'shalom.* Now comes the present principle of *emunah,* and teaches us that we have a relationship with Hashem through serving Him.

11. *Tehillim* 145:18.
12. Commentary on the Mishnayos, *Sanhedrin* 10:1.
13. *Beis Elokim, Sha'ar HaYesodos,* chap. 14.

First we will explain the part: "It is not fitting to pray to another."

Mentioning the Angels in Our Prayers

A question commonly asked is: Why do certain prayers address the angels, if we have the principle of "It is not fitting to pray to another"? On Shabbos night, when we sing *Shalom Aleichem,* we say *barchuni l'shalom,* asking the angels to bless us. In *Selichos,* we recite *Malachei rachamim chalu na pnei Keil,* asking the angels to plead for us. And at the end of *Selichos,* we recite *Machnisei rachamim...* Does this mean that we are praying to the angels?

Indeed, there are people who refrain from saying these particular prayers because they do not want to appear as if they are praying to angels. In regard to this, it is fitting to mention what the Rambam wrote to his son:[14]

> Sometimes you will come upon a... perplexing statement... and it will seem to contradict the principles of Torah.... Do not move from your beliefs.... Put the statement on the side... and do not contaminate all your beliefs because of a certain wise teaching that you failed to understand.

If you don't understand something, just put it on the side for the time being, and go forward with what you know to be true. Accordingly, when we find certain prayers in the siddur that seem to address the angels, we maintain our *emunah* that we should pray only to Hashem. If someone is disturbed by such prayers, he doesn't have to recite them, as long as they are not prayers which are strictly obligatory. In any case, we should hold onto the principles of *emunah.*

It has been suggested that we are not really praying to the

14. *Rambam, Iggeres HaMussar* (written to his son R. Avraham).

angels in these prayers. We are merely asking the angels to bring our prayers up to Hashem. But this doesn't answer the question. As we will explain, we cannot request anything at all from the angels!

The issue of praying to angels leads us to a further question: Why is it permitted to address a request to a live human being? If it is forbidden to request something from an angel, and this is considered a form of *avodah zarah,* then why is requesting something from human being perfectly acceptable?

The answer is simple. We cannot request anything from the angels because there is nothing they are capable of giving us. In *Yechezkel* chap. 1, angels are referred to as *chayos*; in davening we call them *chayos ha-kodesh,* "holy animals." Just as there are men, animals, and birds in our world, correspondingly there are "holy animals" in Heaven. What does this mean? It means that despite the great loftiness and spirituality of the angels, in a way they are like animals: They do not possess the faculty of free choice. They cannot decide anything.

To request something from an angel is like requesting from a stick held in someone's hand that it should not hit you. Angels cannot say yes or no. They cannot fulfill our requests, because they do not have the ability to make a decision of any sort. Thus it is useless to pray to them. This is what Judaism believes.

We may request something from a human being for the simple reason that he possesses the free choice to grant our request. But it contradicts the Jewish faith to believe that an angel can grant a request.

Angel Power Is Avodah Zarah

Now that we know why it is not *possible* to request anything from angels, we can also understand why it is *forbidden* to do so. It is forbidden to request anything from the angels, even that they should pray for us. Yet, we may make a request of a tzaddik, and ask him to pray for us.

An angel is a Heavenly being. It is on a very high spiritual level, and to make even the smallest request from it would be to worship it. This is because the power that expresses itself through an angel is Divine. Angels don't really do anything; Hashem does it all, as we will explain. So if we would request something from an angel, we would be attributing to it free choice, and thereby making it into a divinity. We would be relating to it as a god that has the power to grant our request.

When we request something from a human being, it is different. We do not think the human being has Divine power. We are not allowed to address a request to beings that are above the framework of our physical world, because such beings have no free choice. The moment we attribute free choice to an angel, we are attributing to it a free choice that has Divine power. This is *avodah zarah*.

Angels are like Hashem's gloves. Hashem does everything, but usually He hides His hands inside "gloves" so we don't see Who did it. When Hashem acts without gloves, it is called a revelation of the Shechinah. We see Who did it.

To make a request from an angel is like making a request from a glove. If someone nevertheless insists on speaking to an angel and making a request from it, he is attributing to it a capability that carries Divine power.

Man, by contrast, is a lowly being. It is *possible* to request something from him because he has the ability to decide yes or no. And it is *permitted* to request something from him because there is nothing Divine about man's power. Making a request from a man does not attribute to him any capability that he doesn't have.

If a person would make a request to an angel, yet think the angel is just some kind of a big bird with six wings, it is likely that this would not be *avodah zarah*. It would, however, be total foolishness. This is because an angel has no power at all. *Avodah zarah* is when a person relates to an angel as possessing Divine power.

And if we would attribute some kind of Divine power to a human being, this, too, would be *avodah zarah*. In fact, it would be an *avodah zarah* on a much greater scale. This is because man has free choice, i.e., he has the ability to grant what is requested of him. To also attribute to him some kind of Divine aspect would be to make him into a god.

Why Some Prayers Address the Angels

In light of all this, why do we have some prayers that address the angels? Why do we say to the angels, "*Barchuni leshalom*," requesting their blessing?

Here is what I think is the best answer: It is clear that angels cannot bless us. Neither can they bring our prayers up to Hashem. Requesting anything of them is *avodah zarah*. The reason we address them is expressed by the following allegory.

A small, lowly man is standing before a very great king. As sometimes happens in the presence of a great, overpowering figure, the man does not have the courage to open his mouth and speak directly to the king. Yet, he must voice his request. So he says to the attendant standing next to the king, "Perhaps you could grant me such-and-such?" Although he speaks these words to the attendant, in truth he is addressing the king.

Prayer is a tool we utilize in order to gain Hashem's favor. When a person needs something, his choice of methods depends on how urgent his request is. If he needs something desperately he will utilize every means at his disposal. That is why during the *Yamim Noraim* we employ all the methods that we have. We engage in all the various forms of prayer, even that of speaking to the angels. But when we speak to the angels, in truth it is just another way of addressing Hashem.

Here is a deeper explanation. Let's say a man's slippers are on the other side of the room and he wants them brought to him. He could ask someone to bring him his slippers. Or he could say to a trained animal, such as a dog, "Bring me my slippers!"

What is the difference between these two methods? When the person brings him the slippers, the person is doing the act. But when the animal brings him the slippers, it is not the animal's act. It is the act of the man who issued the order to the animal. Since the man activated the animal's automatic responses, it is considered the man's act.

This answers our question. We do not request of the angels that they should act on our behalf. Rather, it is completely our act. When we "request" something from an angel, we are just "activating" the angel.

The Rambam says that this principle of "It is not fitting to pray to another" forbids us to address any force or Heavenly sphere. If so, how could Yehoshua say: *"O sun, stop in your course in Givon"*?[15] The answer is that Yehoshua did not request of the sun that it should stop. He simply stopped it!

If we see the angels as entities to which requests can be made, this is indeed *avodah zarah*. But we can rather view them as "holy animals," and activate them.

The same applies to praying at the graves of tzaddikim. The correct approach is to request from Hashem that He should help us, in the merit of the tzaddikim. This is what it says in all the halachic sources.[16] There is absolutely nothing we can request from the tzaddik who is buried there. However, according to what we have explained, it is possible that we can "activate" the tzaddik, just as we activate the angels.

As Far as the Eye Can See

When an adult looks out the window he sees people walking by, he sees telephone poles, he sees cars, etc. But when a baby looks out the window he sees undefined images. He does not see a "telephone

15. *Yehoshua* 10:12.

16. See *Mishnah Berurah* 581:27.

pole" or a "car." In one sense, he sees everything the adult sees. In another sense, he sees nothing. He takes it all in but distinguishes nothing.

And what do we see? Let's say we see a child playing. This child contains within him worlds upon worlds. But we see only a simple child, no more.

Let's say we see a sky full of stars. What do the stars contain? Do we appreciate what they are? There is a Chassidic story about a Rebbe who was traveling in a wagon with his *shochet*. There were two bulls there and the Rebbe asked the *shochet*, "Which one is a *treifah* and which one is not?" The *shochet* said, "I don't know." The Rebbe exclaimed, "*Ribbono shel Olam!* You gave man the sense of sight. How could it be that a little skin and meat can cover so much?"

Nowadays we see about as much as a one-month-old infant. It used to be that when people would look at the Heavens above, they would know that the sun, moon, and stars are conduits by which the flow of blessing descends to the world. People realized how the world works. If a man would walk through the market and find a silver coin, he would realize that a lot is contained within this coin. What this coin went through until it reached his hand! Hashem decreed on this coin that it should be found by him, and it traversed the levels of *galgalim* and *ophanim* and then *malachim* until it came to him.

In fact, the Rambam writes:[17]

> All the stars and Heavenly spheres are live beings. They possess intelligence and understanding. They are alive and they recognize He Who spoke and created the world… The stars and Heavenly spheres have less knowledge than the angels do, but more than human beings do.

17. *Mishneh Torah, Hilchos Yesodei HaTorah* 3:9.

People of old lived with this awareness. They knew that each star is a living being and possesses tremendous depth of understanding. They knew that the stars and Heavenly spheres are no less alive than they are. Thus, they faced a tremendous *nisayon*. Despite their knowledge of how the system works, despite their recognition of its incredible power, they had to believe that all these Heavenly entities have no free choice whatsoever, and operate like inanimate objects which are empty of all knowledge and personality.

For us this is not a *nisayon* because we don't even realize what is up there. It is not an issue for us. We should know, however, that everything we receive — no matter how small — comes to us directly from the hand of Hashem. We should be aware that Hashem directs everything personally. His involvement is one hundred percent.

What Is Avodah?

Now we will explain the first part of the principle, "It is fitting to pray only to the Creator." Prayer is defined by *Chazal* as *avodah*: [18]

> What type of *avodah* is performed in the heart? It is prayer.

The word *avodah* actually has two meanings. The first is "work," as in: "*You shall do no crafted work* (*avodah*),"[19] and as in: "*They embittered their lives with hard work* (*avodah*)."[20]

The second meaning of *avodah* is "servitude," as in: "*Whoever does the work of servitude* (*avodah*), *and the work of carrying*."[21] Accordingly, *Chazal* say[22] that the slaughtering of a *korban* is not

18. *Taanis* 2a.
19. *Vayikra* 23:21.
20. *Shemos* 1:14.
21. *Bemidbar* 4:47.
22. *Yoma* 42a.

considered *avodah*. Casting the blood on the Altar is *avodah,* but slaughtering is not *avodah,* even though the slaughter is much harder work. This is because *avodah* in this sense means servitude. It means being completely subject to someone more powerful.

Casting the blood on the Altar is servitude to Hashem, as will be explained. Thus it must be done by a Kohen, it requires *bigdei kehunah,* it has all the other special halachos pertaining to *avodas Beis HaMikdash.* But the *korban*'s slaughter is not an act of servitude to Hashem. The animal is slaughtered only so that its blood may be properly received in a consecrated vessel and then brought to the Altar. Since the slaughter is merely a preparatory step, it does not need to be performed by a Kohen. Neither does it have the other halachos of *avodas Beis HaMikdash.*

When man expresses his recognition of the greatness of God by completely nullifying his own importance, this is *avodah. Avodah* is intensely expressing man's self-nullification before an entity that is so much greater and more powerful than he — it is Divine. Consequently, this type of self-nullification can only occur before Godly greatness. By contrast, when a person requests help from his friend or a wealthy man, he is not nullifying his importance before this individual. He retains his self-importance even though he appears subservient. This is because he knows that the only advantage the wealthy man has over him is a sum of money, and that's why he's able to assist him. But *avodah* of Hashem, on the other hand, is an act of total self-nullification.

An excellent example of *avodah* is when a person bows down on the ground and prostrates himself. This pose demonstrates total self-nullification.

Normally, a person's head is higher than his feet. In fact, there is nothing in the world that is greater and more powerful than man's mind. The lion is the strongest of the animals. Physically, a lion is much stronger than a man. But when man uses his mind he can capture a lion.

Yet, when compared to infinity, the head and the feet are at the same height. They are equally distant from infinity. When someone bows down on the ground and prostrates himself, he is showing that in comparison to God's infinite greatness, a person's head is the same as his feet. A person's mind, despite all its intelligence and human uniqueness and dignity, is no more than a toe when compared to Hashem.

Another excellent example of *avodah* is *korbanos*. In this form of servitude we express our self-nullification before Hashem by means of spilling blood. There is nothing that shakes a person up more than spilt blood. When a person wishes to demonstrate his self-nullification before Hashem, he spills blood. In this way he expresses how powerful his feelings are regarding Hashem.

Take, for example, a flower. When a person wishes to convey his love for someone, he gives the other person a flower. Obviously, it is not just the flower that he is offering — how much is a flower worth? Rather, he is expressing an emotion. This can be seen from the following verse, with *Chazal*'s comment on it:

> *For the performer on Shoshanim* [lit., roses], *by the sons of Korach, a Maskil, a song of friendship.*[23]
>
> This may be compared to a king who entered a city and the people of the city came to crown him with a crown of gold inlayed with jewels and precious stones. The king's servants went out and told them, "The king asks of you only a crown of roses."[24]

Roses more eloquently express a person's appreciation than all the silver and gold in the world. A wealthy man who has ample means to buy his wife an expensive diamond is not embarrassed to bring her a bouquet of roses. What are roses worth, compared to a fine diamond? The answer is that a diamond,

23. *Tehillim* 45:1.

24. *Midrash Tehillim* ad loc.

despite its great value, is an inanimate object. It does not express a live, flourishing relationship. But roses are alive, and they express this much better.

An even better gift than a rose is a *korban*. It expresses how our love for Hashem is in our very life-blood. A person is willing to give silver and gold to his fellow, but he will not spill his own blood for anyone. Only for Hashem! The most powerful expression of *avodas Hashem* is by spilling blood.

[Actually, there is an even better gift than this: *Akeidas Yitzchak*. Our lives today depend on this gift. But this does not relate to the present subject.]

Tefillah without Avodah...

Since *avodah* means expressing our self-nullification before Hashem, the greatest drawback to *avodah* is failing to nullify ourselves before Hashem. Let us understand how this applies to *tefillah*.

A person is ill. He prays the *Shemoneh Esrei* and comes to the blessing of *refa'einu*. He recognizes that Hashem is great, and can heal him even better than can all the medical specialists whom he has consulted. Alternatively, let's say a person is facing a *parnasah* issue. He prays the *Shemoneh Esrei* and comes to the blessing of *bareich aleinu*. He recognizes that Hashem gives *parnasah*, and that He can bestow upon him more wealth than can the richest philanthropists. Why should he run across town trying to secure a loan, when right in front of him is the One Who possesses all wealth?

As the *Mesillas Yesharim* puts it, *tefillah* should be "like a man speaks to his friend, and his friend listens attentively to him."[25] Accordingly, if a person needs a loan he should just speak to Hashem and request it from Him, as simple as that. If you need something, just ask Hashem for it!

25. *Mesillas Yesharim*, chap. 19.

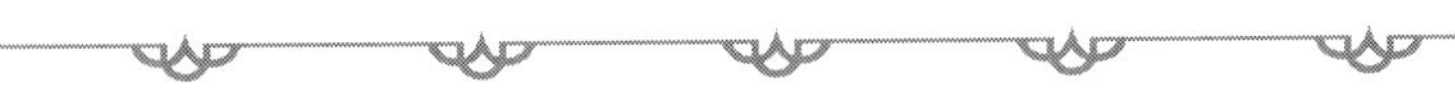

This is all very nice. If a person prays to Hashem as a great Doctor, it is good. If he prays to Hashem as a great Financier, it is even better. However, a person's prayer cannot be called *avodas Hashem* unless it relates to the Divine, to the Godly. A person can offer wonderful requests to Hashem. And it is likely that he will receive what he asks for. But this is not *avodah*. It is missing the main thing! *Avodah* starts when a person completely nullifies himself before Hashem, and recognizes that everything is only from Hashem.

The Rambam and the Ramban have a disagreement over *tefillah*.[26] The Rambam holds that there is a Torah-ordained mitzvah to pray every day. The Ramban holds that from the Torah, there is only a mitzvah to pray in a time of trouble. The *Sefer HaChinuch* writes: "He who transgresses this mitzvah and does not pray in a time of trouble has abrogated a positive Torah mitzvah, according to the Ramban."[27] The *Sefer HaChinuch* is teaching us that according to the Ramban, there is an obligation from the Torah to pray in a time of trouble.

Practically speaking, it comes out like this: Let's say someone finishes *Shacharis* prayers and is suddenly confronted by trouble. For instance, his child fell down and got a nasty bang on his head, and looks like he might need to be rushed to the doctor. The Rambam says that the parent does not have an obligation to pray now. He already fulfilled his obligation in *Shacharis*. But the Ramban says that it is incumbent on the parent to pray at this point in time. A mitzvah has just come to him which is no less obligatory than shofar and mezuzah. *Shacharis* only fulfilled his Rabbinic obligation. The child's medical care should not be delayed, of course, but there is something the parent must do as well: daven!

26. See *Rambam, Sefer HaMitzvos, Aseh* 5.

27. *Sefer HaChinuch, mitzvah* 433.

Before the Brisker Rav would speak with someone, he would say the verse (*Bereishis* 49:18), "*I hope for Your salvation, Hashem!*" I always thought this was a sign of his constant *deveikus* with Hashem. However, there is a much simpler explanation: Any conversation with the Brisker Rav invariably entailed his giving advice on the matter at hand. Because the Rav felt a tremendous responsibility to answer correctly and properly, this was an *eis tzarah* for him — a time of great need for Divine help and guidance. Thus, he had a Torah obligation to daven!

The Rambam states:

> The obligation of this mitzvah is as follows. A person should supplicate and pray every day. He should recount the praise of *HaKadosh Baruch Hu*, then ask for what he needs with begging and supplication, and then give praise and thanks to Hashem for the goodness He has bestowed upon him. Each person should do this according to his own abilities.[28]

The Rambam is saying that a person's requests to Hashem should be prefaced by praise, and followed by praise. And this praise is part of the Torah-ordained mitzvah of *tefillah*. Why is this so? How did praising Hashem get into the Torah obligation of prayer?

The answer is that a person's *tefillah* needs to be *avodah*. If a person merely requests his needs from Hashem, this is not yet *avodah*. True, he is requesting it from the One Who can fulfill his requests. He recognizes that only Hashem can help him. But if that is all he is doing, it is not *avodah*. This person is simply turning to a source of help.

In order to turn our prayers into *avodah*, the Rambam says that the mitzvah of *tefillah* begins with knowing Who we are speaking to: "The great, mighty, and awesome God," as we say

28. *Mishneh Torah, Hilchos Tefillah* 1:2.

at the beginning of the *Shemoneh Esrei*. We need to take a moment and feel the significance of addressing God. We need to stop and recognize that Hashem is capable of absolutely everything, and that He loves us to an infinite degree. He takes care of us, He is close to us, He is Divine. He is our God!

Otherwise it is not *avodah*. It is just making a request. *Avodah* means self-nullification before God.

And after making our requests, we conclude our prayer by giving thanks. We are thereby saying to Hashem: I requested these things specifically from You, because You have always given me what I need. You are Hashem, You are the Almighty God, and Your kindness is infinite.

We begin our prayer with praise, saying: You are Hashem. We continue by making our requests; we say to Hashem: we request these things from You because You have always helped us. And we conclude by thanking and praising again, as we began.

These are the three parts of *tefillah*. Without them, our prayer is missing the main thing. It is not *avodah*.

You Are What You Pray

This fifth principle of *emunah* is to believe that Hashem created us in such a way that we can serve Him. Serving Hashem, *avodah*, means to stand before Him and relate to Him, as it says, "*To stand and serve.*"[29] We perform our *avodah* in His presence.

This aspect of *avodah* is unique to *tefillah*. It does not exist with the other mitzvos. Let's say we affix a mezuzah to our doorpost, or put on tefillin. We have thereby performed an act of a mitzvah. Although we did a mitzvah, we did not become a part of the mitzvah itself. With *avodah* it is different: the person who performs it becomes an essential part of the *avodah* itself.

29. *Devarim* 18:5.

When it comes to *avodah,* an essential part is the *oveid,* the person who performs the *avodah.* Regarding other mitzvos, there are no halachos pertaining to the one who performs the mitzvah. For instance, there is no halachah stating that someone who affixes a mezuzah must be standing, or sitting. (Although there are three mitzvos that require a person to stand, these mitzvos are not invalidated even if the person was sitting.)

With *avodah,* however, there are all sorts of halachos pertaining to the person who performs it. Just as an animal offered as a *korban* must not have a *mum* (physical deformity), the Kohen, the person offering it, also must not be a *baal mum.* The *oveid* is a part of the *avodah* itself, no less than the *korban* is. *Avodah* is a state of praising Hashem and of nullifying oneself before Hashem. The *oveid* is at the center of the *avodah* — you will never find "*avodah*" without an "*oveid.*" There are numerous halachos pertaining to the Kohen who is offering a *korban,* no less than the myriad details pertaining to the actual *korban.*

This is no less true when it comes to *tefillah.* The *Tur* dedicates entire chapters (*Orach Chaim* 94–98) to defining the state a person should be in when he prays: "When he comes to pray he should pause for a short while... he should line up his feet next to one another... this is how his thoughts should be..." There is no other mitzvah with halachos such as these.

Our true relationship with Hashem expresses itself in *tefillah.* The fact that we can transform ourselves into an *oveid* means that we have a connection with Hashem. We can be in a state of "standing before Hashem." Only through *tefillah* can a person achieve a state of "standing before Hashem," to be in Hashem's presence and serve Him.

Prayer Is Contact

The Rambam tells us the way to be connected with *HaKadosh Baruch Hu*:

> The mind, which God has graced us with, is the connection between us and Him. We have a choice before us. If we wish

> to strengthen this connection, we can. And if we wish to weaken it little by little until we sever it, we can. The only way to strengthen this connection is by developing our love of God and focusing ourselves on it. And this connection is weakened by putting our thoughts on something other than God.
>
> We should know that even were we the wisest of men, possessing true Godly wisdom, we nevertheless would cut the connection between us and God if we would turn our thoughts to the food that we need, or to the affairs that we need. We are not with Him then, and neither is He with us. This is because practically speaking, our relationship is cut at that time.[30]

The Rambam is saying that when a person thinks of Hashem, he is with Hashem. And when he does not think of Hashem, he is not with Him. The Rambam makes this point quite clearly.

The *Tur* describes prayer as follows:

> This is how his thoughts should be: The person who prays should focus his heart… until his thoughts and intentions are purified while he is praying… surely it is true that before the King of all kings, *HaKadosh Baruch Hu*, a person needs to focus even his thoughts… This is what the pious men of good deeds would do. They would sit in solitude and concentrate on their prayer until they would reach a level of transcending physicality and of strengthening the intellectual soul, until they would be close to the level of prophecy.[31]

Why does the *Tur* have to tell us what the pious people of ancient times used to do? Because he is thereby explaining to us what *avodas ha-tefillah* looks like. He is telling us that *avodah* is a

30. *Moreh Nevuchim* 3:51.

31. *Tur, Orach Chaim* 98.

touch of prophecy. And what is prophecy? It is a connection to Hashem so strong that one hears Him speak. The nature of *tefillah* may be described as a touch of prophecy. Just as prophecy is a close relationship with God, so *tefillah* is a close relationship with God. Thus, when a person prays, he is with Hashem. The pious men of ancient times were not the only ones who could reach a state close to prophecy when they prayed. Anyone who prays to Hashem, and thinks about Him while doing so, is on a similar level.

This is something we are required to believe in. We must believe that it is possible to reach such a state of great closeness to God, for this is one of the thirteen principles of *emunah*.

When a person has proper *kavanah* in only part of his prayer, it does not mean that for five minutes he prayed properly and for five minutes he did not pray properly. Rather, it means that ten minutes of *avodah* took place, and five minutes of it was performed by a *baal mum*. As we mentioned, the *avodah* of bringing a *korban* comprises both the *korban* and the one who offers it. If there is no Kohen, there is no *avodah*. The same applies to the *avodah* of *tefillah*. If we are not as we should be, the *avodas ha-tefillah* is absent.

We need to understand the truth about ourselves, about Hashem and about the connection between us. This is what the "principles of *emunah*" are all about. One of the basic points here is *avodah*, since our relationship with Hashem is expressed through *avodah*.

Prayer Fills Us

A Jew needs to get in the habit of constant prayer. This is alluded to in R. Yochanan's teaching: "If only a person would pray all day long."[32] Whenever something happens, we should turn to the One above,

32. *Berachos* 21a.

and daven. This is a practice to acquire and make into second nature.

If Shabbos is a Jew's heart, and *emunah* is a Jew's mind, then *tefillah* is a Jew's blood. What is blood? It is a fluid that connects a person with the source of life. While *emunah* is in the head, and Shabbos is just one day of the week, *tefillah* needs to fill a person's entire being. It is like blood, which flows throughout a person from head to toe.

The *Anshei Knesses HaGedolah,* who composed the *berachos* and *tefillos* we recite today, instituted that nothing should come without *tefillah*. Our connection to food, to walking, to learning, to *parnasah,* and to everything else comes only through *tefillah*. Everything needs *tefillah,* because *tefillah* is the blood that flows in our veins. If a person's body has an area to which the blood does not reach, that area dies away.

If a person will adopt the habit of constantly requesting from Hashem what he needs, this will qualitatively change his whole way of life. However, when we request something, it is very important to stop for a moment and think about from Whom we are requesting it. We must be aware that we are praying to "the great, mighty, and awesome God," Who is infinite. Only after this lofty thought should we make our request.

This transforms our request into something totally different. We are not just speaking to someone who can help us out with a problem we have. We are standing before God, Whose power and kindness is infinite. If we would take all the love in the world that any father ever had for his only son, and put it all together, it would be a drop in the sea compared to how much Hashem personally loves us and personally takes care of us.

If we will take a second to think about this, it will arouse our hearts and move us to real feeling for Hashem. This is what *tefillah* means.

It is not enough for us just to know generally that we are praying to God, without thinking about it at the time we pray.

Rather, while we request something, it must be crystal clear to us that we are addressing the One Who has the ability to take care of all our problems; we are speaking to the One Whose abilities are on a Divine scale, not a human scale. He can do much more than just provide the $5000 we happen to be lacking at the moment. Providing $5000 is not a Divine ability. There are plenty of people who can write out checks for much more than this, but it doesn't mean they are God.

Furthermore, it is not enough for us just to request things from God. We also need to thank Him. Doing this is a lightning flash of *avodah* that lights up our lives. And it doesn't require more than a second of thought. It calls for a mental act of prostrating ourselves and nullifying ourselves before Hashem.

As we know, our morning prayers are prefaced by *pesukei d'zimrah*. When we reach the middle part of *pesukei d'zimrah,* we recite the first Psalm of *Hallelukah,* which begins *Halleli nafshi es Hashem,* "My soul praises Hashem." Then we go up a step, to *Ki tov zamrah... Boneh Yerushalayim Hashem*. Now it is not just me. Hashem builds Jerusalem for all of *Klal Yisrael*; here we recite *nidchei Yisrael yechaneis*. Then we go up another step, to *Hallelu es Hashem min ha-shamayim*. Here we speak of the angels in Heaven above. And then we ascend a further step: *Shiru laShem shir chadash,* which refers to the World to Come. Finally we reach *Hallelu Keil b'kodsho,* "Praise Hashem in His holiness," which relates to Hashem's infinity. Now we can truly say *Kol ha-neshamah tehalleil Kah,* "The entire soul praises Hashem."

The *pesukei d'zimrah* start low and go high. They are a ladder we are meant to climb. We begin with the praise sung by our own personal soul, we ascend to the level of *Klal Yisrael,* we reach the World to Come, we touch on infinity, on God in His holiness. This level is higher than Heaven, higher than the World to Come.

Only when our prayer is *avodah* are we able to reach such heights.

Kavanah in Prayer

Here is another practical point we should know about. What does it mean to have *kavanah* when we are davening? Let's say a person is praying for a sick family member. While he is reciting *Tehillim* that the sick person should have a *refuah sheleimah,* he comes to a moving verse that touches his heart. He shuts his eyes and prays intensely. What makes this prayer especially powerful? Is it his concentration on the words?

In truth, the extra concentration the person has on these moving words in *Tehillim* hardly adds anything to his prayer. Even before he came to this verse, he desired with all his heart that the sick family member should have a *refuah sheleimah,* and he was praying for this.

We are accustomed to think that when we pray with more emotional energy, and with heightened concentration on the words, we are praying with more *kavanah*. But this is not so. It is true that prayer is enhanced by putting more heart into it, as *Rabbeinu Yonah* says.[33] However, increasing the intensity of our emotion is not what it means to have more *kavanah* in prayer.

This is what a *tefillah* looks like when extra *kavanah* is added: "Hashem, You are so great! Your kindness is literally infinite. There is nothing that can stand in Your way. No *aveirah* can stop You; whatever it is Your will to do, You do it. In a single moment You could… You control and direct everything that happens to us. And You care about us so much. So please heal the sick person!"

Let us understand this point. Increasing our *kavanah* means increasing our awareness of Hashem's infinite greatness and unlimited abilities. In the example given above, it does not mean that the person intensifies his desire for the sick family member to be speedily healed. The person has this desire even without praying.

33. Commentary of *Rabbeinu Yonah* on *Pirkei Avos* 2:13.

Increasing *kavanah* in *tefillah* means to consider how incredibly kind and caring Hashem is, how His *chesed* is available in infinite amounts. And since this is so, He surely will send a *refuah sheleimah!* After all, His kindness knows no bounds.

Tefillah is *avodah*. Increasing *kavanah* means increasing *avodah*. It means increasing self-nullification, increasing our understanding of Divine power; it means being truly moved by Hashem's greatness and kindness. This is what *tefillah* is all about. If the person does not realize that he is dealing with the Divine, it simply is not *avodah*.

The standard form of *avodah* to Hashem is the offering of *korbanos*. When a person slaughters a *korban* and casts its blood on the Altar of the *Beis HaMikdash,* he is intending that he is spilling his own blood to honor Hashem. This is because there is nothing else in the world for which it is fitting to spill one's blood, other than for Hashem. Let's say a person would be promised a truckload of silver and gold if he gives up his life. Will he do it? Of course not. If he doesn't have life, what will he do with silver and gold? Only for the sake of God is it fitting to give up one's life. This is because after one's life is over, one lives on — just somewhere else.

This is the idea underlying *avodas ha-korbanos*.

And we have also the "*avodah* performed in the heart," which is *tefillah*. The *korbanos* express such powerful emotion, such perception of the Divine, such thanksgiving to Hashem! How can all this be contained within a person's heart? Through *tefillah*.

Avodas ha-tefillah is something we acquire through practice. We try again and again until we acquire the skill. It is not a special *madreigah*, elevated *yiras Shamayim*, or *deveikus*. In a certain sense it could be compared to learning to ride a bike, *l'havdil*. To learn how to ride a bike one simply tries again and again until he gets the hang of it. From then on, he need not exert a special effort to make sure not to fall. It has already become a part of

him, an ordinary activity he has no trouble at all executing.

So it is with *tefillah.* It is something that everyone can attain, through constant practice, working on it until he gets it. If a person works on *tefillah,* his life will be transformed into something else altogether.

Sometimes a person prays with great feeling and fervor, thinking intensely about all the important things he wants to request from Hashem — but without thinking for even a second about God Himself. He knows clearly that Someone hears him, but while he is praying he does not think about the fact that this Someone is Divine. Such an approach takes all the beauty out of the *tefillah.* A vast distance separates this from *avodas ha-tefillah.*

The *avodah* of *tefillah,* and its beauty, is total self-nullification before *HaKadosh Baruch Hu.* This is what it means to "stand and serve" before Hashem.

הָעִיקָּר הַשִּׁשִּׁי

8

The Sixth Principle

אֲנִי מַאֲמִין בֶּאֱמוּנָה שְׁלֵמָה, שֶׁכָּל דִּבְרֵי נְבִיאִים אֱמֶת.

I believe with perfect faith that all the words of the Prophets are true.

Prophecy Is God's Connection with Mankind

JUDAISM IS BUILT ON the idea that God relates to people and communicates with them. This was one of the key points debated by Judaism's opponents. They did not deny the existence of God. Rather, they denied that He relates to people and communicates with them. This issue forms the basis of all *Sefer Iyov,* and in fact the entire Torah stands on this point. Hashem did not create us and just leave us in the dark; He is here with us, and He gave us clear instructions of what He expects of us. We heard Him express His will, and we know His will.

God relates to human beings through prophecy. This is direct communication between God and us. Without prophecy we cannot know God's will. Judaism believes that God clearly and explicitly told us His will through the Prophets, and thereby dictated how our lives should be. The giving of the Torah was itself a general prophecy experienced by the entire Jewish people.

Judaism and Theology

Today, thousands of years after prophecy has ceased, it is hard for us to understand what it is all about. This is for the following reason. Classically speaking, there are seven fields of general (non-Torah) wisdom, which include: mathematics, medicine, and music. Another of these seven fields is theology, which involves itself with understanding God.

Judaism, on principle, contains very little theology. I heard an explanation for this in the name of R. Shimshon Raphael Hirsch *zt"l*. He said that the difference between Judaism and Christianity is as follows: Christianity is a religion which man created in order to understand God, whereas Judaism is a religion which God created in order to understand man.[1] This is a magnificent insight into the nature of Judaism.

All other religions center on knowledge of God. To this purpose they create man-made theologies. They do so freely, saying as they wish about God and His nature, with none to contradict them.

Judaism involves itself very little in the theological issues of understanding God's nature. *"For God is in Heaven and you are on the earth. Therefore, your words should be few."*[2] We know very little about Hashem. We believe that He exists, that He is "great and exceedingly praised, and His greatness is unfathomable."[3] However, we do not spend our days and nights pondering over these issues. We rather spend our time sitting in the *beis midrash* involved in Gemara topics such as *shnayim ochazin b'tallis*.

Even Kabbalah, which seemingly examines and describes God's nature, is completely different from theology. Kabbalah

1. See commentary of R. Shimshon Raphael Hirsch on the Torah, *Shemos* 19:10.

2. *Koheles* 5:1.

3. *Tehillim* 145:3.

cannot be called the study of that which is Divine because it does not involve itself with God's actual nature. It rather focuses on the ways by which God relates to the world, describing the occurrences of this world in terms of their source in the upper worlds and spheres.

This is because it is Hashem's will that we should perfect *ourselves*, rather than study His nature. Hashem and His Torah are true, and His will is that we should involve ourselves in Torah. As *Chazal* say, "If only they would have abandoned Me and kept My Torah."[4] Of course, this is all based on belief in Hashem's existence. And we are meant to love Hashem, fear Him, etc. But the emphasis in *avodas Hashem* has to be on that which involves *us*.

In light of all this, our understanding of prophecy is very limited. Because before we can understand prophecy, we have to know a little about what God is.

Prophecy Is Clarity

All the prophets were connected to the Being of God when they prophesied. This is how the Rambam describes it:[5]

> At the time when the spirit rests upon him, his soul joins with the level of the angels, who are called *ishim* (men), and he becomes a different man.

In short, prophecy is a reality totally beyond all the concepts we are accustomed to.

Prophecy means "seeing." It is written, "*That which today is called a prophet, once was called a 'seer.'*"[6] Without prophecy we are groping in the dark.

4. *Eichah Rabbah, Pesikta* 2.
5. *Mishneh Torah, Hilchos Yesodei HaTorah* 7:1.
6. *I Shmuel* 9:9.

If we want to gain some idea of what prophecy is, let us close our eyes for a moment and feel with our hands what is in front of us. Without seeing, our perception is very limited. We can feel a book with our hands but we have no idea what book it is and what is written in it. It could be a storybook, or it could be a *sefer.* We perceive only the book's shape and have no idea about its true nature.

This is surely true of an object that is a yard beyond our reach. We know nothing about it. Without seeing, we don't even know if it is day or night, if there is light or darkness, whether we are alone in the room or there are other people here with us. We know hardly anything at all.

The moment we open our eyes, millions of things are revealed to us that we never noticed before. In that split second we perceive astonishing sights: people, faces, content, depth, breadth, colors… We observe that the room we are in is constructed from bricks, for example. We perceive what is standing a few feet away from us. We can see the sky, earth, and stars. With our eyes we see entire worlds that cannot be perceived at all by the sense of touch. And even the things we can perceive by touch, it would take us years to understand, whereas by looking at them we grasp it all in a second.

Prophecy is a Divine ability. We cannot conceptualize what was seen by those who achieved prophecy. However, based on the above analogy of eyesight, we could say that whole worlds were opened up before them and they saw the truth in its entirety. They saw to the bottom of all the philosophical questions and various approaches to matters of *emunah.*

The Rambam says[7] that prophecy, when compared to philosophical investigation, is like trying "to pour all the water in the world into one little jug." Just as we cannot fit the Atlantic

7. *Iggeres to R. Chisdai HaLevi.*

Ocean into a cup, so we cannot contain the understanding afforded by prophecy within the bounds of philosophical investigation. Everything we are capable of understanding with our intellect, as deep as it can be and as "scientific" as it can be, is like a cup of water. But prophecy is like the ocean, for it is connection and communication with Hashem Himself. Through prophecy, the prophet enters a whole different world of perception and of truth. At that point, there are no more philosophical questions.

Before meriting prophecy, there is room for a person to investigate whether God exists. A person can ask where He is, what is His will and in which way He relates to us. There are a million questions that can be asked. There is no end to points that can be investigated and issues that can be debated. Human civilization has produced tall piles of books on such subjects.

There are even holy books on these subjects: we have the Rambam's *Moreh Nevuchim,* we have the *Sha'ar HaYichud* in *Chovos HaLevavos,* we have *Sefer HaKuzari, Sefer HaIkkarim,* and so on. These are all books of philosophical investigation. Yet, even if we would comprehend the full depth and significance of everything written in these great works of Torah philosophy, it would be a mere cup of water compared to the mighty ocean of understanding that prophecy reveals. In a mere moment of prophetical contact with Hashem, one sees entire worlds. One sees the truth as it really is.

Among the things we constantly deal with in our lives is *safeik,* uncertainty. Returning to the example mentioned above, if a person feels an object with his hands and decides according to its shape that it is a book, he remains uncertain about the book's nature and contents. After he opens his eyes, though, he sees things clearly. He can read the book's cover and know what it is about.

Yet, there is still room for error. Let's say he glances at the cover and then his friend comes and asks him what book it is. He answers: "It's *Maseches Berachos.*" His friend picks up the book, looks at it and says, "I don't think you saw it so clearly. This is *Maseches Bechoros!*" Sometimes we don't see clearly, and sometimes we misinterpret what we see. This is compounded by the fact that someone can come along and claim that we might not have seen anything at all — perhaps we were just dreaming or imagining that we saw it. Can we prove otherwise?

Prophecy is not like this. It is a perception of reality that is beyond any *safeik*. The Rambam says[8] that prophecy is seeing with absolute certainty and clarity. I again emphasize that we have no idea what prophecy is really like, because we never experienced such a thing. It is like trying to explain to a blind person what it means to see. Nevertheless, Judaism believes that there is such a thing as prophecy.

Furthermore, over the course of generations the Jewish people have had millions of prophets. "Many prophets arose for Israel — twice the number of those who left Egypt."[9] This is not referring to hidden prophets known only by a handful of people. Rather, all these prophets served as practical guides for the people, as this is the simple meaning of prophecy. This is what Judaism believes, and no one ever questioned it.

Prophecy is not something that a person does of his own volition. Rather, God grants him prophecy. It expresses the connection between God and man. Prophecy is a passage from one world to another. It is a passage like that of a baby becoming an adult. It is opening one's eyes and seeing a completely different world.

8. *Moreh Nevuchim* 3:24.

9. *Megillah* 14a.

Seeing Things Clearly

The Rambam writes:[10]

> We should know that there is a level of knowledge above that of the philosophers: It is prophecy. Prophecy is a different world. It is not subject to proofs and discussions. Once it is clear that something is prophecy, there is no room left for proof. Accordingly, we find that a proof would be requested from a prophet only regarding whether he had prophecy or not. This is called giving a *mofeis* (sign). But a proof would not be requested as a higher verification of the prophecy itself. This is because prophecy is higher than proof, and proof is not higher than prophecy.

The Rambam is saying that the clarity of prophecy is a totally different kind of clarity. It affords a level of certainty much greater than anything logical proofs can provide. When it comes to prophecy the only point that needs investigation is whether the person is a true prophet or not. Once it is established that he is a true prophet, there is no need to bring a proof to what he stated in his prophecy. Any proof we could possibly bring is nothing compared to the clarity of prophecy.

Perceiving Divinity

As we mentioned before, Jews do not spend much time on theology, and this makes it hard for us to understand what prophecy is, since knowledge of God is a prerequisite to understanding prophecy.

> *So said Hashem: "The Heavens are My throne and the earth is My footrest."*[11]

Hashem is above all. He is great and awesome. The power expressed by the term "God" is beyond words. This is not a

10. *Iggeres to R. Chisdai HaLevi.*
11. *Yeshayahu* 66:1.

subject that we delve into, but we must know that God is God. His ability and capability is infinite. There is no end to His power and glory. When a person connects with God, at that moment a Godly type of expansiveness enters him, and he suddenly understands what God is.

The difference between how God comprehends things and how we comprehend things is tremendous. It is beyond our ability to grasp. It is not something we have been trained to think about, and in fact, knowledge of it is not what Hashem expects of us. Hashem expects of us to "*Carry out justice and acts of lovingkindness*."[12] We are to learn Torah and keep its mitzvos, thereby perfecting ourselves.

But the day will come when we will know God. This will be after our 120 years in this world have come to an end: "*For no person can see Me and [still] live*."[13] Only at the time of a person's death does he see God, for when a person dies he sees the truth in its entirety.

It is written, "*A man does not know his time... an evil time when it befalls them suddenly*."[14] This verse is saying that the day of death comes suddenly. The question is asked: Why is it called "suddenly"? A person should be preparing for this moment his whole life!

It has been answered that the transformation a person goes through at the moment of death is so drastic that no matter how much he prepares for it his whole life, he will not be ready for it. There is no way to truly prepare oneself for it, so it is called "suddenly." We live in a world of deep darkness. And there, it is a world of shining light.

Let us close our eyes for a few moments and then open them.

12. *Michah* 6:8.
13. *Shemos* 33:20.
14. *Koheles* 9:12.

The difference between our world and the world of truth is like the difference between closed eyes and open eyes. It is like a blind person suddenly starting to see. No matter what we do to prepare him for this moment, even if we explain to him with the utmost detail what is going to happen, it will not be enough.

And so it is with the perception of wisdom that the prophets had. The level they achieved, as the Rambam describes, was above anything we can imagine.

The Rambam explains it as follows:

> Prophecy rests only upon a sage who has great wisdom and who is in control of his character. His *yetzer hara* must not overpower him regarding anything in the world. Rather, he always uses his mind to overpower his *yetzer hara*. And he must have great breadth of knowledge and clarity of thought.
>
> A person who is filled with all these qualities, and who is whole of body, then enters the "orchard" of hidden wisdom. He involves himself with the great, distant matters [i.e., he must have knowledge in the topic of *Maaseh Merkavah*]. And he attains correct knowledge, to understand and to comprehend. He sanctifies himself, and separates himself more and more from the ways of the common people who go in the darkness of temporal matters. He grows continually more zealous, and teaches his soul not to have any thought of idle matters or of the vanities and guiles of temporality.
>
> Instead, his mind is continually focused on that which is above. It is connected to that which is under the Heavenly Throne, to understand those holy and pure forms. He meditates on the entire wisdom of *HaKadosh Baruch Hu,* from the first form until the navel of the earth, and he realizes from them His greatness. When he does this, the spirit of holiness immediately rests upon him.[15]

15. *Mishneh Torah, Hilchos Yesodei HaTorah* 7:1.

The prophet is required to have astounding insight: "He meditates on the entire wisdom of *HaKadosh Baruch Hu,* from the first form until the navel of the earth," i.e., he sees all of Hashem's wisdom, starting with the first reality that Hashem created, before materiality even existed, until the "navel of the earth," which is the earth's lowest point. This means that if the prophet is not familiar with a certain fish somewhere on the ocean's floor, and he does not know the reason why it has such-and-such number of scales, or he does not know why an ant has specifically six legs, and why a lion's mane has a certain number of hairs, then he is disqualified from being a prophet.

"And he realizes from them His greatness." If there is a single star that he is not familiar with — if he does not know its size, form and content — he is disqualified from being a prophet. This is because his knowledge of the size and nature of the stars teaches him about the greatness of *HaKadosh Baruch Hu*.

Then, and only then, "the spirit of holiness immediately rests upon him." He begins to see with prophetic sight.

We live in our small, closed-in world like a chick inside its shell, unaware of the great wide world that surrounds us. Hashem created a tremendous world. He created it according to His dimensions, so to speak. There were great people in this world who had profound understanding, and saw the entire immense extent of Creation.

Prophecy is a concept above and beyond anything we can understand. And it was not just one or two people in a generation who achieved it: "Many prophets arose for Israel — twice the number of those who left Egypt." Judaism believes that Hashem spoke with more than a million prophets. Also in the future, there will be millions of prophets.

The Prophet Sees Everything

When a prophet is in a state of prophecy, everything is open before him and he sees the future. We can explain this as follows: Kings have a certain system for carrying out their actions. Let's say a king wants to make an announcement. He decides on its content and wording, and then the message is delivered — beginning with the most eminent citizens and ending with the unimportant masses. First the king's ministers are informed, and then it passes to the officers, the messengers, the town criers and eventually to the people.

A Heavenly decree follows a certain process as well. Hashem fixes the decree behind the *pargod*, the partition, and then the announcement goes out. This announcement passes from the highest Heavens through all the worlds until it reaches us. The prophet knows what was announced.

Prophecy is the connection of a mortal being to matters of *kedushah*. If so, how does a prophet know what will happen in the future if the matter in question is not specifically related to *kedushah*? We can understand this by comparing it to an apple seed. The potential of the entire future tree lies within a tiny apple seed. Similarly, when a prophet is connected to the root, to the source, he sees and knows everything. Every detail of world events is spread out before him.

Take the following story as an example: It is recounted[16] that Shaul, before he was anointed to be king, was sent by his father to look for some lost mules. Shaul took along a lad and scoured the countryside for three days but could not find them. When they came to Shmuel HaNavi's town, they went to ask him the whereabouts of the mules. Even before Shaul had a chance to ask his question, Shmuel HaNavi informed him that the lost mules had been found. Shmuel HaNavi was connected to the source of everything, so he knew everything. For him, knowing the whereabouts of the missing mules was nothing.

This story of Shaul and Shmuel can be compared to two

16. *I Shmuel*, chap. 9.

people sitting in the same room and listening to a *shiur.* One of them is blind. He asks the other, "What color are the walls here?" The other tells him, "Excuse me, but we came here to learn Torah. Don't worry about the color of the walls!" He answers, "True, but for you it is so simple and easy. If you take just one quick glance you can tell me everything I need to know."

A prophet is connected to Hashem in order to hear Hashem's word, not in order to know where someone's missing mules might be. Yet, at the same time, it was no problem at all for Shmuel HaNavi to know where they were. The entire world was spread out before him like the palm of his hand. It was like taking a quick glance at the wall and noting its color.

The Difference between a Dream and Prophecy

When a person is awake, all his senses are focused on this world. But when he is asleep, his senses are not focused on material reality. That is why his senses can perceive things that are a little more elevated than this physical world. Then he is capable of knowing the Heavenly announcements before they reach our physical world. This is expressed in a foretelling dream.

Let's say Hashem decrees that a certain event will take place. In Heaven it is announced: "On such-and-such a day, such-and-such will happen." This announcement is made in all the worlds, even in the lower ones. There are people whose senses are naturally able to pick up this announcement. This occurs in a foretelling dream.

But not all dreams are the same. Pharaoh had a dream. He called in his sorcerers, who were people with sharpened senses and were capable of understanding dreams. But none of them grasped the true message of the dream. Then Yosef came. He told Pharaoh that with regular human wisdom it is impossible to penetrate the meaning of this dream. It calls for something much deeper than that: "*God will [provide an] answer [that will be*

for] Pharaoh's welfare."[17] Yosef was saying that this was not an ordinary announcement, which was revealed in the lower worlds. It was an announcement that only a prophet can understand.

When Pharaoh heard this, *"Pharaoh said to Yosef, 'Since God has made all this known to you, [then] there is no one as intelligent and wise as you.'"*[18] This is in line with what the Rambam said: a person cannot be a prophet unless he is wise, strong, and wealthy. Since Yosef was a prophet, perforce he was very wise.

There are a lot of people who dream all sorts of things. But a prophet has extra-sensory perception. It is something else altogether. When a prophet is in a state of prophecy he grasps Hashem's word in all its power.

Chazal say:

> Since the day the *Beis HaMikdash* was destroyed, prophecy was taken from the prophets and given to fools and children.[19]

This is because a child's physical senses are not truly activated. It is not just when he is sleeping that his senses are not focused on the physical world. They are never properly focused on materiality. His spiritual senses are still pure, and they can pick up certain Heavenly announcements. This is true not just when a child is asleep. His waking faculties are able to pick up on deep things that only a prophet can perceive. However, while a prophet can perceive the entire system, a child only grasps a word here and there, and he repeats it to others.

The Prophets Were Guides

The worst tragedy that ever happened to the Jewish people was when prophecy ceased. It was worse than the destruction of the *Beis HaMikdash*

17. *Bereishis* 41:16.
18. Ibid., 41:39.
19. *Bava Basra* 12b.

and all the calamities that have befallen our people throughout the generations.

Why? The Vilna Gaon writes that Hashem created us for one purpose: to perfect ourselves. The *Beis HaMikdash* and everything else are just tools to help us perfect ourselves. Every person has his own task and purpose in life. So writes the Vilna Gaon:

> Each and every person has his own path to traverse. This is because people's minds are not similar to one another. Just as their faces are not similar to one another, the natures of no two people are alike. When there were prophets, people would go to the prophets to seek Hashem. According to the judgment of prophecy, the prophet would tell the person which path he should take, according to the root of his soul, and according to the nature of his body.[20]

When we still had prophets, they would guide each person how to achieve his task and purpose in life. The prophet would tell each Jew, "In order to fulfill your purpose, you need to live in such-and-such place, while your friend should live in such-and-such place. There you will find the marriage partner Hashem planned for you before you were born, and you will rear children who are tzaddikim and prophets. That is where your *chavrusa* is. And that is where your *parnasah* is."

Hashem would guide every step of our lives by means of the prophet. The prophet would tell us what *masechta* to learn, and with which *chavrusa*. He would tell us how to raise the children, etc. Not only that, but when Shaul's father lost the mules, Shaul went to ask the advice of the prophet. If they would ask the prophet about mules and donkeys, surely they asked the prophet which *chavrusa* to learn with, what *masechta* to learn, and what is the correct *derech ha-limud*. And there is no

20. See commentary of the *Gra* on *Mishlei* 16:4.

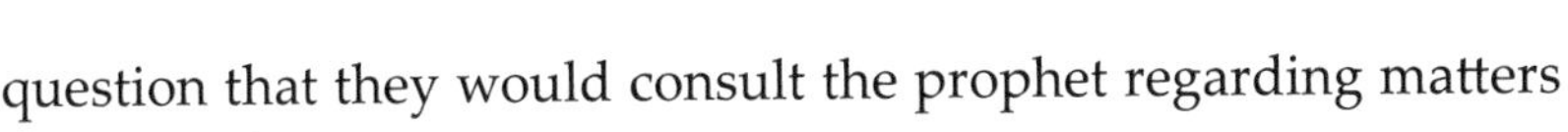

question that they would consult the prophet regarding matters of *shidduchim*.

As long as there were prophets, the Jewish people were with Hashem. Hashem would dictate to us how to live our lives and would guide our every step. Now, without prophecy, we are living in the dark.

Yet, even though prophecy has ceased, Hashem is still with us. We can be connected to Hashem even without a prophet, but it is a different kind of connection. In a certain way, the connection we have to Hashem in our generation is more beautiful because it is a connection that takes place within *hester panim*, within the framework of Hashem's concealed nature. Hashem is with us, just as always. But we experience it as a different kind of connection.

The Torah was given to us through prophecy. This is how we reached the state of, "Who gave us a Torah of truth and planted eternal life within us."[21] Through prophecy and receiving the Torah, we merited eternal life.

We live our lives today according to what Hashem told us at Mount Sinai. Similarly, when there still was prophecy, Jews would live their everyday lives with tangible closeness to Hashem and personal guidance from Him. It was truly a state of, "*Hashem your God is your King*."[22] Hashem was our rebbi, so to speak, and also our *chavrusa*, and He gave us advice how to manage our lives in the best way.

This is the sixth principle: to believe that there is such a thing as prophecy. Why is it so crucial to believe this? Because it is the foundation on which the whole Torah stands. Hashem revealed His will and specifically guided us how we should live our lives.

21. The blessing the *oleh le-Torah* recites after the Torah portion has been read.
22. *I Shmuel* 12:12.

We Must Know What Hashem Wants of Us

One of the main points we emphasize when we engage in outreach to estranged Jews is that Hashem, Who created us and put us here in the world, has a clear set of expectations from us.

When I want to explain Judaism to non-religious people, I compare the world we live in to a five-star hotel. Here we are in a fancy hotel, eating gourmet meals; there is delightful music in the background, and we are provided with fascinating tours and outings. We have a luxury suite in the hotel, which is cleaned daily. In short, it is a life of pleasure. We are in this hotel for a week, two weeks, a month, a year…

When will the day come when we notice the reception counter? When will we go over and ask the clerk, "Excuse me, whose hotel is this? What am I doing here? And what does it cost?" The sooner this day comes, the better.

We live in a very wonderful world. We have the background music of the birds that Hashem created. There is always a beautiful, impressive view. All we have to do is stop and take a look, and we will see the beauty of the world. As we drive along in a car there is not a moment when the view repeats itself.

Why do children love to be in the outdoors? Because every moment there is something new happening in Hashem's world. The pleasure of air, the pleasure of a cup of water, the pleasure we derive from our children, etc. But when will we have the sense to ask, "What do I have to pay for all this pleasure?"

Judaism believes that Hashem told us explicitly what His will is. Sometimes we meet people who say that they are traditional but not orthodox, and that it is enough to contribute to the synagogue. This is very nice, but how do they know that this is Hashem's will?

Hashem revealed His will to us, and we know exactly what He requests in return for the wonderful world He puts at our disposal. He does not need our "gifts" in the form of contributions to the synagogue. Judaism believes that God told us what He wants, and we must fulfill His will exactly as He told it to us.

Hashem indeed created a wonderful world for us. Let's take for example a simple apple. What is contained within one apple? A small, unripe apple has an unattractive, green peel. Its color is giving us the message, so to speak: Don't eat me now. You are liable to get a stomach ache. But when the apple is ripe, its peel is red and attractive. It tells us: Come and pick! Come and eat! Aside from the message the peel sends us, it also keeps the fruit fresh, and the fruit itself contains seeds from which more apple trees can grow.

What is the price that Hashem asks us to pay for this apple? A *berachah*. All we have to do is say, *Baruch Atah Hashem… borei pri ha-eitz*.

Hashem told us the price of an apple, the price of a glass of wine, the price of living, the price of getting married, and the price of supporting children. He told us how much each thing costs. He stated His will explicitly, and all this was through prophecy.

Prophecy means: Hashem spoke to us. He did not leave us in the dark. He has direct, close contact with humanity, and He told us: This is My will. If you want to live here, be My guest. But everything has a price. In payment for what I give you, I desire that you should receive more gifts from Me, gifts which are even greater than those I already gave you. In other words, in payment for the apple you must recite a *berachah*. And this *berachah* will make you a million times wealthier than the apple did.

This is the meaning of, *"His palate is sweetness and He is entirely pleasant."*[23] In order to pay for the apple, we are required to receive an even greater gift.

Returning to the allegory of the five-star hotel, it is like we

23. *Shir HaShirim* 5:16.

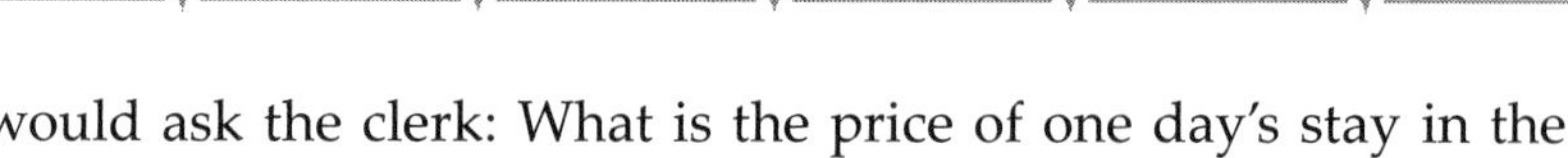

would ask the clerk: What is the price of one day's stay in the hotel? And he would answer: In exchange for your hotel stay, I require you to receive a gift of a million dollars. As payment for the apple, we recite a *berachah,* which is wealth a million times greater than the apple's worth.

Prophecy means that Hashem asserted to us in a clear way what He wants of us. We have clear dictates for each and every step of life.

Connection with Hashem must be with complete clarity. It must be one hundred percent clear and unequivocal. This is because every contact with Hashem is in His dimensions. Between people, there are various avenues of communication. There is direct conversation, there is letter writing, etc. Communication with Hashem has the quality of clear truth, of absolute clarity, far from any trace of uncertainty.

Our relationship with Hashem is not like a human relationship. It is a relationship of a Godly type — it is prophecy.

העיקר השביעי

9

The Seventh Principle

אֲנִי מַאֲמִין בֶּאֱמוּנָה שְׁלֵמָה, שֶׁנְּבוּאַת מֹשֶׁה רַבֵּנוּ עָלָיו הַשָּׁלוֹם הָיְתָה אֲמִתִּית, וְשֶׁהוּא הָיָה אָב לַנְּבִיאִים, לַקּוֹדְמִים לְפָנָיו וְלַבָּאִים אַחֲרָיו.

I believe with perfect faith that the prophecy of Moshe Rabbeinu, may peace be upon him, was true, and that he was the father of the prophets — of both those who preceded him and those who followed him.

The Uniqueness of Moshe's Prophecy

THIS PRINCIPLE OF *EMUNAH* tells us that Moshe Rabbeinu was the father of all prophets. That is to say, his prophecy was in a realm of its own. It had a completely different level of clarity and was not like the prophecy of other prophets.

Still, we must keep in mind that both Moshe Rabbeinu's prophecy and the other prophets' prophecies are prophecy. When we attempt to understand the unique level of Moshe it is crucial not to minimize the importance of the other prophets' prophecy.

What made Moshe's prophecy different? The Rambam[1] and

1. *Mishneh Torah, Hilchos Yesodei HaTorah* 7:6; *Rambam's Commentary on Mishnayos, Sanhedrin* 10:1.

other Rishonim mention a number of practical and qualitative differences. One of them is that all other prophets attained prophecy by falling on their faces and losing all their strength and faculties. But Moshe Rabbeinu would prophesize while standing on his feet.

What does this difference signify? A metaphor illustrates the point: When someone tells a shocking piece of news, the listeners open their mouths and gape in astonishment. But why do they let their jaws drop like this? It is embarrassing for a grown person to let his mouth hang wide open in public! The answer is that when a person is overwhelmed by astonishment he loses control of himself. His mouth opens by itself. When a person holds his mouth shut it is a sign that he still has control over himself.

While someone is witnessing an utterly astonishing event you could take money out of his pocket without him even feeling it. He is so unaware that he even forgets where he is.

A person cannot stand up while he sleeps. This is because standing up calls for a certain amount of self-control. When a person sees something totally astounding he falls off his feet because he does not have enough self-control to remain standing.

This is what happened to the prophets. When they received prophecy they saw such powerful wonders that they fell off their feet and lost control of themselves, so to speak. It is written about Shaul HaMelech that when he prophesied he was without clothes,[2] but this did not concern him at all. At the time he was like someone fleeing from fire, who is interested only in saving his life and does not care about his appearance.

This is because the prophet is overwhelmed by the supreme power, wonder, and delight of his prophetic vision. It is so strong that he loses all his human faculties. When a prophet

2. *I Shmuel* 19:23–24; see *Radak* ad loc.

experiences prophecy, he has no interest in what is taking place around him, to the point that people would call the prophets insane.

Elisha HaNavi sent Yonah HaNavi to anoint Yehu as king. After Yonah left Yehu's house, Yehu's servants asked him, *"Why did that insane man come to you?"*[3]

People would call the prophets insane because an insane person does whatever he likes without regard for his surroundings. If he feels like laughing, he laughs. If he feels like crying, he cries. He does whatever he wants. A person in possession of his senses does not do whatever he feels like, because he realizes that there are people around him who are looking at what he does. If someone is alone at home he allows himself to do all sorts of things that he would not do in front of people.

When a prophet enters a state of prophecy he feels that there is no one in the world who sees him. There is only he and Hashem, and no one else. He does things that would seem fitting for insane people to do. Accordingly, Yehu answered his servants, *"You know the man and his speech."*[4] As Rashi there explains, "You know that the man is insane."

This is how prophecy was for all prophets, with the exception of Moshe Rabbeinu. Moshe did not lose his senses. Why? Because for other prophets, their prophetic perception stood in contradiction to their natural way of perception. Their prophetic state contradicted their normal human state. But with Moshe Rabbeinu this was not so. His natural personality was on such a high level that the prophecy affected his entire being, to the extent that he was called "Moshe, the man of God."[5] There was no contradiction between the "man" in him and the "God"

3. *II Melachim* 9:11.
4. Ibid.
5. *Devarim* 33:1.

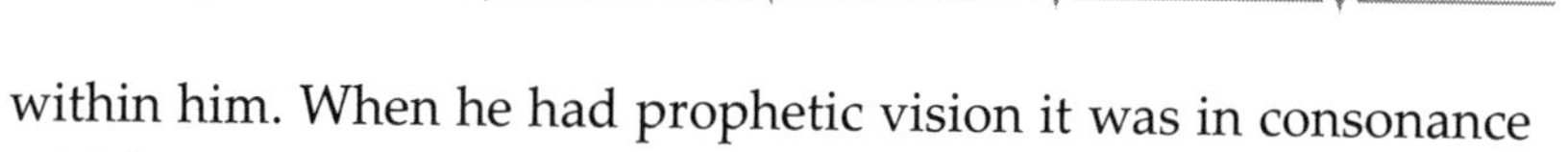

within him. When he had prophetic vision it was in consonance with his personality. This was due to the greatness of the "man" in him.

The Midrash says about Moshe Rabbeinu:

> He never had a foul odor, nor worms and maggots.[6]

It is hard to explain this but we will try to understand it as follows. When we put a slice of bread in the oven, its state is enhanced and a delightful fragrance wafts from it. Whereas when we put a piece of bread in our body, it decomposes and starts to stink. And what happened when a slice of bread entered the body of Moshe Rabbeinu? It came out as if from an oven. That was how his waste products were.

We can see something akin to this phenomenon in our own world. A newborn baby has a good smell. Even though he produces secretions, they are not repugnant, and the halachah permits us to learn Torah and recite *berachos* in their presence.[7]

Moshe Rabbeinu's natural state was akin to this.

Moshe Rabbeinu's Clarity

Now that we have discussed the difference between Moshe's prophecy and that of other prophets, we need to explain an enigmatic teaching of *Chazal*:

> *"A prophet like Moshe never again arose in Israel."*[8] Such a prophet did not arise among Israel, but among the nations of the world, one did arise… What prophet did they have, who was like Moshe? It was Bilaam ben Be'or.[9]

6. *Devarim Rabbah* 11:10.
7. *Shulchan Aruch, Orach Chaim* 81:1.
8. *Devarim* 34:10.
9. *Bemidbar Rabbah* 14:20.

What does it mean that Hashem gave a prophecy resembling Moshe's to a prophet from among the nations of the world?

R. Yehoshua Leib Diskin[10] explains that the difference between all the prophets and Moshe Rabbeinu is illustrated by the principle that "No two prophets prophesize with the same words and expression."[11] The following allegory illustrates this principle.

A rosh yeshivah delivers a *shiur*. Two students hear the *shiur* and understand it perfectly. They grasp the *kushya* and the *terutz* with great clarity. Yet, when they say over the *shiur* they heard, they do not state it exactly the same. And it is inevitably so, because each student absorbed the ideas using his own mind, and transmitted them using his own senses and faculties.

This explains the difference in style between the various prophets. When Hashem grants prophecy, the prophet comprehends Hashem's message with absolute clarity. In the previous chapter we cited the Rambam as saying that prophecy is a form of seeing that has perfect certainty and truth. Nonetheless, the prophet relays this message in his own style, expressing the message as he comprehends it through his own faculties and traits, through his own senses. That is why no two prophets, even if they would receive the same prophecy, would prophesize using identical language.

But Moshe's prophecy was not this way at all. If we would have two Moshe Rabbeinus, they would both relate the same prophecy using identical language. This is known as *aspaklaria ha-me'irah*, "clear mirror." *Chazal* say:

> All the other prophets saw by means of an unclear mirror. Moshe Rabbeinu saw by means of a clear mirror.[12]

10. Responsa of *Maharil Diskin*, p. 142.
11. *Sanhedrin* 89a.
12. *Yevamos* 49b.

Chazal are telling us, in the language of metaphor, that all the other prophets were looking at "an unclear mirror" when they perceived their prophecy. They indeed saw the image, but it was distorted.

Moshe Rabbeinu saw as in a clear mirror when he perceived his prophecy. Moshe saw things totally clearly. The image was not affected in any way by the "glass." The integrity of the image was so high that if there would be two Moshe Rabbeinus, they would transmit their prophecy to us with the same wording.

Now we can understand the prophecy of Bilaam. If Hashem would give Bilaam a prophecy like that of the other prophets, what would happen? Since Bilaam's character was riddled with wickedness he would distort the prophetic message when he absorbed it. In this way he would wreak damage on the Jewish people. Therefore, the prophecy granted to Bilaam was of Moshe Rabbeinu's type. This way Bilaam transmitted Hashem's word purely, exactly in the same style and manner that he received it.

This is the idea that R. Yehoshua Leib Diskin was expressing.

This explains why we say in the *Haftarah* blessing: *Asher bachar binvi'im tovim v'ratzah v'divreihem ha-ne'emarim be'emes* — "He selected *good* prophets, and He was pleased with their words which were said *in truth*."

The prophets of Israel are "good" of character, unlike Bilaam, who was a prophet of evil character. "Their words which were said *in truth*," means that the prophets of Israel truly conveyed the word of Hashem as heard in prophecy. Although each had his own *signon*, his own manner and wording, according to his specific intellect and capabilities, they communicated their message faithfully.

This is one of the basic differences between Moshe's prophecy and that of the other prophets. Indeed, the other prophets faithfully transmitted Hashem's word to us in absolute truth, but this transmission bore the prophet's own style. It was like someone saying over a *shiur* that he heard. Even though he communicates the same exact idea that he heard, he does it based on his own perception and comprehension. Hearing Moshe's prophecy, on the other hand, was like hearing Hashem's word directly. *Chazal* tell us, "The Shechinah spoke from Moshe's throat."[13]

Straight from Hashem's Mouth

Torah and mitzvos were communicated to us through Moshe Rabbeinu, and this was the only possible way it could be done. There is a rule in Torah explication that "We cannot use the words of the Prophets to make an interpretation of words of Torah."[14] This is because Torah must be with the level of clarity afforded by Moshe Rabbeinu alone. Ordinary prophecy is not enough. The nature of Torah and mitzvos is that they come to us directly from Hashem's mouth.

This forms the introduction to the ninth principle of *emunah,* "This Torah will not be exchanged and there will not be another Torah from the Creator, may He be blessed." How so? Because if the Torah had been given to us through one of the other prophets, it would bear his own style. And had it been given to us through two of the other prophets, it would have had a different style the second time. This would create the reality that, in a certain sense, there would be two Torahs. If so, the Torah could be exchanged for another, *chas v'shalom.*

But the Torah was given to us through Moshe. Thus it is the actual word of Hashem, no more and no less. And just as Hashem does not change, as it says, *"I, Hashem, have not changed,"*[15] so

13. *Zohar, Pinchas* 232a.
14. *Chagigah* 10b.
15. *Malachi* 3:6.

the Torah does not change. The reason that the Torah does not change is because it is the direct word of Hashem.

> They were glad and joyous when they heard words to be accepted from the mouth of Moshe, like hearing it from the mouth of *HaKadosh Baruch Hu*.[16]

Hearing from the mouth of Moshe is just like hearing from the mouth of *HaKadosh Baruch Hu*. This is because of the clarity of Moshe's prophecy.

Style versus Clarity?

Before we go on to the next principle of *emunah*, we have to settle a disturbing issue that we just raised. On the one hand, we emphasized the tremendous clarity of the phenomenon called prophecy. In the previous chapter we cited the Rambam as saying that matters communicated through prophecy have no need for further proof. The Rambam says that prophecy carries such a high level of truthfulness that any attempt to bring proof is meaningless: prophetic knowledge is as great as the ocean, while the powers of human investigation are like a small jug. All the logical, philosophical and empirical proofs we could possibly muster are nothing compared to the clear vision called prophecy. All we need to check out is whether this indeed was prophecy or not. Once we know it was prophecy, its level of certainty is Divine. There is no trace of doubt.

But on the other hand, we just finished saying that ordinary prophecy passes through the tinted glass of the personal traits and faculties of that particular prophet. And this impacts the prophetic message so much that no two prophets express their prophecy with the same style. If this is so, what happened to the absolute clarity of prophecy?

16. *Yalkut Shimoni, Tzav* 519.

This question leads us to a very important and basic point on which the entire Torah stands.

When Hashem created the world He had a certain purpose in mind. He created worlds upon worlds, with the goal of reaching the lowliest, bottommost point. Not lowliness in its negative sense, but lowliness in terms of hierarchy. Our physical world is the lowliest and bottommost of all the worlds created by Hashem. And it is the purpose of them all: Hashem's will is that within this world which is farthest from Him, there should be creatures who recognize Him and make contact with Him, despite this world's great lowliness.

Just as man's peak of greatness is to be in contact with God, so God's peak of greatness (if we could speak of such a thing) is to be in contact with man. It is written:

> *As the Heavens are high above the earth, so are My ways high above your ways, and My thoughts above your thoughts.*[17]

The angels are closer to Hashem than we are. All the worlds that Hashem created are closer to Him than our world is. There is nothing farther from Hashem than man is. A man is dust from the ground, which is as far as can be from Hashem's loftiness. A man is the ultimate in materiality, whereas Hashem is One, beyond all comprehension.

What about the animals? We do not speak about them in this connection because they are not something on their own; they were created only to serve man. They do not have independent significance, just as a man's clothing, or his eyeglasses, do not have independent significance.

Hashem's goal in all of Creation was to make man — in order that man, from the point of greatest possible distance, will make contact with Him. What is the purpose of this contact

17. *Yeshayahu* 55:9.

between lowly man and lofty Hashem?

It is not to uplift and transform man, nullifying his human level of perception. It is not to infuse him with super-elevated intellect so he may truly understand the Divine. In fact, Hashem does not desire that man should be metamorphosed in this way. A person will reach this state after his death. But as long as a person is still alive and living on earth, having a super-elevated state runs against the whole purpose for which Hashem created His world.

The purpose is exactly the opposite. It is not to take man out of his gross, physical body (which is death) but rather to purify and refine him while he remains a human being. If he would be stripped of his human characteristics he would be an angel. Hashem did not create His world for angels.

The purpose is for man, in his lowly human state, to perceive Divinity with his own human senses and faculties.

To this end, Hashem prepared for us a Torah. In His infinite genius, Hashem created the Torah in a way that enables man to do this. The Torah consists of a system of down-to-earth, humanly comprehensible concepts. It speaks about a bull goring a cow. It speaks about two people holding onto a shawl, disputing its ownership. At the same time, it is Hashem's word, with all the depth and power this implies!

Through Torah, man can actually comprehend Hashem's will. This is the highest possible level, and the ultimate goal of all. *Chazal* express this point as follows:

> Words of Torah are more beloved to *HaKadosh Baruch Hu* than are all those who ever lived, and are all the works of His hands that He created.[18]

Hashem loves Torah so much because the ultimate goal is

18. *Tanna D'vei Eliyahu Rabbah*, chap. 14.

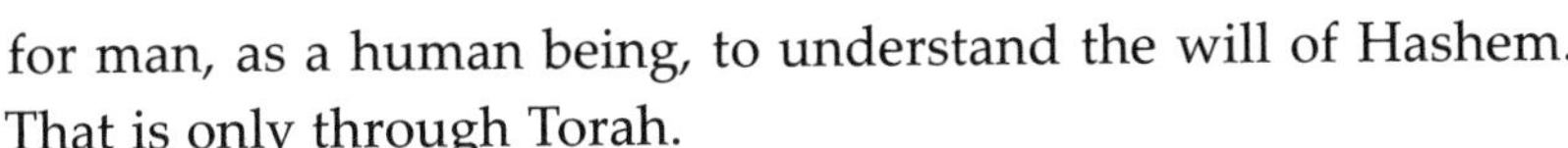

for man, as a human being, to understand the will of Hashem. That is only through Torah.

When a prophet perceives Divinity, when he rises to the tremendous level of grasping Hashem's infinity, at that moment he attains the absolute clarity of which the Rambam spoke. But in a certain sense he becomes "insane." He loses his humanity. In order to attain prophecy he has to give up all his simple, lowly faculties that characterize him as a human being.

As we explained before, prophecy and humanity cannot go together. The prophet cannot stand on his feet and see with his physical eyes when he grasps super-elevated matters. He needs to lose himself, in a certain sense. In this way he nearly becomes an angel, as the Rambam says: "At the time when the spirit rests upon him, his soul joins with the level of the angels..."[19]

This is indeed the highest level that a mortal being can attain. However, it goes against the purpose for which Hashem created the world. That is why the prophet does not remain in this state. After prophesizing he needs to awaken and return to a human state, and thereby transfer to his everyday senses what he saw with absolute prophetic clarity. And since his everyday senses are not those that perceived the prophetic vision, this is called "an unclear mirror." In this aspect, every prophet has his own perception.

R. Yehoshua Leib Diskin, mentioned above, goes on to say:

> Prophetic visions take place in the upper worlds. Nevertheless, these visions slowly descend and take on physical form until their interpretation is within the comprehension of the prophet and he understands what they allude to in this lowly world. At that point, the prophet's spirit almost returns to him... and he beholds his soul, and knows the interpretation of the prophetic vision.

19. *Mishneh Torah, Hilchos Yesodei HaTorah* 7:1.

> Nevertheless, it is like looking through glass. If the glass is tinted green… all that he looks at has a green tone even though he sees the things without deviation… Even so, the ordinary prophets did not prophesize falsely, far be it… The interpretation of the prophecy then exists in this lowly world just as it was imprinted on his soul.[20]

The prophet's understanding during his prophecy has absolute clarity. The way we see a table standing right in front of us in a well-lit room is like foggy darkness compared to the clarity of the prophets during their prophetic visions. But the "interpretation" of the prophecy, after being translated into the language of everyday senses, is on the level of "an unclear mirror." This is because the prophet does not perceive with absolute clarity while using his everyday senses.

Hashem set up prophecy to function in this manner because there is no true value to lofty perceptions if they are totally cut off from the normal human state.

Moshe's Portrait

We will conclude this chapter with a tangential topic, but one that is well worth mentioning.

A story is related in a certain *sefer*[21] about a king who sent an expert artist to make a portrait of Moshe Rabbeinu's face. This artist went out to the Wilderness, sketched Moshe's portrait, and brought it back to the king. The king then gathered all his sages to analyze Moshe's face and determine Moshe's temperament and character based on physiognomy. His sages told him that according to the portrait, Moshe was a man of exceptionally corrupt and deplorable character.

The king was very surprised. He went out to the Wilderness and asked Moshe Rabbeinu himself for an explanation of the

20. Responsa of *Maharil Diskin,* p. 142.

21. *Tiferes Yisrael, Kiddushin* 4:77.

matter. Moshe answered that indeed, his nature had been very bad and negative. However, he worked on his character and perfected himself to the point that he became Moshe Rabbeinu. But had his character been sterling from the outset, there would be nothing laudable about his reaching the level he did.

R. Yehoshua Leib Diskin said that the above story is absolutely false. Since he rejected the story, I too allow myself to find fault with it.

First of all, it is not plausible that an artist succeeded in going out to the Wilderness to draw Moshe's portrait. The Midrash clearly states, as cited in the *Chizkuni*'s commentary on the Torah, that the Clouds of Glory completely surrounded the Israelite camp. Even Yisro could not get in. Surely, an ordinary person would not be able to enter the camp and approach Moshe.

Second of all, this story is clearly contradicted by a verse in the Torah. It says about Yocheved, Moshe Rabbeinu's mother, that when Moshe was born, *"She saw that he was good."*[22] And *Chazal* explain this as follows:

> When Moshe was born, the whole house filled with light.[23]

Thus we see that even at birth, Moshe was already on such a high level that the house filled with light. *Chazal* say further:

> There was a woman in Egypt who gave birth to six hundred thousand at one time. There was a disciple named R. Yishmael son of R. Yosi who asked, "Who was this woman?" The answer was given, "It was Yocheved. She gave birth to Moshe, who was equal to the six hundred thousand Israelites."[24]

Thus we see that Moshe was born with a righteousness and

22. *Shemos* 2:2.
23. *Shemos Rabbah* 1:20.
24. *Shir HaShirim Rabbah* 1:3.

greatness equal to the entire Jewish people. *Chazal* say further:

> Moshe Rabbeinu said to him [to the angel Samael who sought to take his soul]: "I am the son of Amram. I was born without a foreskin, and I did not need to be circumcised. The day I was born I began to speak, and I stood up and walked, and spoke with my father and mother, and I did not even suckle milk. When I was three months old I prophesized and said that I am destined to receive the Torah from among fiery flames."[25]

We see that Moshe Rabbeinu was on an astoundingly high level from day one. So when we hear a story saying that he was born with a poor temperament and negative character traits, we know it is absolutely false. And it is folly for the following reason, as well:

Let's imagine someone would come and ask us how America managed to send a rocket to the moon. And we would answer that they built a high base from which the rocket was launched. Thanks to the high base, the rocket was already much closer to the moon!

The above-quoted story seeks to bolster the image of Moshe Rabbeinu. But in order for Moshe to seem great, do we need to say that he started at zero and got where he did? The story implies that had Moshe started out life with a good nature, it would not be so much of a surprise that he reached the heights he did! This is folly.

In order to reach the supremely exalted level of speaking face-to-face with the Shechinah, and all the other utterly amazing things that Moshe did, even the best character traits in the world would not begin to do the job. They would not bring Moshe noticeably closer to the great heights he achieved, just as

25. *Devarim Rabbah* 11:10.

a high base for launching a rocket does not bring it noticeably closer to the moon.

Moshe was not great because he overcame negative character traits. Moshe Rabbeinu was born with a righteousness and a greatness that was comparable to that of the whole Jewish people combined. The house shone with light when he was born! And after that beginning, he began working in an unparalleled way. Indeed, he reached awesome heights that we cannot even imagine.

10

The Eighth and Ninth Principles

אֲנִי מַאֲמִין בֶּאֱמוּנָה שְׁלֵמָה, שֶׁכָּל הַתּוֹרָה הַמְּצוּיָה עַתָּה בְיָדֵינוּ
הִיא הַנְּתוּנָה לְמֹשֶׁה רַבֵּנוּ עָלָיו הַשָּׁלוֹם.

I believe with perfect faith that all the Torah we have now in our hands is what was given to Moshe Rabbeinu, may peace be upon him.

אֲנִי מַאֲמִין בֶּאֱמוּנָה שְׁלֵמָה, שֶׁזֹּאת הַתּוֹרָה לֹא תְהֵא מֻחְלֶפֶת
וְלֹא תְהֵא תּוֹרָה אַחֶרֶת מֵאֵת הַבּוֹרֵא יִתְבָּרַךְ שְׁמוֹ.

I believe with perfect faith that this Torah will not be exchanged, and there will not be another Torah from the Creator — may His Name be blessed.

Only the Main Points

THESE TWO PRINCIPLES OF *emunah* go together: The Torah we have today is the same as what was was given to Moshe Rabbeinu. And it will never be replaced.

We will start with the first of the two principles. When a rabbi transmits what he knows to his disciple, he does not transmit his entire body of wisdom, but only as much as the disciple is capable of receiving. The disciple always has less than the rabbi. The more the rabbi transmits to the disciple, the greater the disciple becomes.

There were certain great Torah figures whose greatness expressed itself not just in who they were and in what they knew, but also in the way they taught others. They had a special way of transmitting their wealth of Torah. They communicated so much Torah wisdom to their disciples that even if all the sea were ink it still would not enable their disciples to write down all the Torah they received from their rabbis. Nonetheless, that which remained with their rabbis was greater than that which was imparted.

These disciples received from their rabbis only a drop in the sea. The nature of things is that the rabbi imparts to his disciple only certain points. As R. Akiva said:

> I learned a lot of Torah, yet I did not receive from my rabbis even as much as a dog licking from the sea.[1]

There is only one case where the rabbi imparted all his wisdom to his disciple. The rabbi was Moshe and the disciple was Yehoshua. *Chazal* say:

> Before Moshe Rabbeinu left this world for *Gan Eden*, he said to Yehoshua, "Ask me everything that is unclear to you." Yehoshua said, "Rabbi, did I ever leave you for a moment and go somewhere else? Did you not write about me, '*His servant Yehoshua son of Nun, a lad, would not depart from the tent*'?"[2]

Yehoshua received all that Moshe had to give. This was due to Moshe's greatness (not Yehoshua's). But aside from this case, every rabbi imparts only part of his wisdom to his disciple.

The greater the rabbi, the more he seeks ways to impart his wisdom to his disciple. Let's take a ten-year-old child as an example. After such a child is taught an *amud* of Gemara many

1. *Sanhedrin* 68a.
2. *Temurah* 16a.

times until he knows it well, is he capable of teaching it to his friend? Surely not. This is because to teach others and impart one's understanding calls for a different type of talent. It is a special wisdom to be able to impart what one knows.

The clearer things are to the rabbi, the better he can explain them. Let's say there is a child with limited comprehension in a class. If the teacher wants to explain a section of Gemara to this child, he first has to make sure he personally understands the Gemara very clearly. Only then will he be able to explain it to the child.

Hashem Gives It All

This principle of *emunah*, "All the Torah we have now in our hands is what was given to Moshe Rabbeinu," is based on the idea that Hashem, Who is our great Rabbi and Teacher, imparted everything to us. By giving us the Torah He transmitted to us His full wisdom, and He even gave us Himself along with it, so to speak. In His infinite greatness He is capable of this extraordinary feat. Hashem in His entirety is contained within the Torah. He held back nothing from us. *Chazal* describe this by saying about the Torah, *"It is not in Heaven."*[3] This conveys that nothing was left in Heaven; Hashem gave us all there is to give.

This idea underlies the ninth principle of *emunah* as well: "This Torah will not be exchanged." It is basic to our faith that Hashem gave us the Torah in its entirety. Otherwise, if He would have given us just half the Torah at Mount Sinai, it could always be claimed that He intended on giving us more parts of the Torah in the future. Or it could be claimed that He taught us the Torah in a limited way that was appropriate for us then, but He intended on changing it to make it appropriate for future generations. On the contrary: we know and believe that He gave

3. *Bava Metzia* 59b; *Devarim* 30:12.

us the Torah in its entirety, and that in His infinite wisdom He put Himself into the Torah, so to speak. Therefore, "This Torah will not be exchanged, and there will not be another Torah." This is because *"I, Hashem, have not changed."*[4] Just as Hashem does not change, so His Torah does not change.

Torah is understanding the ways of Heaven. At Mount Sinai we understood everything. Moshe Rabbeinu understood the entire Torah. About this it says, *"In all My house, he [Moshe] is faithful."*[5] There was nothing about the ways of Heaven or of this world that Moshe did not understand. How much we understand of the Torah today is another question. "The Torah… is rolled up and sitting in the corner. Whoever wishes to come and learn, he may come and learn."[6] It is all there, despite the fact that we do not understand it in its true depth.

Every person is obligated to know the Torah according to his own power of comprehension. Yet, Hashem did not give us the Torah in a limited way, according to our ability to receive. He did not confine Himself to our level of intelligence and comprehension. Rather, Hashem gave us the Torah on the level of His ability to teach, so to speak. And since His capabilities are unlimited, He has the ability to teach absolutely everything in its full depth and breadth!

If we would be asked to "give the Torah" to someone, we would teach him only the parts that are relevant to him, that he is capable of understanding and implementing. By way of example, we do not go and buy a full set of *Shas* for an eight-year-old boy who is just starting to learn Gemara. We buy him only the little section that he is studying in school. Why does he need a full *Shas* if he won't use it?

4. *Malachi* 3:6.
5. *Bemidbar* 12:7.
6. *Kiddushin* 66a.

Hashem, however, gave us the entire Torah in one unit. He did not give us only those parts that are immediately relevant to us.

About the Torah it says, *"Its measure is longer than the earth and wider than the sea."*[7] The Torah is infinite because Hashem is infinite. And Hashem's infinity is expressed in the Torah. "He chose us from among all the peoples and gave us *His* Torah."[8] The Torah we received is not tailored to our size. Hashem tailored the Torah to fit Himself, so to speak. The Torah is according to His dimensions, with all His infinite depth and breadth. Also the mitzvos are according to His dimensions. So to speak, Hashem learns Torah and keeps mitzvos. For instance, *Chazal* say: "From where do we know that *HaKadosh Baruch Hu* puts on tefillin…"[9]

Torah within Torah

We might wonder how *HaKadosh Baruch Hu* did it. How did He give to us, who are small beings, a Torah possessing His lofty dimensions which are totally out of proportion to human measurements? Could one take the hat of the legendary giant Og Melech HaBashan and put it on a dwarf's head? And here the difference is even more striking. So to speak, it is like putting *HaKadosh Baruch Hu's* shoes on our tiny feet.

The answer is: *HaKadosh Baruch Hu* knows how He did it, but this is not a subject for us to delve into because it is far beyond our ability to understand. The very fact that Hashem gave us the Torah expresses His infinite, unlimited ability. It is not for us to ask *how* He did it, but rather, *what* did He do. To this question, the answer is: Hashem transmitted to us *His*

7. *Iyov* 11:9.

8. *Birkas HaTorah.*

9. *Berachos* 6b.

Torah, and since it is His, it never needs to be added to or exchanged. Hashem acted as a rabbi who transmits everything to his disciple, holding back nothing.

The real question we should ask is: What are we supposed to do with all this Torah we have received? Why do we need it all? The answer is: so that with our own senses we may grasp the Divine greatness, dimension, and depth that is contained within the Torah. This idea is shockingly profound. Hashem puts on tefillin, and we also put on tefillin. Hashem eats matzah, and we also eat matzah. Hashem learns Torah, and we also learn Torah.

Practically speaking, our tefillin are not Hashem's tefillin. Our matzah is not His matzah, as ours is made of flour and water. But within our matzah is the content of Hashem's matzah. Within the *batim* of our tefillin is the content of Hashem's tefillin.

This means that we gain a hold on Hashem's tefillin by means of our tefillin. Someone who puts on tefillin has thereby put on the tefillin of Hashem. Someone who eats matzah is eating the matzah of Hashem. And someone who learns Torah is learning the Torah of Hashem, so to speak. In truth, this is what he is learning.

It is all contained within, just compressed. When something of large quantity is compacted, the resulting substance contains all the original content but in compressed form. Nothing is missing, but it is miniaturized. When someone swallows a concentrated pill, it has the same effect as if he ingested the original, uncompressed substance.

Hashem took His tefillin and "compressed" them into our tefillin, so to speak. But essentially they are His tefillin; nothing is missing. When we learn Torah, it is the same Torah that Hashem learns.

In the future we will be able to handle things in their large, uncompressed state, but we already have received it in all its power, just in concentrated form. A day will come when

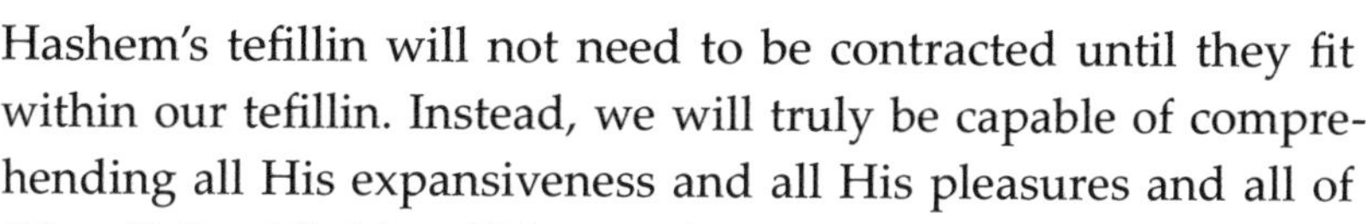

Hashem's tefillin will not need to be contracted until they fit within our tefillin. Instead, we will truly be capable of comprehending all His expansiveness and all His pleasures and all of *Olam HaBa*. All this will be ours!

Moshe Rabbeinu Is the Bridge

In the seventh principle we explained why the Torah was given specifically by Moshe Rabbeinu. And what we explained here adds further depth to this point.

The distance between Hashem and human beings is tremendous. But Moshe Rabbeinu bridged this distance. This underlies the eighth principle, "All the Torah we have now in our hands is what was given to Moshe Rabbeinu, may peace be upon him." Hashem utilized a certain "tool" in order to take His unlimited greatness and Godliness, and invest it into a system that we can relate to with our finite, human senses. That "tool" was Moshe Rabbeinu.

When Moshe Rabbeinu would have prophecy he would remain standing on his feet. He would not tremble and collapse like the other prophets would. Only he was capable of bringing us the Torah. In order to understand what Torah is, we must believe that Torah could not have been given by another prophet. This is because when an ordinary prophet prophesizes, to a certain extent he loses his normal, everyday senses. And the purpose of Torah is the opposite of this: it is for Hashem's word to enter the realm of our finite, human senses. This can be done only by Moshe Rabbeinu.

Only Moshe spoke to Hashem "like a person speaks to his friend,"[10] that is, in possession of all his human senses. This was not due to Moshe himself. Rather, Hashem in His kindness granted him this ability. And Moshe Rabbeinu brought us a

10. *Shemos* 33:11.

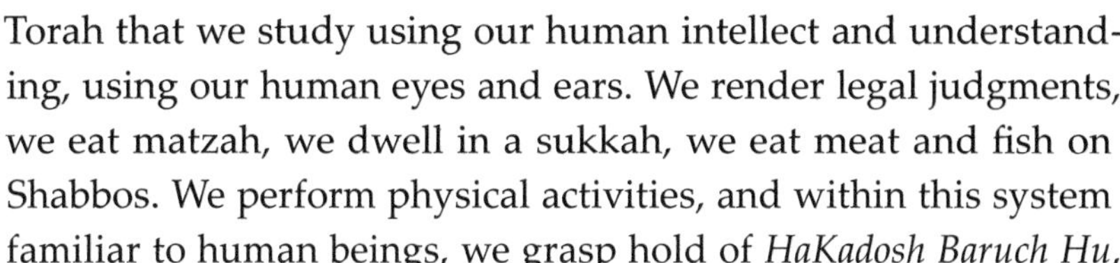

Torah that we study using our human intellect and understanding, using our human eyes and ears. We render legal judgments, we eat matzah, we dwell in a sukkah, we eat meat and fish on Shabbos. We perform physical activities, and within this system familiar to human beings, we grasp hold of *HaKadosh Baruch Hu*, so to speak. This is Torah.

Judaism believes that the Torah will never be exchanged. If the Torah is *HaKadosh Baruch Hu*, how could it possibly be exchanged? If the Torah is the ways and attributes of Hashem, how could it be exchanged?

Hashem did not tailor a set of mitzvos to fit us. Hashem did not tailor a system of behavior to fit us. Instead, it is as *Chazal* say, "I sold you My Torah, and, so to speak, I was sold along with it"[11] — "Torah is *HaKadosh Baruch Hu*."[12] Just as we believe that *"I, Hashem, have not changed,"*[13] so we believe that the Torah will not change. This is the entity known as Torah.

"This Torah will not be exchanged," and it will never be added to or subtracted from. This is the key principle of *emunah*. Someone who does not know this principle does not know what Torah is.

Hashem Is within the Torah We Learn

There are those who claimed that if one studies a Gemara topic dealing with mundane monetary issues, such as "*shor she'nagach es ha-parah*," and does not have in mind that the subject under study is the physical manifestation of Heavenly matters in the upper worlds, this is not called learning Torah.

Such a claim runs against belief in Torah and against all understanding of what Torah is. We believe that every section

11. *Shemos Rabbah* 33:1.
12. *III Zohar* 73a.
13. *Malachi* 3:6.

of Torah learning, such as "*shor she'nagach*," contains within it all the Divine power of Torah. Let's say a person learns "*shor she'nagach*" and for him the *shor*, bull, represents one of the *chayos hakodesh* of Hashem's celestial Chariot. But when it comes to the pragmatic issue of how much the owner of the bull must pay the owner of the *parah*, cow, in damages — whether the payment is half damages or full damages — this person does not find meaning and satisfaction in his learning. This person is denying the truth of Hashem's unlimited capabilities.

Why? Because for him, the *sugya* in the Gemara dealing with the bull and the cow is just a means to speak about matters of the upper worlds. This is a serious error. Hashem has the ability to bring Himself into the *sugya* as it is learned and understood here, in this lowly world. If someone thinks that Hashem is not found within the *sugya* as it is here in this world, he is denying the very nature of Torah. (See *Nefesh HaChaim*, sec. 4, where this point is elaborated.)

This underlies the difference between Torah learning and *tefillah*. How long can a person pray with *kavanah* and *deveikus?* An hour, two hours, three hours… but no more than that. This is because *tefillah* is *deveikus.* It is attachment to Hashem. A person normally cannot remain in such an elevated state indefinitely. A person can only eat so much honey! But Torah learning is different. A person can learn a *daf,* and another *daf,* and discuss the topic back and forth, and put forward a *svara,* and yet another *svara,* for it is all within the realm of our concepts.

Torah is the greatest gift that Hashem gave man. Through Torah, Hashem brought all His power and all of Himself, so to speak, down into our world.

Judaism believes that "This Torah will not be exchanged." Everything is contained within the Torah. *Deveikus* to Hashem in all its power is right here, in the Torah. Learning a *daf* of Gemara leads to learning another *daf,* and another *daf,* and to attaining *deveikus* in all its power.

The Tenth and Eleventh Principles

אֲנִי מַאֲמִין בֶּאֱמוּנָה שְׁלֵמָה, שֶׁהַבּוֹרֵא יִתְבָּרַךְ שְׁמוֹ יוֹדֵעַ כָּל מַעֲשֵׂה בְנֵי אָדָם וְכָל מַחְשְׁבוֹתָם, שֶׁנֶּאֱמַר הַיֹּצֵר יַחַד לִבָּם הַמֵּבִין אֶל כָּל מַעֲשֵׂיהֶם.

I believe with perfect faith that the Creator — may His Name be blessed — knows all the deeds of human beings and all their thoughts, as it says: "He fashions their hearts together; He comprehends all their deeds."

אֲנִי מַאֲמִין בֶּאֱמוּנָה שְׁלֵמָה, שֶׁהַבּוֹרֵא יִתְבָּרַךְ שְׁמוֹ גּוֹמֵל טוֹב לְשׁוֹמְרֵי מִצְוֹתָיו וּמַעֲנִישׁ לְעוֹבְרֵי מִצְוֹתָיו.

I believe with perfect faith that the Creator — may His Name be blessed — bestows good upon those who keep His mitzvos, and punishes those who transgress His mitzvos.

Omniscience and Free Choice Are Intertwined

THE TENTH PRINCIPLE OF *emunah* teaches us that Hashem knows everything we think and do. He is omniscient. Since He knows all, His knowledge is not limited to the past and the present. He knows the future, too.

It is notable that this principle of *emunah* is the only one for which a *pasuk* is cited as support: "I believe with perfect faith… as it says (*Tehillim* 33:15): '*He fashions their hearts together; He comprehends all their deeds.*'" Why does this principle need a *pasuk*? I heard it explained that Hashem's omniscience seemingly contradicts the next principle that Hashem rewards and punishes. Why is this so? Because if Hashem knows what we will do in the future, apparently we do not have free choice. And if we are not free to choose our deeds, we can be neither rewarded nor punished for them.[1]

Yet, the eleventh principle of *emunah* states that Hashem "bestows good upon those who keep His mitzvos, and punishes those who transgress His mitzvos." Since the tenth principle seems to contradict the eleventh, and we might not readily accept its truth, a *pasuk* is cited in support of it.

In other words, we have stumbled upon a great philosophical issue that has perturbed people over the millennia: Divine omniscience versus human free choice. After we explore this issue a little, we will better understand what the *pasuk* is coming to tell us.

It is basic to our *emunah* that a person has free choice. What he does is completely in his hands, for better or worse. He can choose to be a tzaddik like Moshe Rabbeinu, or as wicked as Yerovam ben Nevat. Yet, God knows the future. He knows that this person will be a tzaddik. If so, in what way is this person free to choose the path of wickedness?

Talking about Things We Don't Understand

The answer to this deep philosophical question is found in the Rambam's words:

> *HaKadosh Baruch Hu* does not know with a knowing that is external to Him, as do human beings, for whom their selves and their knowledge are two. Rather, He and His knowledge are one; may His Name be exalted.

1. See Rambam's introduction to *Pirkei Avos*, chap. 8.

However, proper comprehension of this matter is not within the realm of man's knowledge.[2]

If Hashem's knowledge were like our knowledge, there would indeed be a contradiction between His knowledge of the future and our free choice. Hashem's knowledge of our future actions would preclude us from doing otherwise. However, His knowledge is completely different. It is not something we can even understand. He and His knowledge are one; Hashem's knowledge is part of Himself. Such a thing is beyond our ability to conceptualize.

This Godly type of knowledge does not conflict with our free choice. Why? The question is irrelevant: we cannot debate things we don't understand. How can we discuss whether A contradicts B, when we know neither what A is nor what B is?

The Raavad[3] leans toward saying that the two points are not in absolute contradiction to one another. He attempts to make peace between omniscience and free choice. But the Rambam was a very great philosopher and he says that knowledge of the future (as we understand it) and free choice contradict each other absolutely.

When Hashem sent Moshe Rabbeinu to bring the Jewish people out of Egypt, He said to him:

I know (Ani yadati) that the king of Egypt will not let you leave.[4]

Based on the above-quoted Rambam, the Brisker Rav[5] explains the repetition in this enigmatic *pasuk*: It says *Ani yadati,* but the word *yadati* includes the pronoun "*ani*" within it. So why is the pronoun "*ani*" necessary as well? The Brisker Rav answered

2. *Mishneh Torah, Hilchos Teshuvah* 2:5.
3. *Hasagos HaRaavad* ad loc.
4. *Shemos* 3:19.
5. *Chiddushei HaGryz al HaTorah,* chap. 47.

that it implies that as far as "*I* know," as far as Hashem's knowledge is concerned, Pharaoh surely will not let the people leave. But as far as free choice is concerned, this is not so.

Hashem was telling Moshe that this is a knowledge only I can know. If you would know it, then it would contradict Pharaoh's free choice. My knowledge is different: it does not negate Pharaoh's freedom to do otherwise.

This idea underlies the tenth principle of *emunah*. "I believe with perfect faith that the Creator — may His Name be blessed — knows all the deeds of human beings...." Hashem's knowledge of our deeds is not the kind of knowledge we are accustomed to. Rather, it is a knowledge of the type, "*He fashions their hearts together; He comprehends all their deeds.*" The Divine knowledge spoken of in this *pasuk* is completely different from our knowledge. It is the unique knowledge of He Who created human beings and thereby comprehends all their deeds. (Later on we will return to explain this point.)

We can understand all the previous principles of *emunah* in our terms. Our declaration of belief that Hashem is the Creator is based on our human perception of the term "creator." When we attest that Hashem is not physical, we perceive this based on our selves, too; contrary to us, Hashem does not have a body. But now we are talking about something beyond our terms of reference. Hashem's knowledge is completely different from human knowledge. This is because if we'd be able to understand Hashem's knowledge based on our personal experience, this would contradict the next principle of reward and punishment.

Reward and Punishment — Beyond Our Comprehension

Similarly, the principle that Hashem "bestows good upon those who keep His mitzvos, and punishes those who transgress His mitzvos" is not measured in human terms. *Chazal* express this point in the following teaching:

He who says that *HaKadosh Baruch Hu* lets things pass [without holding one responsible for one's deeds], his life will be let to pass.[6]

If someone says that Hashem will not hold a person responsible for his deeds, even if he says this regarding a small misdeed, *Chazal* tell us that he will receive a punishment of Divine dimensions. This sheds light on the meaning of Divine reward and punishment, as we will explain.

When Hashem bestows good, He does so in His measurements. For instance, Hashem once gave us a kiss, so to speak. This was when we stood at Mount Sinai, about which it says, "*He will kiss me with the kisses of His mouth.*"[7] And what did we receive through that one kiss of Hashem? The answer is found in the *Sim shalom* blessing recited at the end of the *Shemoneh Esrei*. "For with the radiance of Your face" — that is, with Hashem's smile — "You have given us… the Torah of life, and love of kindness..."

Mount Sinai was a one-time event. But from it we received "the Torah of life, and love of kindness, and charity and blessing and mercy and life and peace," all of which are forever and ever. Once upon a time we received a kiss, and the tremendous reward imparted through that kiss is kept for us for the future to come, for eternity.

Similarly, Hashem punishes in His measurements. Let us attempt to understand what punishment is in Hashem's terms. Imagine a father hitting his child. How much does it hurt the child? It depends how big the father's hand is. After a light slap from the palm of the legendary giant Og Melech HaBashan, nothing would be left of an ordinary child.

6. *Bava Kamma* 50a.

7. *Shir HaShirim* 1:1; *Midrash Rabbah* ad loc.

When a Being of immense dimensions gives a little "scolding" once in a thousand years, we call it an Inquisition, or a Holocaust… Of course, also His patience and forbearance is according to His dimensions, as we will explain.

Why Measure for Measure?

Chazal say:

> All Israel have a portion in *Olam HaBa* … And these are the people who do not have a portion in *Olam HaBa*: He who says there is no source in the Torah for the resurrection of the dead…[8]

Someone comes along and claims that the Torah does not speak about *techiyas ha-meisim*. What is his punishment?

> It was taught: Since he denied *techiyas ha-meisim*, he will not take part in *techiyas ha-meisim*, for all the measurements of *HaKadosh Baruch Hu* are *middah k'neged middah,* measure for measure.[9]

Why is it that all the measurements of *HaKadosh Baruch Hu* are "measure for measure"? What is so special about *middah k'neged middah*?

The concept of *middah k'neged middah* appears often. When Yisro went out to the Wilderness to meet Moshe, and heard all that Hashem did for His people Israel, he said: "*Now I know that Hashem is greater than all the gods, for by the very thing that they plotted against [Yisrael were they punished].*"[10] Rashi there explains that Yisro was speaking of Hashem's trait of *middah k'neged middah*. The Egyptians had plotted to destroy the Jews through drowning their newborns in the water. Hashem punished the Egyptians through drowning them in the water, at *Yam Suf*.

8. *Sanhedrin* 90a–b.
9. Ibid.
10. *Shemos* 18:11.

This *middah k'neged middah* was so overwhelming that it brought Yisro to exclaim, *"Now I know that Hashem is greater than all the gods."* What amazing thing did Yisro now realize about Hashem that he did not know before?

Every force in the world acts within a limited area. For instance, someone turns to his rabbi and discusses a personal problem with him. The rabbi responds, "I am a rabbi, not a psychologist. I can help you, but only within the realm of my expertise."

And what about Hashem? He, too, acts within the special area that is His. What is Hashem's "specialty"? Being one and only. That there is nothing besides Him.

Let's take Haman as an example to illustrate the point. If we would be asked what to do with Haman, we would say: "Chop off his head." If an international lawyer would be asked, he would say: "Bring Haman to the court in Hague to be tried for genocide." Everyone has his own way of doing things, his own realm of action.

And how does Hashem deal with Haman? Hashem uses Haman's own means to fight against him — this is Hashem's trait of "one and only." Everyone else who fights with Haman pits his realm of power against Haman's. But Hashem is the one and only. His field of action is not limited to the sword or the subpoena. Hashem can deal with Haman within Haman's own field of action, and so He does. This is because Hashem is "one and only." There is no one else.

Therefore, Hashem arranged that Haman himself should be the one to bring Esther into the home of Achashveirosh, since he was the one who advised Achashveirosh to kill Vashti. Furthermore, Haman himself built the gallows on which he was hung. He himself sent the letters telling people to be ready "for this day."

And with Pharaoh it was the same. Pharaoh reared Moshe Rabbeinu, the redeemer of the Israelites, in his own home. He even paid for Moshe's wet nurse.

This is the trait of "one and only." Absolutely everything is Hashem's.

This explains why *middah k'neged middah* is so special. It is something that no "god" can do. "A" uses his own means to attack "B," and "B" uses his own means to fight back against "A." Let's say someone's strength is with water. I can fight him with fire. He attacks me with water, and I retaliate with fire. But with Hashem, if you attack Him with water, He retaliates with water. If with fire, then with fire. Since He is "one and only," He can match your means, no matter what it is.

Hashem does not retaliate with a different means because then people will say that Pharaoh's strength is with water, and Hashem's strength is with fire. But when do people know that "*Hashem is greater than all the gods*"? When He responds with the same means.

Nature Is Made of Yiras Shamayim

As we mentioned before, one of *emunah*'s basic concepts is expressed in the teaching: "He who says that *HaKadosh Baruch Hu* lets things pass [without holding one responsible for one's deeds], his life will be let to pass." Hashem does not let anything pass by unaccounted for. Not any point, or a thousandth of a point or even a millionth of a point. He responds to everything, and according to His scale of measurements.

This seems puzzling. What is this principle that Hashem doesn't let things pass? What could be wrong with letting things pass? Wouldn't it be more magnanimous of Hashem to let the little things pass by?

Even more puzzling is the fact that some of Hashem's ways are indeed based on letting things pass. For instance, "*I will be gracious when I choose to be gracious*"[11] teaches that Hashem bestows

11. *Shemos* 33:18.

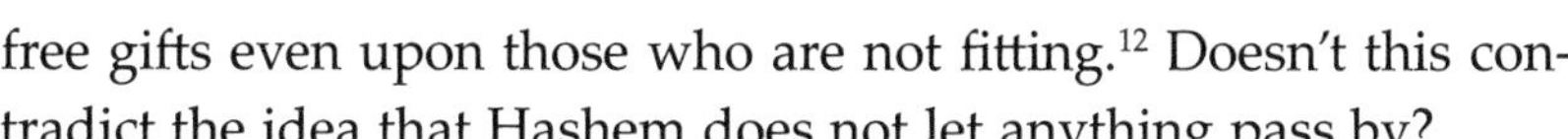

free gifts even upon those who are not fitting.[12] Doesn't this contradict the idea that Hashem does not let anything pass by?

To understand this matter, we must know that Hashem has a trait of *chesed* and a trait of *din*. Avraham Avinu exemplified the trait of *chesed*, and Yitzchak Avinu, the trait of *din*. We cannot truly understand the spiritual level that the *Avos* were on, but in our terms we would say that Avraham Avinu looked upon the world and saw a world of *chesed*. Man is surrounded by so many aspects of *chesed*. Hashem saves him from so many kinds of illnesses. The body functions just as it should, and he is healthy. What is air? What is sunlight? What is food? What is eyesight? What is hearing? They are all *chesed*!

There are millions upon millions of points of *chesed* within our daily lives. We express this in the *Nishmas* prayer: "If our mouths were full of song as the sea, and our tongues with praise like its myriad waves... we would not be able to thank You for even one thousandth of the countless millions of kindnesses that You did for our forefathers and for us."

That is how Avraham Avinu saw the world, and that is how he lived. He went through the world singing of *chesed*. In everything, he saw the *chesed* of Hashem.

Yitzchak Avinu saw the world completely differently. He did not see the world and all its natural laws from the perspective of *chesed*.

Let's use a table to illustrate the difference between Avraham and Yitzchak. A table is standing in the middle of the room. It has a certain length, and there it ends. It is covered with lacquer, it is stained to a certain shade, it has millions of other particulars. What holds all these particulars together?

In other words, regarding the millions upon millions of particulars that Avraham saw as *chesed*, Yitzchak posed a deep

12. *Berachos* 7a.

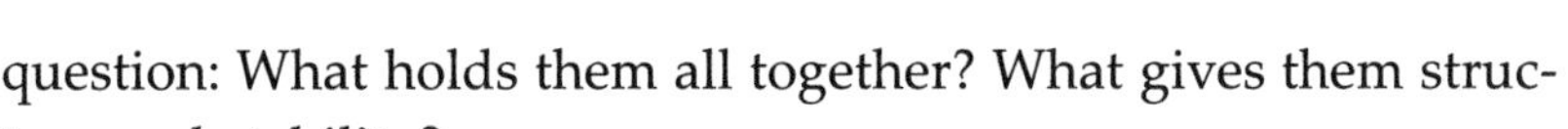

question: What holds them all together? What gives them structure and stability?

The answer is: *yiras Shamayim. Din. Chazal* say:

> When *HaKadosh Baruch Hu* created the world, it was continually expanding like the two loops of a loom, until *HaKadosh Baruch Hu* rebuked it and stopped it, as it says (*Iyov* 26:11): *"The pillars of Heaven were slipping; they froze up from His rebuke."*

And it says, *"In the beginning, Elokim created...."*[13] *Elokim* is a Divine Name denoting the trait of *din*. This is *yiras Shamayim.*

We see from all the above that the very existence of the world depends on *yiras Shamayim,* on *din*. *Ahavah* is associated with *chesed,* and *yirah,* with *din*. *Chazal* say as follows:

> *HaKadosh Baruch Hu* said to Moshe: "Say to Israel, 'Look at the Heavens that I created to serve you. Do the Heavens deviate from their ways? Did the orb of the sun ever come up from the west? For it says (*Koheles* 1:5): *"The sun shines in the east, and the sun sets."* Look at the earth that I created… did it ever deviate from its way? Did you sow, and it failed to sprout? Or did you sow wheat, and it put out barley?'"[14]

There is something that keeps the sun running on the same course every day. And not just the sun. All the billions upon billions of particulars in the world maintain their structure and stability thanks to this something. What is it that makes an apple tree keep producing apples and not oranges? It is *yiras Shamayim.* The sun fears Hashem, and stays on course. The apple tree fears Hashem, and produces the kind of fruit it is supposed to. The whole world is composed of *yiras Shamayim,* of *din*. Just as the world shouts out *chesed,* so it shouts out *yiras Shamayim.*

13. *Bereishis* 1:1.
14. *Yalkut Shimoni, Ha'azinu* 942.

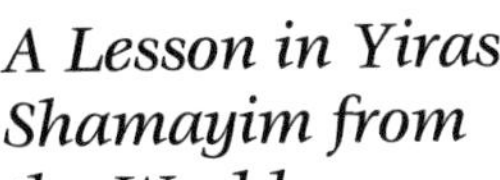

A Lesson in Yiras Shamayim from the World

A table remains a table and does not change itself into a star in the sky. Why? Because the table has *yiras Shamayim.* Despite the fact that it is an inanimate object, it does Hashem's will. When Hashem requests of a flesh-and-blood person to be a *talmid chacham,* surely he should do so, keeping true to his nature. Just as a table is meant to be a table, so he is meant to be a *talmid chacham.* That's the way Hashem made him. If he does not have *yiras Shamayim* and decides to be an ignoramus instead, this is just the same as a table deciding to be a star in the sky.

The moment there is no *yiras Shamayim,* a donkey can be a cow and cow can be a donkey. And a *talmid chacham* can be a musician or a doctor or anything else.

Yet, a table is inanimate. It does not think and does not have free choice. How can we say that it has *yiras Shamayim*? How can a table teach us a lesson in how to behave, when we are intelligent beings and are free to choose our deeds, while a table is far from this? The answer is that a table is not as inanimate as we imagine it to be. It is not an object bereft of all expression. Even inanimate objects "speak," for it is written, *"The Heavens recount the glory of God, and the firmament proclaims His handiwork."*[15] Everything has a soul, and everything sings a song to Hashem. There is nothing truly silent and inanimate.

When we call an object "inanimate," really we mean that we do not understand its way of expression. But nothing is truly inanimate. Hashem created nothing without a soul, because without a soul it cannot exist. Certain things are categorized as "inanimate" because their role in the world is to act as if they were inanimate.

Let's take the Queen's Guard in England for instance. They stand for hours and hours without moving a muscle. What if

15. *Tehillim* 19:2.

someone would come along and claim, "I said 'good morning' to him, and he did not respond. He did not even bat an eyelash. It must be a wax statue!" This claim is false because the guard's job is to remain silent and motionless.

And so it is with the sun, and so it is with the stones, and with everything else. They are called "inanimate" because their job in the world is to be inanimate. All of Hashem's creations — mineral, vegetable, animal, and human — express His existence. Everything exists only to the extent that it is connected to Hashem. The true *neshamah* of each and every thing in the world is the word of Hashem that gives it life.

We pay no attention to this matter because we have grown so accustomed to it. We are used to seeing everything follow "natural law." We don't pay attention to what is really going on, just as we don't pay attention to the remarkable and wondrous fact that we see and hear. But every time two rocks strike one another and produce a sound, this is an expression of Hashem's command. The rocks emit a certain noise upon contact because they are obeying Hashem.

The fact that the rocks make a sound is not something that "just is." If it were true that this existed on its own, independently, then there would be two gods, *chas v'shalom*. There would be Hashem, and the sound that rocks make. This is not so. The sound rocks make is something created by Hashem, just like all the other creations of Hashem that we see. Hashem created rocks and gave them a command to behave as they do.

The entire world teaches us what *yiras Shamayim* looks like. It shows us that there is no deviating from Hashem's will. The whole world gives us a live demonstration of the power of Hashem's will. Hashem determined that two and two should make four. Try to change it!

In exactly the same way, Hashem determined what our actions should be. He commanded a table to be a table, and a Jew to be a Jew. Therefore, when we do something against Hashem's will, it is not conceivable for this to pass by unaccounted for. A deed such as this is an affront to all of reality. It is in contradiction to everything that exists.

To allow a deed to be done against Hashem's will, to let it pass by, is like allowing two plus two to equal fifteen — nothing more and nothing less.

When Miracles Happen

Now we understand more about the concept of reward and punishment. When a person sins, by definition he is deviating from his nature and from that of the entire world. Perforce, this calls for a reaction.

Now let us look at the other side of things. We all know that two plus two equals four. It cannot be otherwise; this is a rule that cannot be abrogated. Yet, Hashem in His great mercy can change around reality and make two plus two equal fifteen!

Within the realm of our world, within the realm of "two plus two equals four," there can be no passing by. Everything we do is part of reality, and it is not conceivable that we should act against Hashem's will. If Hashem would let a misdeed pass by and not hold us responsible, it would mean that Hashem's will is not what determines reality.

Nevertheless, Hashem can work miracles. Just as He can make two plus two equal fifteen, so He can go against reality and let our sins pass by.

"He who says that *HaKadosh Baruch Hu* lets things pass…" does not mean that in practice, Hashem always holds a person responsible for his sins. There are many *pesukim* that say otherwise. Hashem is very forgiving and forbearing. For instance, it says: "*If your sins will be like scarlet, they will turn white as the snow.*"[16]

16. *Yeshayahu* 1:18.

Nevertheless, Hashem has a trait of not letting things pass. In other words, things are not loose. Our deeds are like every other aspect of reality. A sin is against Hashem's will, and reality does not tolerate deviance from Hashem's will. Just as the physical world we live in does not tolerate an apple turning into an orange, so the spiritual world we live in does not tolerate sin. It is a world of "He bestows good upon those who keep His mitzvos, and punishes those who transgress His mitzvos," as the eleventh principle of *emunah* teaches us. Anything that is against Hashem's will is in contradiction to Hashem's *yichud*.

On the other hand, Hashem has thirteen lofty traits called the *yud gimel middos shel rachamim*, which include the middah of *chesed* and the middah of *rachamim*.

For example, in the world of ordinary reality, which is the reality of "two plus two equals four," it is not possible for the entire Jewish people to stand within the narrow space between the two poles of the *aron ha-kodesh*. Yet, *Chazal* tell us that this is exactly what happened.[17] How did it work? Very simple: Hashem made a miracle. He went against reality.

First we need to recognize how the natural world functions — how reality is held together by inexorable *yiras Shamayim*. Then we need to recognize that Hashem in His great mercy can do miracles and go against reality. Hashem says, so to speak, "I am the Boss here, and I can do what I want."

It is written, *"I will be gracious when I choose to be gracious,"*[18] teaching that Hashem bestows free gifts, even when they are not deserved.[19] How can Hashem give undeserved handouts? Because He is the Boss.

Yiras Shamayim is what holds reality together. The world's

17. *Bemidbar Rabbah* 19:9.

18. *Shemos* 33:18.

19. *Berachos* 7a.

very existence depends on it. But it is not the last word. After *yiras Shamayim* comes an even deeper concept: Hashem sometimes lets sin pass by, miraculously.

We should not let this deeper concept of "Hashem letting sin pass by" make us think that Hashem does not run things in a thorough and exacting way. This would negate the very concept of God, and for this reason, "He who says that *HaKadosh Baruch Hu* lets things pass, his life will be let to pass." Thinking that way contradicts the idea that Hashem is the "one and only." Judaism believes that there is nothing other than Hashem, and He is involved with every single matter in the world. He is in control of every point everywhere, no matter how big or small. To say that Hashem simply allows certain things to pass and slide by is to say that there are certain particulars with which He is not involved. And that denies the basics of *emunah*. The fact that Hashem is the "one and only" means that every single detail is within His realm and under His direction.

However, we know that Hashem has a lofty and wondrous trait of "letting sin pass." And He sometimes acts with this trait. This does not contradict *yiras Shamayim*. It does not negate the trait of *din*. The problem is if we think that Hashem isn't involved with certain particulars, and lets them slip by. This is not so. Hashem takes account of everything, but sometimes chooses to employ His miracle-working trait of letting sin pass.

Hashem Enables Our Actions

We have explained how reward and punishment, the eleventh principle of *emunah*, is a basic component of reality, and is as inescapable as two plus two equals four. The tenth principle of *emunah*, that Hashem "knows all the deeds of human beings and all their thoughts," is along the same lines.

The way that Hashem knows our deeds is not the way we know things. It is radically different. It works like this: Hashem makes everything exist. He created the world, and at every moment He makes the world continue to be. In other words, Hashem continually creates reality. Furthermore, all of reality is nothing but the fulfillment of His will. Reality is His. The mitzvos are His, and the Divine commands that structure the natural world are His. Since man's deeds are part of reality, Hashem automatically knows every deed that man does. Hashem knows what He is creating. Thus, it is basic to reality that Hashem knows all of man's deeds.

Who is it that creates the reality enabling a person to do any certain deed? Hashem. He knows all of man's deeds because He *created* them.

Free Choice versus Hashem's Will

After all we have explained, one might ask how free choice could exist. Hashem creates, knows and is in total control of every detail in the world. Hashem creates reality, which includes man's deeds. Where is there room for free choice?

The answer is: *"He made man in the image of God."*[20] Hashem created man to be similar to Him. This means that just as God can do as He wishes, so can man, so to speak. The free choice that man possesses is strikingly powerful. It is a testimony to Hashem's unlimited capability that He granted it to man. Within the wonder of His total Oneness and absolute control of all reality, Hashem worked a double wonder: He gave man the ability to act freely and do exactly as he wishes.

In order to illustrate how much power man was given, we will bring three examples of sins.

The first example comes from one of the three cardinal sins: adultery. *Chazal* say:

> If a man has relations with his fellow's wife, in principle she should not conceive, but… Hashem said: "Not only do the

20. *Bereishis* 9:6.

> wicked people treat My stamping tool as if it were public property, they also trouble Me to place My stamp against My will."[21]

When a new person is made, *Chazal* describe this as Hashem taking His stamping tool and impressing the raw material in order to give this person his shape and form. The greatest and most beautiful thing that Hashem created in His world is man. And now, an adulterer comes along and "forces" Hashem to make an ugly person, a *mamzer*. Hashem is agitated by this, so to speak: "I gave you the ability. Everything is in your hands. But why do you force Me to do something I don't want to do?" If *Chazal* would not have said such a thing, we would never say it.

The second example is the sin of *bitul Torah*. *Chazal* say:

> Just as the reward for Torah study is greater than that of all the mitzvos, so the punishment for disregard of Torah study is greater than that of all the sins.[22]

Bitul Torah carries the most severe of punishments. Why? If someone neglects his learning, what terrible thing is he doing? Is he killing somebody? Is he sacrificing to an idol? He is just sitting around and doing nothing!

To understand this matter, let us start by considering an ordinary mitzvah. Someone fails to take a *lulav* on Sukkos. What punishment is he liable for?

Let's say this person not only fails to take a *lulav* on Sukkos but goes over to the *Sefer Torah* and rips a piece out of it. He completely uproots the *pasuk* of *lulav* from the *Sefer Torah*. Now what punishment is he liable for?

21. *Avodah Zarah* 54b.

22. *Sifrei, Parashas Eikev,* cited by *Rabbeinu Yonah, Sha'arei Teshuvah* 3:14.

Chazal say:

> If someone disregarded one word of the Torah, this is as if he burnt it.[23]

Chazal are telling us that when someone disregards a mitzvah and fails to fulfill it, he is uprooting that mitzvah and making it cease to exist, so to speak. He "burnt" it, and now it is destroyed. This is far more severe than simply ripping a *pasuk* out of a *Sefer Torah*. It is uprooting a mitzvah from the very Torah itself. Man has such an ability!

It comes out that a person who failed to take a *lulav* on Sukkos has actually done much more than that: he has burnt and destroyed one of the Torah's mitzvos. Now what punishment is he liable for?

Let us extend this idea and apply it to Torah study. Hashem gave man the ability to develop *chiddushei Torah*. He enabled man to delve into Torah learning, which is a level of reality all on its own. When a person disregards this reality, when he does what is called *bitul Torah*, he is doing much more than just wasting a little time. He is making the Torah itself cease to exist, so to speak. He could have learned Torah. And instead, he has turned the Torah into nothingness!!

And we know what Torah is: He and His word are one.

Here is the third example. Take any halachah, be it a Torah law or a Rabbinic decree or a binding Jewish custom. Along comes a person who does not keep this halachah. As we explained, all of reality expresses Hashem's will. Hashem set and stated His will in the Torah, and He wants this halachah kept. But the reality is that this person did not keep the halachah. When he acts against Hashem's will, he is actually changing reality, and Hashem's will, so to speak.

23. *Ruth Rabbah* 2:4.

One might ask how such a thing is possible. Isn't it written, *"I, Hashem, have not changed"*[24]? We should not ask questions. All we know is that *"He made man in the image of God."*[25] Admittedly, we don't understand how it works, but we must realize that we can do anything. And when we act, we should be aware of what we are doing. We have the ability to change the nature of reality, and this power can be horrendous.

It is a reality that we must eat *maror* on Pesach. This is a reality that stems from *yiras Shamayim,* fear of Heaven. If someone refuses to eat *maror* on Pesach, he is acting against Heaven. Simply speaking, one cannot act against Heaven. Yet, the All-Powerful One came and said: "I give you the ability to act against Heaven." What does it mean to "act against Heaven"? It means to change the nature of reality.

Chazal say:

> Someone whose merits are greater than his sins... resembles someone who burnt the entire Torah and did not leave a single letter from it.[26]

Chazal are telling us that if someone's merits are barely greater than his sins, he needs a real lot of atonement. Therefore he is treated in this world like "someone who burnt the entire Torah." Here again, *Chazal* do not say, "Someone who burnt a Torah scroll." They rather say, "Someone who burnt the entire Torah" — i.e., he burnt the Torah itself and destroyed it.

"Against Your Will, You Are Born"

The repercussions of our power are awesome. We might ask why Hashem gave us such power, if it enables us to hurt ourselves and the whole world. Even little sins have giant

24. *Malachi* 3:6.
25. *Bereishis* 9:6.
26. *Kiddushin* 39b.

consequences, and *HaKadosh Baruch Hu* does not let things pass!

On the other hand, the potential for good is so tremendously great that it is all worth it. Just as we spoke of the impact of every sin, let us imagine just how great is the impact of every mitzvah! Every word of Torah that we learn, every act of *chesed* that we do... The good is so overwhelming that it makes our walking on the cliff's edge worthwhile.

While the benefit is by far greater, it does not appear that way within man's small frame of reference. *Chazal* say, "Against your will, you are born."[27] A person does not want to come into this world at all. But in the greater frame of reference, which is beyond our conception, the good is many times greater.

The Significance of Our Actions

We need to get used to the idea that every act we do, no matter how small, has tremendous significance. And nothing is lost, for better or worse. This idea is part of the thirteen principles of *emunah.*

An acquaintance once told me of a conversation he had with someone who works in Israel's nuclear reactor in Dimona. He asked this person, "How many years have you been working there?" He answered, "Seventeen years." He asked further: "They say that Israel has the atom bomb. Did you hear anything about it?" He answered: "Believe me, for the seventeen years I have been working there, not only don't I know whether there is an atom bomb or not, I don't even have a clue what I am working on. I sit in a cubicle with a window, and they stick some object for me through the window. It comes along with instructions: 'Rub here, do this, do that, etc., and pass it on to the next window.' I have no idea whether the piece is for

27. *Pirkei Avos* 4:22.

a table, or for the factory manager's system, or for an atom bomb."

My acquaintance then asked him, "Don't you go crazy from boredom working that way?" He answered, "It's the very secrecy of the whole thing that energizes me. Not only that, there are penalties. If someone doesn't follow the instructions, he gets penalized. He could even be imprisoned. We're not playing games there. The very secrecy and precision of everything is what makes it interesting. I receive a piece and they tell me, 'Work on it exactly like this, and if not, know that you were the cause of a tragedy.' I have not lost interest in my work for seventeen years!"

This is just what our role in this world is like. They tell us, "Take a *lulav* and shake it to the right, now to the left… and know that if you don't follow the instructions exactly, Divine punishment awaits." Another night arrives and we receive new 'instructions': "Sit down, lean to the left, and eat a *k'zayis* of matzah… and know that if you fail to eat it within the required time, you have destroyed entire worlds."

We have no idea what it is all about. We don't know what we are building. But we know that we are working within a large, complex system, and any deviation from the instructions damages the entire system.

It Doesn't Matter What Happens

I will sum this all up with a simple story, as I heard it from R. Chaim Kamil *shlita*. The message of this story is straightforward, and is not a new one. But I never heard the message stated so clearly.

This is what R. Chaim Kamil told me, in the name of R. Chaim Zeitchik, who heard it from R. Reuven Grozovsky *zt"l*. It was a time of imminent war. The situation was catastrophic. No one knew what to do. They had no idea if war would break out and when, or what the Germans would do and what the

Russians would do. Many fled from Germany to Russia, and others from Russia to Germany. People were consumed by uncertainty, and did not know to where their own family members had fled.

In the middle of all this terrible tumult someone went up to the Brisker Rav *zt"l* and asked him, "What will be?" This is what the Rav replied: "What will be does not matter to me. I only need to know what is permitted to do, and what is forbidden to do."

In our generation we often ask ourselves what will be. The answer is: It is not our business. That is up to Hashem to decide. Hashem makes the world go round. There is only one thing that is our business: what is permitted to do, and what is forbidden to do.

Understanding the whole system and its workings is not our job — we are not obligated to understand it. All we need to know is that we are part of a great, Divine system in which every single person has a certain task assigned to him, and he must fulfill it. If a person properly fulfills his task, there is a reality of "Bestows good upon those who keep His mitzvos." And if, *chas v'shalom*, a person is negligent in his task, there is a reality of "Punishes those who transgress His mitzvos."

Through this, we can understand the deeper meaning of the tenth principle: "The Creator — may His Name be blessed — knows all the deeds of human beings and all their thoughts, as it says: *"He fashions their hearts together; He comprehends all their deeds."* By the same token that Hashem created us, He knows and comprehends our deeds. Our deeds are tied to Him no less than is our very existence. Just as our existence reflects Hashem's deeds, so our deeds reflect His deeds. And that is why "The Creator — may His Name be blessed — bestows good upon those who keep His mitzvos, and punishes those who transgress His mitzvos."

Whatever we did, we did. We cannot escape our actions

and their consequences. If we transgressed Hashem's will, if we turned two plus two into thirteen and a half, then there are repercussions. Should we expect *HaKadosh Baruch Hu* to just let it pass? Do we realize what will happen if two plus two is allowed to equal thirteen and a half? The San Francisco Bridge will fall down! The engineers who designed this bridge employed mathematical calculations that depend on two plus two equaling four. Similarly, all of reality is based on Hashem's word.

With this outlook, we start to realize what kind of a place the world has become. We live in a "modern" world, but with all its technological advances, including audio recording devices and cameras, etc., the results are shockingly poor. Everything is put to use for the bad. The world was a more beautiful place without modern cameras and their streams of indecent images that now flood the world. And so it is with technology's other products. There is no modern invention that did not do harm to the world, without exception.

Here is one example of the disasters brought by modernization. It used to be that when a Jew would desecrate Shabbos, it would be by stoking a fire or walking in public domain carrying something in his pocket. Now, he gets in his car and drives. Every time he steps on the gas pedal he creates thousands of sparks per second. A single trip from New York to Baltimore causes more Shabbos desecrations than took place from the beginning of the world until the invention of the automobile!

We believe that every little misdeed damages the whole world. For every sin a person does, Hashem punishes. No point passes by without a reaction.

The main thing is for us to be aware that Hashem knows all our deeds. For every action, there is reward and punishment. This is because our deeds are an integral part of reality. They are part of the world that Hashem created. We should live our whole life with this awareness.

"A Good Reward for the Keepers of His Mitzvos"

When it comes to the reward that Hashem bestows on the keepers of His mitzvos, there is an unsettling issue we must face. This issue was raised by great Torah figures, primarily by R. Yisrael Salanter and his disciple R. Yitzchak Blazer.

We are led to believe that reward and punishment works something like this: On the Day of Judgment, we go before the Heavenly court. If we are found to be carrying bundles of *aveiros*, it will be very bitter because nothing will be passed over or forgotten about. There is a price to pay for sin. Nevertheless, even this has a limit. After we go through all the cleansing and purification, after *Gehinnom* scrubs away all the filth that sullies our soul, we will go to *Gan Eden* and receive eternal reward for the mitzvos we did in this world.

But this scenario is not for sure. It is not clear that in the end we will receive our reward for the mitzvos we did. Here is the catch: R. Yisrael Salanter used to say that even if a person did mitzvos, he is likely "to eat the mitzvah he did, through the tasty '*tzimmes*' (dessert) he is eating."[28] In other words, it sometimes happens that a person receives all his reward in this world, leaving nothing for the next world. R. Yitzchak Blazer said[29] that this is the meaning of the following *pasuk* and *Chazal*'s comment on it. After Avraham defeated the four kings and rescued Lot, it is written:

> *Avram, do not fear.*[30]

Chazal explain why Avraham was worried, even though he had returned from battle as a successful victor.

> Avraham Avinu was afraid, and said: "I went into Nimrod's

28. *Chochmah U'Mussar*, vol. I, p. 19.
29. *Ohr Yisrael, Kochvei Ohr*, chap. 2.
30. *Bereishis* 15:1.

> fiery furnace, and I was saved. I went into battle against the kings, and I was saved. Perhaps this means I received my reward in this world and will have nothing in the next world!" *HaKadosh Baruch Hu* said to him, *"Avram, do not fear. I am your Protector.* All that I did for you in this world was done for free. Your reward is ready and waiting for the future."[31]

This is astounding. Avraham Avinu did so much in his life. He passed ten tests, he put his own son on the altar, he taught the world about Hashem. Yet he was worried: "Perhaps I received all my reward..."

R. Yitzchak Blazer brings another teaching of *Chazal* that makes a similar point:

> When R. Eliezer fell ill, his disciples went to visit him. He said to them, "A fierce sun is beating down on the world." [He was referring to his own state, intimating that Hashem had become angry with him and made him severely ill.] They began to cry, but R. Akiva laughed. They said to him, "Why are you laughing?" He replied, "Why are you crying?" They said, "A *Sefer Torah* is in suffering. How can we not cry?" He replied, "That is why I am laughing. As long as I saw how my rabbi's wine did not sour, his flax did not spoil, his oil did not grow putrid, and his honey did not decay, I said to myself: 'Perhaps my rabbi received his reward in this world, *chas v'shalom*.' But now that I see my rabbi is suffering, I am happy!"[32]

When we think about our own situation, we realize that even bigger than the problem of our sins is the problem of our mitzvos. What about their reward? Will we get it in the end?

There are indeed certain things we can do to protect our good deeds from being eaten up. We will discuss some of them.

31. *Bereishis Rabbah* 44:4.
32. *Sanhedrin* 101a, *Rashi* ad loc.

But first, let us understand how it is even possible for a person to "eat up" his mitzvos in this world. Don't *Chazal* say, "There is no reward for mitzvos in this world?"[33] Doesn't a mitzvah carry eternal reward? If so, how could it possibly get used up in this short lifetime? We will explain this with an allegory.

Someone is driving an old beat-up car through the desert on a hot day. He drives for miles and miles down a deserted road. He is thirsty and sweaty. In the middle of nowhere he comes across a snack stand. He stops his car, goes up and asks, "Do you maybe have a can of soda?"

"Yes."

"With a kosher certification?"

"Yes."

"Can I look?"

"Go right ahead, sir."

"Wow, it has a good hechsher. This is Gan Eden!" he thinks to himself. "How much does it cost?"

"A quarter."

He searches his pockets and does not find a quarter. But he has a check for ten thousand dollars folded in his wallet. He asks, "Do you have change for ten thousand dollars?"

"No, I am very sorry. Nobody has that kind of change out here in the desert."

"So what should we do?"

"There is nothing to do, sir. If you want the soda, leave me the ten thousand dollars. Otherwise, drive on. It is as simple as that. I cannot give away my merchandise for free."

Is the can of soda worth ten thousand dollars? Of course not! But there isn't any way to make change. Neither is there any way to "make change" for our mitzvos in this world. Our mitzvos are worth eternity, and all the riches of this world are

33. *Kiddushin* 39b.

not enough to make change for a single mitzvah. Furthermore, nothing here in this world is for free. If we want to stop on the way and enjoy ourselves here and now in this world, if we are "thirsty" for pleasure, we must leave our mitzvos as payment. We won't get anything unless we pay for it.

The point is that the pleasures of this world are not a true payment for our mitzvos. In no way are these pleasures worth the price in mitzvos that we pay. But nothing is for free. The decision is in our hands: We can drive on, glued to our destination. Or we can stop on the way and indulge ourselves in pleasure, thereby parting with the ten-thousand-dollar check in our wallet. It is fair, and the choice is ours.

R. Yisrael Salanter used to say: "This world is a very expensive hotel." For one serving of "*tzimmes*" we can use up all our mitzvos. An ordinary person staying at the hotel will get a bill detailing everything he received, and he will find it very hard to pay. He is likely to walk out penniless.

However, said R. Yisrael, there is a way to stay at the hotel completely for free! This is the way to protect our mitzvos. R. Yisrael would explain that if the hotel guest is there not for his own personal pleasure and leisure, but because he was sent by an overseas firm to act on their behalf as a marketing representative, then things are very different. This person can stay at the hotel, eat and drink as he pleases, and it all goes on the company bill.

So it is, says R. Yisrael Salanter, when a person is not in this world for his own sake. If he devotes his whole being to the mission Hashem sent him on, if he feels that every moment of his life belongs not to him but to Hashem, then none of this world's many pleasures go on his bill. The "Boss" pays for everything. Practically speaking, R. Yisrael's advice was to become someone needed by the community. This way, a person does not live for his own sake.[34]

And this is R. Yitzchak Blazer's approach: *Chazal* say that *chillul Hashem* is the severest sin; all the suffering that there is in this world is not enough to atone for it. Nevertheless, Rabbeinu Yonah wrote that *chillul Hashem* may be atoned for by *kiddush Hashem*. Based on this, R. Blazer reasons as follows: All the suffering of this world cannot wipe away one *chillul Hashem*, but one *kiddush Hashem* can. If so, surely it is true that all the pleasures of this world cannot wipe away one *kiddush Hashem*. This is because Hashem's trait of kindness is greater than His trait of punishment.[35]

Accordingly, the way to protect our reward and save it for the next world is by doing *kiddush Hashem*.

I heard a third way, from R. Chaim Shmuelevitz *zt"l*. He draws an example from the story of the "poor man's lamb." Nasan HaNavi comes to David HaMelech to reprove him for the incident with Bas Sheva, and begins his reproof with an allegory about a poor man who had a lamb:

> *"There were two men in one town; one rich and one poor. The rich man had very many flocks and cattle, and the poor man had nothing except for one little lamb that he bought... A wayfarer came to the rich man, who was reluctant to take from his flock and cattle to make a meal for the guest who came to him, so he took the poor man's lamb and made a meal from it, for the man who came to him."*
>
> *David grew very angry with this man, and said to Nasan HaNavi: "By Hashem's life, the man who does this is deserving of death..."*[36]

34. *Chochmah U'Mussar*, vol. I, p. 19.
35. *Sotah* 11a.
36. *II Shmuel*, chap. 12.

The end of the story is that Nasan says to David, *"You are that man!"* Simply speaking, he meant that David's taking of Bas Sheva was comparable to the rich man's taking of the poor man's lamb.

But R. Chaim Shmuelevitz asks as follows: Why did Nasan need to use an allegory when he spoke to David? Why didn't he just come in and say, "Your Majesty, I was sent by Hashem to inform you that you have sinned and are deserving of such-and-such a punishment"?

The answer is: A price must be fixed for David's sin. How much should he pay for it? No one can fix this price other than David HaMelech himself.

The same is true with our mitzvos. A price must be fixed for them: how much reward should we receive for our mitzvos? Let's say someone is sitting and learning a *daf* of Gemara, and he has a half an hour of learning to go until he finishes the *daf*. But it seems to him that he is hungry. He closes the Gemara and goes off to buy himself something to eat.

What did this person just do? He fixed his price for a *daf* of Gemara. He decided how much it is worth to him. During that half hour he could have finished the *daf*, but he sold it for the price of a slice of pizza. In other words, he showed through his actions that learning the *daf* is worth no more to him than a hot slice of pizza.

"You are that man." You fix the price yourself. If this is how much a half hour of Gemara learning is worth to him, then this is what he will receive for it. He will pay with half an hour of Gemara learning for every serving of food to which he helps himself during his lifetime.

By contrast, let's say someone is sitting and learning Gemara, and the fellow next to him tries to engage him in conversation about worldly matters: news, politics, and the like. He politely declines, saying to himself: *"When I am sitting in front of a Gemara, the world does not exist for me."* What has he done? He has fixed his price for a *daf* of Gemara. He has shown that his learning time is worth more to him than the entire world. From now on, for every *daf* of Gemara he learns he will receive as reward no less than an entire world.

What lesson do we learn from this? That if we set an appropriate price for our mitzvos, we can save and protect them from getting used up in this world.

Hashem promises us that He will "bestow good." But to whom? To "those who *keep* His mitzvos." We must "keep" our mitzvos intact, and hold on to them, making sure we don't lose them through the "*tzimmes*" we eat.

העיקר השנים־עשר

12

*The Twelfth Principle**

אֲנִי מַאֲמִין בֶּאֱמוּנָה שְׁלֵמָה בְּבִיאַת הַמָּשִׁיחַ, וְאַף עַל פִּי שֶׁיִּתְמַהְמֵהַּ, עִם כָּל זֶה אֲחַכֶּה לּוֹ בְּכָל יוֹם שֶׁיָּבוֹא.

I believe with perfect faith in the coming of the Mashiach, and even though he may tarry, I will still await his coming every day.

The Mashiach: Future or Present?

THE CHASAM SOFER WAS puzzled that the Rambam counts the coming of the *Mashiach* among the thirteen principles of *emunah*. He writes:

> It is impossible for me to believe in any way that our *geulah* is one of the principles of *emunah*. Let us suppose there would be a serious downfall, God forbid. And let us say that our sins would bring Hashem to banish us forever, *chas v'shalom,* as happened with the Ten Tribes, according to R. Akiva who holds that they are forever rejected. Would this permit them to throw off the yoke of Heaven's sovereignty, or to make even the tiniest change in the Torah, in even a

* This chapter is taken from the introduction to *Tiferes Torah* on the Torah, written by Rav Pincus *zt"l.*

> Rabbinic ordinance? Far be it! We shall not serve Hashem in order to eat the fruits of the Land and be satiated by its goodness. Rather, *"O God, my desire is to do Your will."*[1]
>
> In every way and in every case, we are servants of Hashem, and He will do with us as He wishes and desires. This [belief in our eventual *geulah*] is not a principle, and not a foundation on which to build anything. Rather, the real foundation of everything is to believe in the Torah and the Prophets. And there our final redemption is stated, in *Parashas Nitzavim* and *Parashas Ha'azinu*, as the Ramban wrote there. Furthermore, the *geulah* is mentioned at length in the words of the Prophets. Therefore, anyone who entertains doubts about the *geulah* is denying the basic principle of *emunah* in the Torah and the Prophets.[2]

The Chasam Sofer is saying that *galus* will not go on forever. The *geulah* surely will come, but this is not one of the Torah's basic principles. If we say it is a basic principle, we are saying that the edifice of the Torah cannot stand without it. And this is simply not true, argues the Chasam Sofer. Even should we suppose that the *Mashiach* will not come, the last generation would be no different from all other generations that did not see the *geulah*. Jews always have and always will serve Hashem, and for this they go to *Gan Eden* and *Olam HaBa*. Our service of Hashem does not hinge on *Mashiach* coming to bring us out of *galus*.

Yet, the Rambam counted the coming of the *Mashiach* among the thirteen principles of *emunah*. How are we to understand this, in light of the Chasam Sofer's powerful argument?

The answer is that the *Mashiach*'s coming is not a principle of faith because of its meaning for the future. The Torah's edifice

1. *Tehillim* 40:9.
2. Responsa, end of *Yoreh Deah*.

does not depend on this event coming true in the end of days. Rather, *Mashiach* is basic to our faith because of its meaning for the *present*. It is part of the essential nature of Judaism as we live it here and now. It represents the true meaning of our experience today, and every day, in *galus*.

What is Judaism? Essentially, it is a covenant of love which Hashem made with the Jewish people at Mount Sinai. This covenant of love expresses itself primarily in Eretz Yisrael, in the *Beis HaMikdash*. The fact that it is a covenant means that it is eternal. Otherwise, it is not a true covenant: if Hashem could rid Himself of the Jewish people, *chas v'shalom*, then Torah and mitzvos would be no more than a business of reward and punishment. And even should we keep the mitzvos in order to fulfill Hashem's will, it still would be bereft of Judaism's essential component. Why is this so?

Non-Jews, too, are obligated to fulfill Hashem's will; they are forbidden to "throw off the yoke of Heaven's sovereignty" and rebel against God. They, too, are forbidden to "make even the tiniest change" in the words of God. The Chasam Sofer speaks of "*O God, my desire is to do Your will.*" He says, "In every way and in every case, we are servants of Hashem, and He will do with us as He wishes and desires." These words of the Chasam Sofer indeed express lofty values, but such values are not yet the defining characteristic of Judaism. Judaism is a covenant of love and connection with Hashem. The fact that Hashem will send us the *Mashiach* reflects this covenant.

We will employ an analogy to explain this point. Let's imagine a father who threw his son out of the house. The father might have done this for one of two reasons: either he is using a tough tactic to train his son to behave properly, or he kicked the boy out because he doesn't ever want to see him again. What is the difference between the two?

The real difference is not in the future, but in the present. The first way, the father is in the very process of training his son. He cares about him and has a relationship with him. The second way…

Let's say for argument's sake that the *Mashiach* will not come, and Hashem kicked us out of His house into our present *galus* because He wanted to be rid of us permanently. What are the implications of this? It would mean that all along, the covenant of Mount Sinai was merely temporary. If so, it was not really a covenant. There never was a true relationship. If so, the very heart and essence of Judaism would be missing! As the Chasam Sofer says, we still would be obligated to keep God's commands. However, this would not be Judaism.

That is why belief in the eventual coming of the *Mashiach* is essential to Judaism. Not for the benefit it will bring us then, but for what it means now.

Without Shame

I would say that *Mashiach*'s coming is basic not only to Judaism, but to the whole reason why the world was created.

As we know, this world was created for the sake of reward and punishment. It exists so the goodness we will receive in *Olam HaBa* will not be an undeserved handout, "the bread of shame," but will come as payment for the work we did in this world. The Ramchal enunciates this well-known principle:

> God, may He be blessed, is surely the quintessence of good. And it is the nature of one who is good to bestow goodness on others. This is why Hashem wished to create people: it is so He may bestow goodness on them. If there would be no one to receive the goodness, it would not be possible to bestow it.
>
> And He knew in His lofty wisdom that in order for the goodness He wishes to bestow to be complete and perfect, its recipients must receive it through their own labor. That way, the goodness will belong to its recipients, and they will not be left with a feeling of embarrassment for having received it, as is the case with someone who receives *tzedakah* from

another. About this it was said in the Talmud Yerushalmi:[3] "He who eats food that does not belong to him is embarrassed to look in the other's face."[4]

The Ramchal seems to be saying that by working hard at Torah and mitzvos in this world, we come to deserve the goodness of *Olam HaBa*. Yet, the *Chovos HaLevavos* writes that no matter how much we do, no matter how hard we work, we will never deserve even a tiny fraction of that goodness:

It is a kindness from God, it is a freewill gift and a favor, as it says, *"Kindness is yours, Hashem, because You pay a person according to his deeds."*[5] This is so because even if man's good deeds were as numerous as the sand of the sea, they still would not be worth a single act of goodness bestowed by the Creator, may He be blessed, in this world. And surely this is so if the person has a sin.

If the Creator would be exacting with man, and require from him thanksgiving for the goodness bestowed on him, then all of man's deeds would be swallowed up and disappear within the smallest of the Creator's acts of goodness to him.[6]

The Midrash, too, makes this point:

Said R. Yirmeyahu son of R. Elazar: A Divine voice is destined to blast out from the hilltops and say, "Whoever acted for God, let him come and receive his reward." And so it is written, *"At that time it will be said to Yaakov and to Yisrael, 'What did one do for God?'"*[7]

The spirit of prophecy says, *"Who preceded Me, that I should*

3. *Orlah* 1:3.
4. *Da'as Tevunos* 1:42.
5. *Tehillim* 62:13.
6. *Chovos HaLevavos, Sha'ar HaBitachon*, chap. 4.
7. *Bemidbar* 23:23, rendering based on the Midrash.

> *pay him?"*[8] Who praised Me before I gave him a soul? Who lauded My Name before I gave him a son? Who made for Me a *ma'akeh* before I gave him a roof? Who made for Me a mezuzah before I gave him a house? Who made for Me a sukkah before I gave him place? Who made for Me a lulav before I gave him money? Who made for Me tzitzis before I gave him a tallis? Who separated *pe'ah* for Me before I gave him a field? Who separated *terumah* for Me before I gave him a harvest? Who separated *challah* for Me before I gave him dough? Who designated an animal as a *korban* to Me before I gave him an animal?"[9]

It is clear that our deeds do not really make us deserving of payment and reward. This being so, how can we say that the world was created for the sake of reward and punishment? In the end, the goodness we receive remains a freewill gift. Why isn't this once again the "bread of shame"?

Indeed, our service of Hashem in this world will spare us from shame, but not because we will have earned what we receive. Everything to be bestowed on us is nothing but Hashem's pure kindness and good will. Yet, as we can see from the following analogy, it will elicit no shame at all.

Let's say a father feeds and cares for his son. He provides him with whatever he needs. When the son grows up and gets married, the father buys him a house and fills it with nice furniture. Is this considered "bread of shame"?

Let's say a wealthy man takes a girl from a poor family as a daughter-in-law. He sets her up in her new household more luxuriously than she could have even imagined. Maids and nannies take care of all the domestic chores, while she sits at leisure. Her husband comes home and showers her with gifts

8. *Iyov* 41:3.

9. *Vayikra Rabbah* 27:2.

of expensive jewelry. Is this "bread of shame"?

No. When there is closeness and love, when there is a true relationship, there is no shame.

This is why we came to this world. Not to "earn" *Olam HaBa* as recompense for our work, but to acquire closeness and have a relationship with Hashem, to the point that Hashem says about us, "My daughter, My sister, My mother" — as written in *Shir HaShirim*. As a result, when we enter into the great, unending banquet of the next world, we will not feel we are eating the "bread of shame," because in this world we attained love and a relationship with Hashem. Thus it says in *Pirkei Avos*:

> He who engages in Torah learning for its own sake… is called "friend," "loved one"…[10]

This is our goal in this world.

Hashem said about Avraham, *"For I 'know' him."*[11] The term *'know him'* implies endearment and affection.[12] It seems that this is what Yirmeyahu HaNavi meant when he declared, *"The Torah sages did not 'know' Me."*[13] He was lamenting the fact that the best men of the nation, the Torah sages, were missing the goal: love, endearment, and relationship with *HaKadosh Baruch Hu*.

What Is There to Give?

A *pasuk* in *Parashas Lech Lecha* teaches us all this. Hashem says to Avraham:

> *"Avram, do not fear. I am your Protector; your reward is very great." Avram said, "Hashem, God, what can You give me, when I go childless?"*[14]

10. *Avos* 6:1.
11. *Bereishis* 18:19.
12. *Rashi* ad loc.
13. *Yirmeyahu* 2:8.
14. *Bereishis* 15:1.

This *pasuk* seems very strange. Why did Avraham say to Hashem, "*What can You give me*?" Hashem's capabilities are unlimited! It is written, "*You can do anything; no plan cannot be executed.*"[15] Hashem has the ability to give things even greater than sons and daughters. What did Avraham mean when he said, "*What can You give me*?"

We may understand Avraham's words as follows. Hashem had informed Avraham that his "reward," his payment for doing Hashem's will, is very great. Avraham responded by saying that if it is reward and payment, then it is lacking all content. Does a father give "payment" to his son? Does a husband say to his wife, "If you cook me a good meal, you will get a nice payment?"

Thus Avraham says, "'*What shall You give me*?' If it is 'payment,' it is meaningless. That is not Judaism! I don't want payment; I want a relationship with You. I want a son from whom will come the Jewish people who will enter into a covenant of love with You, thereby fulfilling the true purpose of everything. Nothing is of value other than this."

Even eternal delight is of no value to us. It is the portion of the non-Jews. Those righteous individuals from among the world's nations who obeyed God's word will receive as their reward eternal delight in *Olam HaBa*. But for a Jew, the only thing that holds any true value is attachment, closeness, and a covenant of love with Hashem Himself.

That is what Avraham Avinu desired, that is what the *Avos* desired, and that is the desire and nature of each and every Jew.

15. *Iyov* 42:2.

העיקר השלושה־עשר

13

The Thirteenth Principle

אֲנִי מַאֲמִין בֶּאֱמוּנָה שְׁלֵמָה, שֶׁתִּהְיֶה תְּחִיַּת הַמֵּתִים בְּעֵת שֶׁיַּעֲלֶה רָצוֹן מֵאֵת הַבּוֹרֵא יִתְבָּרַךְ שְׁמוֹ וְיִתְעַלֶּה זִכְרוֹ לָעַד וּלְנֵצַח נְצָחִים.

I believe with perfect faith that there will be a resurrection of the dead at the time the Creator so wills it — may His Name be blessed and may His remembrance be exalted forever and for all eternity.

Man by Nature Is Connected to Eternity

"ALL ISRAEL HAVE A portion in *Olam HaBa*."[1] A Jew's *neshamah* is a creation of Hashem. "The *neshamah* that You placed in me — You formed it, You created it, You breathed it into me..."[2] Judaism believes that every Jew who is born has a *neshamah* which, by its very nature, is attached to Hashem. That is what *Olam HaBa* is all about: attachment to the Source of life, to the One Who exists forever and for all eternity.

In stark contrast to this, Christianity claims that every person who is born is inherently doomed to annihilation. He needs

1. *Sanhedrin* 90a.
2. *Elokai neshamah* blessing.

to be redeemed from his state of original sin. He needs "salvation" in order to be delivered from his fate. And if he makes a significant donation to the Church, the priest will "absolve" his sins so that he may receive "eternal life." According to Christianity, man is not born with a natural connection to eternal life.

Judaism believes the opposite: Man by nature is born for *Olam HaBa*. His very being is eternal. Even after he dies, he will come back to life. The Christians opposed this Jewish belief and thus denied the key concept underlying *techiyas ha-meisim*. They claimed that man's nature, as he was created by God, is that he will come to an end and cease to exist.

The Deniers of Techiyas HaMeisim

In fact, the heretics who denied the Torah focused mainly on the issue of *techiyas ha-meisim*. This is because they adopted our Torah, but only the Written Torah. All the disputations they held with the Jews centered on the question: what is written in the Torah?

These disputations go back a long time. Here is one that took place in the time of the Gemara:

> The heretics asked Rabban Gamliel: "What is the source that *HaKadosh Baruch Hu* will resurrect the dead?" He answered them by citing from the Torah, the Prophets, and the Writings, but they did not accept his answer.
>
> He cited from the Torah: *"Hashem said to Moshe, 'Behold, you will lie with your forefathers, and will arise…'"*[3] They responded: "Perhaps it means, *'And this people will arise and go astray…'*"
>
> He cited from the Prophets: *"Your dead will come to life, my corpses will arise. Awake and shout for joy, those who rest in the dust, for Your dew is a dew of light. You will make the wicked ones fall to the ground."*[4] They responded: "Perhaps it speaks of the

3. *Devarim* 31:16.
4. *Yeshayahu* 26:19.

dead who were resurrected by Yechezkel HaNavi."

He cited from the Writings: *"Your palate is like good wine. It goes straight to my Beloved. It causes the lips of the sleeping to move."*[5] They responded: "Perhaps the only thing that will happen is that their lips will quiver."

Then he quoted this verse to them: "'*...The land that Hashem swore to your forefathers to give to them.*'[6] It does not say, '*To give to you,*' but rather, '*To give to them.*' This is the source in the Torah for *techiyas ha-meisim.*"

Some say that he quoted this verse to them: "'*You, who cleave to Hashem your God. You are all alive this day.*'[7] Just as you are all alive today, so too will you all be alive in *Olam HaBa.*"[8]

We see that the heretics did not believe in *techiyas ha-meisim,* and Rabban Gamliel cited them verse after verse, while they rejected each proof since it was not explicitly written in Scripture. Every time Rabban Gamliel cited a verse they disputed its meaning, until he cited a verse that expressed the point unequivocally, and then they accepted the proof.

Those heretics were not like the heretics of our day, who claim things as ridiculous as two plus two equals thirty-five. The heretics back then did not deny the obvious. They were not blind to that which was standing in front of their eyes, like modern heretics are, but rather accepted the premise that Torah is reality. They did not deny that the Jewish people stood at Mount Sinai and received the Torah, since there were three million people there to testify about it. They had no dispute over this point. But there were certain points that escaped them, points over which Judaism seems to contradict itself. They were

5. *Shir HaShirim* 7:10.
6. *Devarim* 11:21.
7. Ibid., 4:4.
8. *Sanhedrin* 90b.

unable to grasp those points properly, and came to deny them.

They believed in the greatest wonder of all: that the Jewish people merited receiving the holy Torah, the teaching of God. But they did not believe that God gave over the Torah's interpretation to the Jewish people.

For instance, there are sins for which the Torah requires forty lashes. The Sages come and say to give a maximum of thirty-nine. It is forbidden to mete out forty lashes, they say! This is something the heretics were at a loss to understand. They did not accept that the Jews have a deep covenant of love, a close relationship with Hashem, in the context of which they have the power to extrapolate the Torah's meaning.

So it was with the disputation between Rabban Gamliel and the heretics. If the Torah says, *"The land that Hashem swore to your forefathers to give to them,"* this is acceptable. What is written is written. But if it says, *"...and will arise,"* and Rabban Gamliel comes and interprets it as referring to that which will happen at the end of time, this is not acceptable. "Who gave you permission to tamper with the Torah's meaning?" they counter. They deny the intimate relationship between the Jewish people and Hashem, which is described at length in *Shir HaShirim* in terms such as, *"My dove, My beloved, My perfect one."*[9] It is simply inconceivable to them that the Jewish people can have a dialogue and a "debate" with Hashem.

Techiyas HaMeisim Is What Makes Us Eternal

Chazal say about those who deny *techiyas ha-meisim*:

> All Israel have a portion in *Olam HaBa* ... And these are the people who do not have a portion in *Olam HaBa*: He who says there is no source in the

9. *Shir HaShirim* 5:2.

> Torah for the resurrection of the dead… It was taught: Since he denied *techiyas ha-meisim*, he will not take part in *techiyas ha-meisim*…[10]

Someone who does not have *emunah* in *techiyas ha-meisim* is disassociated from *techiyas ha-meisim*, just as someone who does not have *emunah* in Torah is disassociated from Torah. This is because *emunah* creates a connection.

Why would a person deny *techiyas ha-meisim?* Only because he does not have *emunah* in Hashem. And if he does not have *emunah* in Hashem, he has no connection with Hashem. Such a person is thus severed from his root above, and is cut off from eternal life. (This point was explained at length in Chapter One, "Preface to the Thirteen Principles of Faith.")

Techiyas HaMeisim and the Queen

We can better understand *techiyas ha-meisim* through a question asked by a non-Jewish queen named Cleopatra.

> Queen Cleopatra asked R. Meir: "I know that the deceased will come alive, as it says, *'They will sprout up from the city like the grass of the field.'*[11] But when they are resurrected, will they be bare or will they be clothed?" He answered her: "This may be learned from what happens to wheat kernels. Wheat kernels are buried bare, but they come out well dressed. The tzaddikim, who are buried in their clothing, will surely be so."[12]

This queen asked R. Meir whether the dead will be dressed when they come back to life, and R. Meir answered her with an example from a wheat kernel. What was she really asking, and what did R. Meir answer her?

10. *Sanhedrin* 90a–b.
11. *Tehillim* 72:16.
12. *Sanhedrin* 90b.

First of all, we must know that when *Chazal* say the tzaddikim will be resurrected with clothing, it does not mean they will simply be furnished with something to wear. It rather means that *techiyas ha-meisim* will take place even for the tzaddikim's clothing.

Why should the great miracle of *techiyas ha-meisim* apply to articles of clothing?

Let us understand the significance of clothing. As is known, the system of worlds that Hashem created divides into four. They correspond to the four letters of Hashem's ineffable Name. These four worlds are: *Atzilus, Briyah, Yetzirah,* and *Asiyah*. Similarly, everything in our world is composed of four elements: fire, air, earth, and water. Man, too, has four parts: soul, body, clothing, and home.

Soul and body, we know what these are. Clothing are the garments we wear. And a person's home, the place that he inhabits, is also a part of him. A man without a home is not a man, for *Chazal* say that a man's home is his wife,[13] and "A man without a wife is not a man."[14]

It is also known that the soul divides into various parts, each deeper than the preceding: *nefesh, ruach, neshamah, chayah, yechidah*.

Clothing and Body

This brings us to a question. The general rule is that the inner part is superior to the external part. For instance, a person has a body, and inside it, a *nefesh*. The *nefesh* is superior to the body. Inside the *nefesh* is the *ruach*. The *ruach* is superior to the *nefesh*. And so on. But with clothing, the opposite is true: clothing adds honor to the person

13. *Yoma* 2a.

14. *Yevamos* 63a.

inside it. "R. Yochanan would call clothing 'honorers.'"[15] This is because a person's unclothed body is a source of embarrassment. Regarding people who go unclothed in the marketplace when they are doing messy work, the Rambam says they are "considered like dogs."[16]

Why is clothing, an external part, superior to the body itself? Theoretically it should be the other way around. Clothing serves the body, and should be less honorable than the body, which is the inner part.

The answer is as follows. Before the sin of Adam HaRishon, man was really his *nefesh* and *neshamah*, and the body was merely an article of clothing that covered them. The body was no more than a garment. Although it was visible to others it was not a source of embarrassment, as shown by the Torah's account of *Gan Eden* before the sin. It was not a part of man himself, so there was nothing embarrassing about it. But after Adam sinned, the body became a part of him. At that point, nakedness became a cause for embarrassment, as the Torah recounts.

But our question is not yet fully answered. Clothing serves the body. Thus, it should be less honorable than the body. Doesn't the inferior usually serve the superior?

The answer is that man has two systems: an internal one and an external one. The body, however external it seems, actually belongs to the internal system. It is part of the person himself. It is the most external part of the internal system. Clothing, however, belongs to the external system. It is outside the person himself. It is the most internal part of the external system.

That is why clothing cannot be judged relative to the body. They belong to two different systems. We can see for ourselves that this is true because when the body is touched, the person

15. *Bava Kamma* 91b.

16. *Mishneh Torah, Hilchos Eidus* 11:5.

himself feels it. But when the clothing is touched, the person does not feel it. The body belongs to the person himself, yet is the lowliest and most inferior part of him. That is why it is a source of embarrassment to him.

Man's Structure

Man's greatest aspect is, so to speak, similar to that of Hashem. This is because man was created in the image of God.

What is Hashem's greatest aspect, so to speak? It is that He is *yachid.* He is the one and only; there is none other than Him. The aspect that best expresses Hashem's greatness is not His wisdom or His grandeur or His compassion. It is His *yechidus*: the fact that He is the only one.

If we say that Hashem is kind and gracious, we have not yet spoken of His distinguishing quality. There are many people, too, who are kind and gracious. If we say that Hashem is wise, then again, there are many people who are wise. All we are saying is that Hashem is wiser than they are. The same is true if we say that Hashem is powerful. We have not yet touched on Hashem's unique aspect.

But when we say that Hashem is *yachid,* that He is the only one, this is an aspect that is uniquely His. Hashem is the only one. No person is the only one. There are many people, but there is just one Hashem! This is the aspect that truly expresses Hashem's greatness.

Man, as well, has this aspect of "*yachid,*" so to speak. The deepest part of man is called *yechidah,* "the only one," and this part expresses a man's true unique greatness. It is his distinguishing quality. At the other end of the extreme, man's body is something he has in common with all others. It is his plainest and most external part, for when it comes to the body, man and beast are essentially equal.

The body has a "spouse" called the *nefesh,* the life force. The *nefesh* gives expression to the body's nature. The *nefesh* is not quite as lowly as the body is, but it is its "spouse." Let's take the eye for an example. The eye's "spouse" is the faculty of sight. It gives expression to the eye's nature. The "spouse" of the ear is the faculty of hearing. And so it is with the body: its "spouse" is the *nefesh,* which is the body's aliveness.

After the *nefesh,* the next part of man is called the *ruach,* the spirit. Its "spouse" is the clothing that man wears. And the next part of man after the *ruach* is called the *neshamah,* the soul. Its "spouse" is the home that man lives in. The clothing gives expression to the *ruach,* and the home gives expression to the *neshamah.* But the two most profound aspects of man, *chayah* and *yechidah,* have no "spouse" at all. In Torah sources they are called *mekifim,* "encirclers." This is because they are not integrated into man's being but rather encircle and surround him from outside.

These are the parts of which man's structure is composed.

The body and the *nefesh* are unified with each other, and this is the cause of man's embarrassment, for in this way he resembles the animals. This *nefesh* is what is known as the *nefesh ha-behamis,* "the animal soul." It comprises the faculties of sight, eating, natural vitality, etc. Thus it is embarrassing for a person when he expresses his *nefesh,* for he is showing his animalistic side. He wants to eat, drink, etc. He wants "creature comforts." This embarrassment is the same as that of the body being unclothed.

When a person expresses his *ruach* he is showing what values he holds. This is externally expressed by his clothing. He may wear the garb of a Torah sage, or the uniform of a policeman. It expresses his uniqueness.

When a man is unclothed he is without his honor. He is only body, for his inner being is not expressing itself right now. Only when his clothing covers his body and gives expression to his inner being do we see, according to his clothing, the man's inner qualities. We see that he is not just a nameless human but a person with an identity.

This is not the end of the story. There is something even more expressive of man's inner being: his home. The nature of a man's home and family reveals more of a man's greatness than his clothing does. Everyone can dress up like a Chassidic Rebbe, but not everyone can establish a home like a Chassidic Rebbe, try as one may. The home reflects much more about a man's inner being.

If we see someone in the bathhouse we don't know much about his identity. When we see him walk out the door in rabbinical garb we know more or less what segment of society he belongs to. But we still don't know if he is a venerable rosh yeshiva or perhaps the grandson of one. When can we know this? When we enter his home. A man's home is where his true nature reveals itself.

It sometimes happens that we enter the home of a man whom we imagined to be a Torah personality only to find his central bookcase displaying Encyclopedia Britannica instead of a *Shas*. More than a man's clothing, his home clearly expresses what kind of person he really is. A person's house, which is seemingly a more external aspect, actually expresses *penimiyus*, internal depth. A person feels tremendously attached to his home. And ultimately, this is where the Shechinah rests. There is something very deep about the home.

Between the Ruach and the Neshamah

The *nefesh* is a person's natural life force, the fact that he is alive. It is something that Jews and non-Jews have in common.

The *ruach* is a person's conscience. It is what makes him inclined to doing good deeds. This, too, is something that non-Jews have as well. Every human being has an inclination to honesty. Even the lowliest person is embarrassed when he is caught telling a lie. This is because of the conscience. Jews place a lot of significance on the *ruach*: doing mitzvos, learning Torah, engaging in worthy activities.

All this is within the natural human framework. But there exists an aspiration to a higher level of *kedushah* that is beyond the natural human framework. For instance, there are people for whom following an upright Jewish life is not enough. They yearn for true spiritual greatness. Sometimes they impose upon themselves physical deprivation. Sometimes they learn for entire nights. This is not something demanded by man's conscience, by his inclination to doing good, as keeping all the mitzvos would be sufficient. This lofty aspiration is above and beyond the standard Jewish way of life.

This is what is called *neshamah*. It is something else altogether, and it too has many levels. The true meaning of *neshamah* is "*ru'ach hakodesh* — the lofty/holy spirit."

Chayah is something even higher than *neshamah*. It has to do with prophecy and total attachment to Hashem.

As we mentioned, the body and the *nefesh* are "spouses." This is because they are the two lowest parts, in the spiritual realm and in the physical realm. Both of them are aspects that all beings have in common, man and beast alike. They do not express man's uniqueness. When the non-unique part of man presents itself, when a person is displayed as a nameless and characterless being, this is embarrassing. But it is not embarrassing for an animal because this is its nature. An animal is no more than a creature. Man, however, was not made to be like everything else; he was made to be unique.

That is why we wear clothing — it emphasizes the uniqueness of man. Every person is special and unique, and he expresses this in the way he dresses. At the beach, we cannot tell if the person in front of us is a rosh yeshiva or a bus driver. As soon as he gets dressed we get some clues about his identity. Now, his appearance starts to reflect his inner being. The *ruach* begins to show itself.

Back to Cleopatra's Question

This explains Queen Cleopatra's question to R. Meir. In this world, the *nefesh, ruach,* and *neshamah* have certain means with which they can express themselves. Man's inner being has outward expression. The Queen wanted to know if it will be that way in the world of *techiyas ha-meisim,* too.

The Queen reasoned as follows: I know that the *nefesh* will be resurrected. The body goes into the grave, and the body comes back to life. The same goes for the *nefesh,* because the body and the *nefesh* are essentially the same.

Related to this, the Ramchal wrote:[17]

> *Techiyas ha-meisim* can be simply summarized and generalized as follows: When *HaKadosh Baruch Hu* created man He gave him both a body and a *neshamah.* Together, the body and the *neshamah* work to bear the Divine service. Together, they observe Torah and mitzvos which man was given. It is thus fitting that they should be together also for receiving the eternal reward. It is not right that the body should labor but not reap the fruits, for "*HaKadosh Baruch Hu* does not withhold reward from any creature."[18]

Thus it is clear that when a person comes back to life in *techiyas ha-meisim,* the *nefesh* will be accompanied by the body. However, queried the Queen, what about the *ruach,* which is a greater and deeper part of man? Will its "spouse" come along with it, too? Will there be clothing in the world of *techiyas ha-meisim*?

This is a good question because the truth of the matter is that the *ruach* has no inherent need for clothing. In fact, the *ruach* never even dies. It is written, "*The ruach returns to God.*"[19] Thus it is pertinent to ask whether the *ruach* will appear in the world of *techiyas ha-meisim* — will the resurrected person be wearing clothing, as an expression of his *ruach*?

17. Ramchal, *Da'as Tevunos* ch. 68

18. *Bava Kamma* 38a.

19. *Koheles* 12:7.

R. Meir answered that man will indeed have his clothing in the world of *techiyas ha-meisim,* as may be learned from wheat kernels. Wheat kernels are placed in the ground bare, yet come out "dressed" with a number of layers of "clothing": tufts, husks, stems, and leaves. Surely a tzaddik, who is buried in clothes, will come out of the ground dressed in clothing. This is because clothing does more than just express the *ruach.* Indeed, if this were its only function, there would be no need for man to be resurrected with his clothing, as the *ruach* does not really need clothing. However, clothing has an additional function: It ennobles the body. Clothing is not merely a window into the *ruach* but is also an independent entity. It dignifies the body by covering it and thereby taking away embarrassment. This is why the tzaddikim will come back to life with their clothing.

Two Techiyos HaMeisim

When we speak of *techiyas ha-meisim* we usually mean the great *techiyas ha-meisim* that will take place prior to *Olam HaBa*. The prevalent view is that of the Ramban: the *Mashiach* will come, build the *Beis HaMikdash,* and bring the Jewish people back to Hashem. We will live long lives but it will still be normal life as we know it. It will be this world, in its rectified state.

And when this world finishes, then *"HaKadosh Baruch Hu* will, in the future, make His world anew."[20] This is *Olam HaBa,* about which *Chazal* say:

> *Olam HaBa* has no eating, no drinking, no procreating, no business dealings, no jealousy, no hatred, and no rivalry. Rather, the tzaddikim sit with their crowns on their heads and enjoy the radiance of the Shechinah.[21]

20. *Sanhedrin* 92b.
21. *Berachos* 17a.

Olam HaBa is a spiritual world without physical activities. And *techiyas ha-meisim* takes place before we enter the spiritual world of *Olam HaBa*. However, the Ritva writes that *techiyas ha-meisim* will occur twice:

> "Regarding someone who eats meat and drinks wine on Tishah b'Av, Scripture says:[22] *'Their sins will be upon their bones.'"*[23] This means his bones will not come alive in the *techiyas ha-meisim* that will take place at the time of the building of the *Beis HaMikdash*. This *techiyas ha-meisim* will be for those who died in *galus* and awaited salvation, regarding whom it says, *"Fortunate is he who awaits and reaches the days."*[24] Yet, it could be that such a person will still come alive at the time of the Day of Judgment, which is after the days of the *Mashiach*.[25]

We see from the Ritva that there will be two *techiyos ha-meisim*. There will be the great one, when all will be resurrected — "These for eternal life, and those for eternal disgrace."[26] And there will be a minature *techiyas ha-meisim* when the *Mashiach* comes. It will be for people who lived their lives awaiting the *Mashiach*.

The following *Chazal* is proof for the minature *techiyas ha-meisim* taking place upon the *Mashiach*'s coming:

> What is the source in the Torah for *techiyas ha-meisim?* It says, *"You shall give Hashem's terumah from it, to Aharon the Priest."*[27] But did Aharon live forever? He did not even enter Eretz Yisrael, that he should be given *terumah*! Rather, it teaches

22. *Yechezkel* 32:27.
23. *Ta'anis* 30b.
24. *Daniel* 12:12.
25. *Ritva, Ta'anis* 30b.
26. *Sanhedrin* 92a.
27. *Bemidbar* 18:28.

that in the future, Aharon will come back to life, and the Jewish people will give him *terumah*. Here we may learn *techiyas ha-meisim* from the Torah.[28]

We see that when Aharon will be resurrected he will receive *terumah* produce. As is known, *terumah* is meant to be eaten. It is the *kohanim*'s food. Thus, this *Chazal* about *techiyas ha-meisim* does not seem to fit with the nature of *Olam HaBa,* in which there is "no eating, no drinking... Rather, the tzaddikim sit with their crowns on their heads..." But it does fit with the days of the *Mashiach,* during which there will be normal life in this world.

Here is another proof:

> R. Simai says: What is the source in the Torah for *techiyas ha-meisim?* It says, *"And also, I will fulfill My covenant with them, to give them the land of Canaan."*[29] It does not say, *"To give you,"* but rather, *"To give them."* Here we may learn *techiyas ha-meisim* from the Torah.[30]

This, too, seems to refer to the little *techiyas ha-meisim* when the *Mashiach* comes, not to the great *techiyas ha-meisim* preceding *Olam HaBa*. This *Chazal* is telling us that Hashem will give the land of Canaan to the *Avos*. It is not saying that they will receive a portion in the land, but rather that the *Avos* will be given the entire land of Canaan.

This *Chazal* seems to be intimating an important point about Eretz Yisrael itself: The land will belong to the *Avos*. It will no longer be the land of "Yisrael," i.e., the land of the Jewish people, but will rather be the land of the "*Avos*." This is a whole new type of *kedushah.*

The difference between the *Avos* and their descendants may

28. *Sanhedrin* 92a.
29. *Shemos* 6:4.
30. *Sanhedrin* 90b.

be seen from the example of a man standing in front of a mirror. There are two images: the man himself, and his reflection in the mirror. This is the difference between the *Avos* and their descendants. Everything that we, the descendants, have today is only from the *Avos*. We have nothing of our own. We are no more than their reflection, while they are the object itself.

It is said about a certain Jew who davened with exceptional fervor, that he was once asked how he came to daven this way. He answered that he was once in a hall where R. Yisrael Salanter spoke. A minyan was held in the hall, and R. Yisrael, standing in front, faced the wall. This Jew was positioned in a spot from where he could see the reflection of R. Yisrael's face while R. Yisrael stood and davened. The image he saw made a profound impression on him.

This is what the Jewish people will be like after *techiyas ha-meisim*, when the land will belong to the *Avos*. The *Avos* will be resurrected, and will serve as a personal example in *avodas Hashem* for all the people. Their *kedushah* will be reflected in the people. We can imagine what tremendous heights the Jewish people will then reach.

All this is the miniature *techiyas ha-meisim* that will take place with the coming of the *Mashiach*. In *Olam HaBa*, we cannot even imagine what it will be like: *"No eye other than Yours, O God, has seen that which God will do for those who await Him."*[31]

31. *Yeshayahu* 64:3; see *Berachos* 34b.

הערה, בענין י"ג עיקרי האמונה

14

*Epilogue to the Thirteen Principles of Faith**

THE THIRTEEN PRINCIPLES OF *emunah* were elucidated by the Rambam in his commentary on the *Mishnayos*. The Rambam ruled that these are the basic principles of faith. This means that someone who does not believe in these principles is separated from the Jewish people. We do not have the same obligations toward him as we do toward other Jews. Furthermore, he has no portion in *Olam HaBa,* as the Rambam states there.

A person who never learned a certain teaching of the Sages, or who never heard about a certain mitzvah, is not thereby separated from the Jewish people. He simply doesn't know, that's all. He has to learn.

But someone who is ignorant of one of *emunah*'s basic principles has missed the boat. It makes no difference why he doesn't know it or doesn't believe in it—the bottom line is that he lacks the basic principles of Judaism. He is missing the basic building blocks of the Jewish soul. (This point was elaborated on in Chapter 1, "Preface to the Thirteen Principles of Faith.")

This underscores our obligation to teach the Thirteen

* This chapter is taken from the end of *Sefer Bereichos B'Cheshbon,* written by Rav Pincus *zt"l.*

Principles of Faith along with their proper explanation. If we are obligated to teach Torah and to bring back wayward Jews, surely we have a great obligation to teach the principles of *emunah,* for even someone who keeps all the mitzvos with great fervor and learns Torah nonstop is separated from the Jewish people if he lacks one of the basic principles of *emunah.* For instance, if he does not know the principle that "This Torah will not be exchanged," or that "Moshe Rabbeinu... was the father of the prophets." These are very deep points even on their simple level. Someone who does not know these things is not missing details. He is missing the main thing.

This brings us to an important question. The second principle states that Hashem is One. There are various aspects to Hashem's unity. Are we required to know and understand all these aspects in order to believe in this principle? Which aspects are bottom-line requirements and which are not?

For instance, the Rishonim explain that Hashem's unity is absolute; He does not divide into various parts. Consequently, explains the Rambam, "Hashem knows, He is that which is known, and He is knowledge itself — it is all one. This is something that the mouth cannot speak, nor the ear hear, nor man's faculty of understanding properly grasp." (This was elaborated in Chapter 4 of this section, "The Second Principle.")

Do we have to know and understand this in order to believe that Hashem is One?

Another aspect of Hashem's unity is that Hashem is the only thing that exists. There is nothing else at all besides Him. (This, too, was elaborated in Chapter 4, "The Second Principle.") Although the *Nefesh HaChaim* warned against the dangers inherent in dwelling on this point, do we have to know and understand it in order to believe that Hashem is One?

If so, the obligation would fall upon us to teach these utterly profound matters to every Jew, whenever it may be possible, in order to save his soul from being cut off.

However, it does not stand to reason that these deep matters are basic, bottom-line requirements of *emunah*. So many good, believing Jews never learned them and never were taught them.

In this vein, *Chazal* said about a person who was reciting the *Shema* and drawing it out for a long time:

> Once you have made Hashem to be King above and below and to the four directions of Heaven, you need not do more.[1]

When we recite *Shema Yisrael Hashem Elokeinu Hashem Echad,* we must have *kavanah* that Hashem is One. The Rambam writes that this *pasuk* teaches us the mitzvah to believe in Hashem's unity. Yet, *Chazal* say that there is no need to draw out the *Shema* too much. The basic *kavanah* is sufficient.

This is somewhat of a proof that delving into the deeper aspects of Hashem's unity is not a basic requirement. We must know that Hashem is the One and Only throughout all the expanses of the world, but we are not obligated to understand that Hashem is above and beyond all reality known to man. Failing to understand this does not prevent us from performing the mitzvah of believing that Hashem is One.

It is said that the Brisker Rav commented on the above-cited Gemara that the place in the *Shema* where one should have *kavanah* that Hashem is above all known reality is when he recites Hashem's Name. This is because Hashem's transcendent and unknowable nature is expressed by His ineffable Name, whereas the word *Echad* merely expresses that He is the One and Only throughout all the expanses of the world.

We can raise the same type of question regarding the first principle of *emunah*: What is entailed by the requirement to

1. *Berachos* 12b.

believe that Hashem exists? To what extent, or if at all, does failing to fathom Hashem's uniqueness detract from our belief that Hashem is One? This matter requires further investigation.

Perhaps we can bring a parallel from the hymn we sing at the end of the Pesach Haggadah: *Echad mi yode'a.* This hymn opens by asking, "Who knows One?" This question implies that the deeper aspects of Hashem's unity are not a basic requirement incumbent on all Jews. Why? The logic is as follows: The author of this hymn would not address his audience, Torah observant Jews, and ask them a question such as, "Is there anyone here who knows that Hashem is One, and not two or three?" Of course everyone knows the simple meaning of One! This cannot be his question.

Therefore, the first question in this hymn must be asking who knows the deeper but non-obligatory meaning of Hashem's unity, over and above the basic knowledge that every Jew is required to have. The hymn is asking: Who knows the principle of the deeper aspects of Hashem's unity? The answer is: "*Echad Elokeinu shebashamayim uva'aretz*" — Hashem is absolute, indivisible unity, and nothing else at all exists besides Him.